Tea and Transition

Nicola Jane Chase

TELEMACHUS PRESS

This is a work of creative non-fiction. While the people, places and events are real; some of the names and descriptions have been changed to protect individual privacy.

TEA AND TRANSITION
This book is licensed for your personal enjoyment only. This book may not be re-sold or given away to other people. If you're reading this book and did not purchase it, or it was not purchased for your use only, then you should return it and purchase your own copy. Thank you for respecting the hard work of the author.

Cover designed by Nicola Jane Chase and Telemachus Press, LLC

Front cover photo by Carolyn O'Neill
Back cover and interior author photos by Jeffrey Goritz
www.JeffreyGoritzPhotography.com

Cover and interior art:
Copyright © iStock/4591781/elly99
Copyright © iStock/31301518/HiRes/Nataleana
Copyright © iStock/33696738/FrankRamspott
Copyright © iStock/29722028/Giraphics
Copyright © iStock/8232434/Johnnylemonseed
Copyright © iStock/30865402/SCHUBphoto
Copyright © iStock/655841/Marje

Fashion in author photo by Express, styling by the author

Published by Telemachus Press, LLC
www.telemachuspress.com

Visit the author website:
www.nicolajanechase.com

Follow the author on Facebook:
www.facebook.com/TeaAndTransition

ISBN: 978-1-941536-99-5 (eBook)
ISBN: 978-1-942899-00-6 (paperback)
ISBN: 978-1-942899-01-3 (hardback)

Version 2015.04.15

10 9 8 7 6 5 4 3 2 1

Tea and Transition

*A story of love, the human spirit,
and how one man became one woman*

To anyone who is questioning their gender: you are not alone.
Although this fact may not affect you as you follow your
path, its reassurance can still be a comfort.

To friends, extended family and all the health professionals
who have been there for me on my journey: thank you.
It would have been so much harder without your support.
Your names have been changed but you know who you are.

To Lori, my editor and cheerleader:
Your belief in my story was the inspiration I needed.

Finally, to my mother, Ann Chase:
I love you more than I have ever said.
This book is dedicated to you.

Nicola Jane Chase
Spring 2015

Tea and Me

All true tales should probably start at the beginning. However in my case, I can't be sure when that beginning was. For the first 40 years of my existence I was a heterosexual man. Now I am a heterosexual woman. This change didn't occur overnight, nor did I flip a switch to make it happen. In fact, I didn't see it coming it at all.

Over the course of several years, I recognized feelings that I couldn't ignore. I started to embrace them. I began a journal. Changes happened and my evolution became a revelation—not least to myself. Sometimes I felt my life was following its own direction and I was just tagging along. But not everyone accepted the new me; some friendships strengthened, and others broke. There was pain. The slings and arrows I suffered were rejection and stigma—every transgender person has experienced those.

The outlines of yin and yang were shifting, with gender and with my sexuality too. What did I expect from intimacy? Would the symmetry remain?

Equipped with my British heritage, Asian connections, and a New York state of mind, I traversed three continents to confront my past life as a DJ and broadcaster and address my future one—with a new voice.

I wanted to better align my inner and outer selves, but to what extent? Would there ever be an end to my journey? It became a unique arc of discovery. There were difficult choices and unexpected rewards. And surprises. So many surprises. Whenever they happened I wrote in my journal. That journal evolved into this book.

Usually, when I wrote, I had a cup of tea by my side—as I do now. Tea was also there at many key moments in my transition, its solace much deeper than coffee could ever have been. In fact the happenstance of tea is referenced far more frequently than I initially appreciated: Darjeeling poured in times of awkward disclosure, a strong brew when support was needed, or tea leaves left behind after inspiration had seeped. Tea has been my muse and my comfort.

Now, as I look over the pages ahead (English breakfast tea steeping) and I recall instances of my male past, it seems I am looking back over someone else's shoulder, not mine. Yet all those memories have contributed to me becoming the woman I am, along with new experiences only a woman can feel.

This is the story that I have to tell.

Part One

Chapter 1

Cause and Effect

Something rattles me out of my restless sleep. Heart thumping, mind racing, thoughts everywhere. Rasping… choking… drowning… death? Trapped inside a plastic bag. No, clammy sheets are twisted around me. Sit bolt upright. Eyes wide open. Pitch black. Gasp of breath. Awake.

Fireflies rage in my head.
Think straight; can't.
Try to focus; can't.
Helpless, vulnerable, 3am.
I am afraid. I feel very, very afraid.
Dark shades of alarm rise up, suicidal thoughts.
No, I just need daybreak. Time, give me time.
Uneasy rest; afraid of sleep's dark specter.
I was upset before I went to bed, yes.
I watched Pretty Woman *last night.*
Her fault. Bloody Julia Roberts.

Sunrise eventually came that September morning. With the light, Nosferatu was no longer perched on my window ledge and I was breathing easier. My pulse was still pounding but now I favored life's light to its darker alternative. So why the fear? Didn't I want to go to Thailand?

Practicalities of the day ahead allowed me to briefly focus elsewhere; I had to be at work in the office in a couple of hours and needed to get ready. But I was exhausted, an utter mental wreck.

Tea helped. I am English and so tea is a resolution for most things. It has started wars and triggered independence, but tea can also calm nerves. Toast makes it even better. Was it Thursday? Yes, so I had a session scheduled with Navi, my head doctor. Perhaps she could find a way to ease my mind. Yet as I reflected on the previous hours, I knew what her advice would be.

I was scheduled to head to Bangkok for Sexual Reassignment Surgery (SRS) a few weeks later. It is a date that many transgender women dream of, and for me it had seemed so certain, so right. But with the panic attack, my conviction evaporated. I tried to reject the evidence but the demons that visited me that fraught night had delivered a stark message: I had to cancel my date with surgery.

"When did you know?" It's something people ask me all the time; when did I know that I was transgendered? Perhaps it sounds strange, but I really don't know. There wasn't one supreme moment of sublime enlightenment, no one morning when I woke up as a woman having gone to sleep as a man, nor even a time when my gender status was beyond cogent doubt. Yet it was an inescapable direction in which I was led. Choice? No, there was no choice involved, only emotions to ignore.

It would have been much easier if TRANSGENDERED had been stamped on my birth certificate or tattooed onto my head after I was born. I remember in one of the Omen movies that Damien had an unfortunate birthmark—a 666 on his scalp—revealed when someone snipped away at his hair as he was sleeping; three digits that confirmed he was the devil incarnate. (Though napping when such an important revelation is pending was surely a character flaw for Beelzebub, especially having lived through the Samson and Delilah era.) Without a doubt it would have been far more convenient if I had similar identifying features on my scalp, if only to save years of confusion and soul searching. However, anyone cutting away enough hair to uncover my thirteen letters would have royally frustrated James, my hairdresser, who'd then have needed to repair the damage.

But there must have been a million clues when I was growing up, right? Red flags that could have at least given me pause for thought that I was a little girl in a little boy's body? Nope, none of the above. I do vaguely remember trying to replicate a sauna in my mum's linen closet when I was 10 or 11 and she was out one evening, but I don't think that being naked in a linen closet with an electric heater was necessarily a warning sign. Weird perhaps, but in itself no indicator of my inner femininity. In fact, all through my 30s I didn't have a clue that the male identity I had grown up with was out of sync with my true self. What amazes me the most now is that possibly, back then, it wasn't—as my male side was still buoyant. So when did the woman inside rise to the surface?

Chapter 2
Welcome to the Pleasuredome

I can't imagine living anywhere other than the crazy, wonderful, legendary place that is New York City. Of course it is not faultless, but those imperfections enhance its spirit. Would I miss bitching about the extremes of weather? Or the frustration of not finding a cab when it's raining? Or the smell of stale urine at the end of subway platforms? I suppose I could live without that last one, possibly the second one too, but this city is my home and I'm an adoptive New Yorker. Like so many others who make up its fabric, I am also an immigrant who was unquestionably drawn here. I used to be a globe-trotting club DJ and then found a niche as a *radio personality* (which sounds so crass) for a radio station in Hong Kong. That seems a long time ago now.

My two bedroom apartment in Queens is blessed with having a small back yard (a real find in this city), and so summers are spent coaxing my gooseberries, harvesting rhubarb, and wondering how the latest family of American robins is doing. They hatch a new brood every spring, though I'm not quite sure where they live. But they feed off my patch of grass and bathe in my bird bath so I feel invested in their future. I always enjoy observing the changing seasons and my garden is a personal oasis in the midst of the hubbub. Beyond my front door is the city of New York.

England is where I grew up, forty-something years ago. As a man. On a peninsula called the Wirral. If you triangulate the beauty of the Welsh hills, history of Chester, and renown of Liverpool on a local map then you will find a small town called Heswall. That is where I was born, and it was home until I got bitten by the travel bug in my 20s. Although I didn't dislike life there, it was not a place for dream building—not that I knew what my dreams were. Heswall was a satellite town for the sprawling mass that is Liverpool, and Liverpool was even less appealing to me. I wasn't into soccer, and while I appreciated the wealth of musical talent spawned from the city I never felt any desire to go see where the Cavern Club once stood or take a ferry 'cross the Mersey—not for musical reasons anyway. When I was growing up, Liverpool meant unsafe neighborhoods, stolen cars and rampant drugs. I wasn't into any of that. Nor did I appreciate the sense of entitlement imbued by the local *Scouse* accent that was deemed working class. The thicker the accent, the more you were a *real* Liverpudlian. Woe betide if you lived anywhere within a car-stealing distance of the city if you didn't *sound* like you grew up there. My parents didn't come from that neck of the woods, had no Liverpool accent, and so neither did I. At school that deemed me as being posh, which made me the ideal kid for bullying. So school days were not too happy, but my home life was. My mum, my sister, and me, that was our family unit. We always did things as a family and I loved vacations and days out to Wales or the Lake District. While other kids went to youth clubs and discos, I remained home to play with my train set. No, it was more than a train set, it was a whole model railway layout that Mum allowed me to build in the spare room. It was grand, and it was all mine. I didn't feel a loner; I just didn't relate with most of my generation.

That sentiment stuck with me through my teens, and it was only when I started working at an electronics store in Birkenhead (an erstwhile shipbuilding town across the River Mersey from Liverpool and even worse than its more famous twin) that I developed a wider circle of friends. These people were outside my safe family sanctuary and they helped me spread my social wings and gave me a new perspective on going out, drinking, and having fun. I even started going to clubs. I dabbled in having girlfriends, though nothing worked out. My plan was to take a year off between leaving school at eighteen and heading to university, but I never ended up furthering my education in that way. Life with a few pounds in my pocket was far more interesting than higher education. I bought my first car, a navy blue Mini—the original model, of course.

With increasing self-assurance and independence I moved on to retail management at an old-fashioned department store called Beatties, still in the cultural black hole that was Birkenhead in the 1980s. The store was based at the end of a shopping precinct (before they were called malls) which was beset by having too many discount furniture stores and too little class. Step through the place after closing time and the ground was strewn with beer cans and fast food wrappers. Outside the couple of pubs, there would be fish and chip remains—with or without a vomit coating.

However, Beatties was a cut above the rest and I worked in that same department store for the next seven years. I was managing a team of more than 20 people and I learned as much about life itself as how to sell greeting cards or market menswear. But I was developing a big interest away from retail: music. I became fascinated by club rhythms and the way DJs would seamlessly mix tracks together. I had to learn the same skills! I built my own DJ rig in my bedroom and spent a vast proportion of my wages on 12" singles. That was during the glory days of vinyl when record stores could be found in every town and were still the main way to buy music. There was something hypnotic and exciting about buying maxi singles that I had listened to in my local music shop or heard on the radio, and then bringing them home to play. The shrink wrap would come off and I was dizzy with anticipation. I was buying into a lifestyle. I would then practice mixing them together to form seamless cassette tapes which I would sell to shops and hair salons for their background music. The cassette mixed tape; who could forget that.

It was the era of Frankie Goes To Hollywood, and T-shirts that told you to relax. I bought multiple remixes of "Two Tribes" and every other single FGTH released. Also the Human League. The one-sided haircut of Phil Oakey and the two striking girls beside him epitomized 80s style; their synthesizers dominated the sound of that era. There was Yazoo and the new romantic sound of Spandau Ballet. Madonna was getting into the groove, Prince was making doves cry, and Sister Sledge was lost in music. However I wanted an edgier collection so I sought out rare imports, usually from a dingy basement in one of the cooler music stores in Liverpool. One time I was there I picked up a hot new single by Meli'sa Morgan from the rack at exactly the same time as someone else. There was only one copy in the store so we did the honorable thing of tossing a coin to see who could buy it. I won, and "Fools Paradise" came home with me with an extra sense of triumph in the bag. These singles often came out of New York and were twice the price but double the kudos. Tracks and remixes by Jellybean or Arthur Baker. Singles by the BB&Q Band, Chaka Khan, and Sheila E. It was all so exotic and I was caught up in the dream.

Eventually the allure of music became more compelling than the routine efficiency of the department store and I threw in the nine-to-five towel of the working man. I enhanced my club skills and went on the road as a DJ. I was also aware of ways that I could scratch my DJ itch and get to see other parts of the world at the same time. So over the next few years I worked for several different agencies, usually headquartered in London, which had contracts with hotel venues around the world. Each agency would supply music and DJs to the venue. To keep the club fresh, the DJs (like the records) would be rotated, usually every four to six months. It seems incredible now, but my first overseas contract was playing at a five star hotel in Egypt literally just across the road from the pyramids of Giza. (Yes there is a road that goes straight to the pyramids, and no, they are not in the middle of nowhere as you might imagine.) It was a cowboy-themed club called The Saddle, though the ridiculous irony was that jeans were not allowed.

Those were incredible times, a world away from the River Mersey, and I made friends with other DJs who were working in different hotels and clubs in Cairo. Sometimes we'd meet up on a shared night off and head to one of the clubs where another DJ was still working. One of my abiding memories of that city was a crazy Monday night at Jackie's, the nightclub at the Nile Hilton, where four of us danced like the possessed to Paul Simon's "You Can Call Me Al." We had not a care in the world. At that time the concept of gender confusion hadn't even popped into my head.

DJs have a stereotypical reputation for being half-wit womanizers, and even though I didn't fit that profile I did meet some interesting people along the way. For instance, there was one semi-groupie who was hanging around the club at Giza near the end of one evening. She seemed interesting enough, so I asked her if she wanted to see the pyramids at dawn. (How wonderful a chat-up line is that, without even being a euphemism!) She said yes and we agreed to meet up two hours later. I didn't consider her a potential sexual conquest but I didn't rule out the idea either. But it soon transpired that that would never happen. When she was in the club, either the lights were low or she was wearing pants. Or maybe I was too distracted by playing music to notice. However when we met up in the coffee shop prior to the expedition to the pyramids, she was wearing shorts. That was when I saw them: the hairiest, scariest legs I had ever seen on man or beast. She would put giant spiders to shame with that black fuzz adorning her legs. Even worse, she almost seemed to take pride in it. I wondered if I should have handed her a comb. Maybe I have that hapless tourist to blame as the trigger for my hirsutism phobia. In fact, once I started my transgender journey body hair was the first to go. Needless to say, that morning ended up being a speedy guided tour around the Great Pyramid of Cheops before I raced off into the distance like the Road Runner. It would have been so embarrassing if my squeeze were confused for a camel.

Body hair played a bizarre role in another of the few times that I hooked up with someone from a club. This time I was working at another Cairo hotel, just near the airport. She was a stewardess from Royal Air Maroc. (They were still called stewardesses at that time, rather than the more politically correct *cabin crew* of now.) This Moroccan girl was certainly attractive, bordering on gorgeous, but she also had a secret that was only unveiled after we got jiggy with it. She had the wiriest pubic bush that I have ever come across. It was like one of those metal scouring pads that you use in the kitchen to remove baked-on stains from ovenproof cookware. It was simply terrifying and I was afraid of getting injured. Still, I survived the encounter without bloodshed. But there were wonderful connections too. If I hadn't worked in Egypt, I'd never have met Louise. She lived in the American Midwest, but was on a group tour of Egypt and came into my club one night. We definitely clicked and a year later I visited her in the United States. A butterfly flaps its wings in Cairo, and I have sex in Minneapolis. We became close, but without email and the Internet, long-distance relationships back then were easily doomed. But if I'd not gone to visit her in Minneapolis then I'd not have had good reason to pass through New York—which forms the cornerstone of my life now.

My DJ jaunts eventually took me to Guangzhou, in southern China, a city once known as Canton. That was in the early 90s when the city was in a confused state of growing pains. The industrial powerhouse that is the Pearl River Delta was just opening up and money was flooding into the city—for some anyway; other residents remained pitifully poor. Before I arrived I had envisioned the place as full of historical temples and men in Chairman Mao suits, but in actuality it was a dirty gray city filled with people who rarely smiled. Men who did wear suits often kept the manufacturer's label clearly visible on the outside of the sleeve to show that they had money, even if those labels misspelled Gucci. The city itself hadn't determined if it had wealth or not. I remember seeing a fire engine speed past the hotel one afternoon, only this one seemed like something out of a black and white Mickey Mouse cartoon. There was no siren, just a man on the front of a ramshackle four-wheel truck clanging a bell. Five other men clung to a small water tank on the back equipped with large buckets. But rampant change was only a matter of time; twenty years later the city had built a 160-mile subway network which would put most of the rest of the world to shame. I expect they have modern fire trucks now too.

I stayed in Guangzhou for three years and played in three different venues, each the best of its class. The clientele was all wealthy Chinese, mostly from Taiwan or Hong Kong, but the music I played was all western, though I'd occasionally toss in a local favorite.

It was there that I developed a long relationship with JJ. She was a young, wonderfully uncomplicated Chinese girl with a captivating smile who spoke as much English as I did Cantonese at the time: none. But against the odds, we connected. We met for tea some afternoons—jasmine or *oolong* usually—or even for a late supper after I finished work at 2am. The city was still bustling then. A couple of times she took me back to her hometown just out of Guangdong province to meet her family; that was how strangely solid our relationship had become. This place was deep in the Chinese heartland where the locals hadn't seen many white people before—if any. I felt I was like a great 19th century explorer discovering *the interior*.

I recall one time standing with JJ in the middle of town, looking over the side of a bridge to the view below. It must have been a beautiful river once, but now it was encrusted with discarded Coke bottles and Styrofoam food containers. Nothing but a small stream struggled through and I guessed it would be just a matter of time before it gave up its valiant fight altogether under the weight of environmental disregard. We were talking (as best we could at the time), but when we turned around there was a huge mob standing right behind us. A crowd of locals, maybe 100 deep, had been drawn to see this strange white beast. It could have been intimidating but I figured this was more curiosity than anything threatening. Even so, we took no chances and JJ whisked me off before the mob could turn ugly. We nearly got married the following year and I actually gave her a ring, so maybe that means we are still engaged. Leaving her in China after more than two years together was heartbreaking for us both, but the pragmatist in me saw no viable future for us. The differences in experience, culture, age, language and virtually everything else would always be too great. Love does not conquer all, but I still feel sad thinking about her.

Next stop was the United Arab Emirates where I DJed for private parties and the occasional nightclub. Abu Dhabi was familiar, as I'd had a DJ tour of duty there a few years earlier. One of my best-ever DJ experiences had been on a packed Thursday night at the Safari Club at the Hilton Hotel around 1989. I had already built up a name for myself, and working in the city's premier club enhanced my draw. I'd occasionally pop outside the club and see a line of people queuing to get in; only a few would make it through the door. That exclusivity made me feel even more special. On that night the dance floor was pulsating and I was in absolute control of the crowd. Every track I picked worked like a charm, and I saw people's exhilaration peak to new levels with successive beats. I'd been playing house tracks most of the evening but I decided to toss in a classic Stevie Wonder number to really mix things up. (I think it was "Superstition" but it may have been "Master Blaster.") The effect was like pressing a button; it lifted the crowd even higher. As a DJ there is always an extra level of anticipation when trying something new or unusual, but seeing the first inkling of recognition—and then approval—of a new track from an already euphoric crowd is incredibly validating. In fact, the sense of power from controlling a packed dance floor is unique. In many ways I miss it, though I know that era has passed.

I had been away from Abu Dhabi for a few years and when I returned, the Safari Club had been redeveloped into a fun pub or fitness center or some other passionless entity. It was good to be back in the city again, especially as I still had friends there. Although the country was not completely westernized, I appreciated a greater level of creature comforts in the U.A.E. than those I had experienced weeks before in Guangzhou. Just as in China, there were pockets of extreme wealth, and that led to another unforgettable DJ experience—this time for one of the prominent sheikhs at an event on New Year's Eve. My DJ rig was set up on the penthouse roof of a skyscraper overlooking the sea, and there must have been more accumulated wealth in the wallets and pocketbooks of the VIP guests than in many a small country. I played for well over eight hours that night but I was high on emotion. When the sun came up over the Corniche I started to wind things down. With the morning call to prayer broadcast over loudspeakers across the city, I was playing a final track from Pink Floyd: "Keep Talking" from *The Division Bell*.

Around this time I was becoming less interested in dance music and more engrossed in alternative, indie types. I wanted to get out of clubs too, if only to see more daylight. I wondered if I would miss the buzz of the beats per minute but knew that I needed to evolve. One of my friends in Abu Dhabi worked on an English language radio station there and I'd occasionally go in and help out. I would select vinyl from the archives and suggest tracks to the other DJs. This was an exciting new direction and I really felt that radio was the way ahead for me. Through a friend of a friend I heard of a radio station in Hong Kong that was hiring, so I sent in my demo tape. It was a pretty optimistic pitch as I'd never even presented a radio program on my own at that time, but amazingly they wanted to know more. Even more amazingly, they hired me.

Moving back to Asia after a year in the U.A.E. was like returning home. Hong Kong felt right and the 12 years I lived there slipped by in a heartbeat. Radio also suited me well, and for most of those dozen years I presented a two-hour music program every weeknight. In the early years it started off being fairly pop, but I managed to slide in more alternative tracks as time passed and my following grew. I developed a reputation for playing cool music that few had heard of. I liked that accolade. I loved Hong Kong too, as it was the ideal blend of east meets west. It was clearly a very Chinese city but with obvious reminders of its colonial past. There were red mail boxes just like the ones in England. Walk into any of the pubs and there would be Brits working there, often working their way to fund the next sector of their global passage. Double-decker buses were normal and the street names were laced with British history; what could be more English than *Wellington Street*.

I bought an apartment in the New Territories that looked over the distant hills of the Chinese mainland, and even though public transport was excellent, I bought a car and shared it with a girlfriend at that time. First I had a rusting black Saab convertible (until it died in a typhoon on the highway driving home and I got drenched), and then a bright red Volkswagen Golf (also a convertible; I'd obviously not learned my lesson).

Times were good but there was something missing and I was yearning for the next step in my life. I wasn't sure what that stage would be. Something needed to change, or evolve, or maybe *I* needed to change or evolve. Even though I didn't know the specifics of what was lacking, I had a strong feeling where I might be able to find it. I was being pulled towards New York. I had stayed in the city for a few days en route to seeing Louise in Minneapolis in 1989, but this time I felt a different sort of attraction far beyond wanting to see the yellow taxi cabs and Empire State Building. Might this be my personal Utopia?

I tested the waters of a global move in 2005 when I lodged for three months in a friend's basement in Park Slope. That period cemented my fondness for the city. However, recognizing the desire to live here and actually making that happen were two different things. It took a further year to negotiate the convoluted United States visa process, but on January 31, 2007 I landed in New York to start my new life. Half a container of furniture and personal belongings followed behind me on a ship also destined for the New World: my new world.

Chapter 3

Brave New World

I t quickly became easy to feel at home here in New York. I've often wondered if the draw of this city was a perceived ease that I could be who I wanted to be—or the gender I was destined to be. Not that I had ever felt stifled living elsewhere, but was my latent feminine side calling me to the world's most famous cultural melting pot?

I had dabbled in cross-dressing when I lived in Hong Kong but I never dared leave my apartment dressed as anything other than a man. Hong Kong was not a city where the transgender community was understood, let alone welcomed. Not that I considered myself transgendered then. I don't know *why* I felt the need to occasionally don women's clothes at home, nor can I explain my urge to dress up or play around with make-up, but I did both, though not as an everyday occurrence. It wasn't for sexual kicks; I just felt good when I dressed up, there was no greater reason than that. However, moving to New York advanced this spark of interest in me. Dare I advance to the next stage and leave the house dressed as a woman? I wasn't quite sure why I wanted to do that either, but I did. Was there anywhere that might accept me dressed as a woman? Naturally, yes, New York City has a place for everyone.

I researched online and found a place on East 20th Street called the Silver Swan, now long gone. It was a restaurant and bar that claimed to have "the finest traditional German-American cuisine." I never ate there so I can't validate its culinary credentials, but its claim to fame from my perspective was that every Saturday night there was a party for the trans community. "Party" is probably overstating the event, however; it was the one day of the week when all were welcomed from within and outside the transgender spectrum. I knew I had to go there, but it took several weeks thinking about it before the allure grew strong enough for me to make that huge first step into this great unknown.

As I prepared to leave my apartment that night, I was filled with an abstract mix of panic, exhilaration, nerves and anticipation. Those sensations were still acute after a few shots of Dutch courage from the Swedish vodka bottle, but at least they were numbed slightly. I can't remember what I wore for this induction but it was probably too small and too tight. I know I felt incredibly self-conscious, especially as I had to wear high heels for the event—as all women wear heels 24/7, of course. I prayed that the shoe gods would smile and not mock me. It would be terrible if I tripped on the sidewalk and fell flat on my face. As I started the 15-minute walk of anxiety to the subway station my adrenalin was pumping. I put my earphones in and chose an album by Underworld to help blot out reality. I had also left late enough so that most people on my block would have turned in for the night; that way I wouldn't be seen by too many inquisitive eyes. In the gaps between music tracks the walk to the station was eerily quiet; all I could hear was my heels clacking on the sidewalk.

I got to the station and fumbled with my MetroCard and swiped it through the turnstile. I noticed the employee in the ticket cubicle look up at me, but then he promptly returned to reading his two day-old newspaper. That was a good sign at least; I wasn't *that* obtrusive. It seemed to take forever for the R train to arrive as I waited awkwardly on the platform. When it did, I found a vacant group of four seats at the end of the subway car where I tried to hide in plain sight. Once in Manhattan my nerves eased; the influence of the city's most famous borough seemed calming after the train had crossed under the East River. My walk from the 23rd Street subway station to the Silver Swan was easier—not just because I was getting used to wearing those heels in public. When I arrived I felt elated; I had done it! There was a $5 cover charge but that seemed like a ticket to refuge.

Inside, I remember feeling strangely at home. There was a main bar area which most people congregated around, and then an open area towards the back which was used for dancing, talking, and I suspected a little groping too. A DJ played music and I briefly wondered what tracks I would have played if I had been working there. I talked with a few people who looked like me, plus a few people who didn't. Maybe I wasn't so different after all.

The return home was less intimidating. There were fewer people on the subway at 3am, and those who were seemed too tired or drunk to notice the relieved person in the corner with the curly wig and deteriorating make-up. I was also empowered from the four or five glasses of wine I'd consumed. But my sense of achievement was palpable. I had made it into the city and back, by subway, as a woman, for the very first time! Examining the reasons *why* I wanted to do this could wait.

The Silver Swan became a regular Saturday night haunt for me after that. It was a haven from my male-centric reality. I sat at the bar and daintily sipped the house Merlot. I could express myself there, albeit in ways that I didn't quite understand. I was just a single lady sitting at the bar nursing a drink; it was liberating in its normalcy. Of course it was clear that I was not born a woman, but this was a place where that fact was overlooked—perhaps even welcomed. Over time I made friends there who I looked forward to seeing each weekend. I was among like minds and similarly caked-on make-up. However the place had its sad side, too. Some of the trans crowd needed to get blind drunk to forget their troubles. There were also the so-called "admirers"—a term out of the transgender dictionary that describes men who like, well, anyone from cross-dressers to transvestites, to drag queens, to full-fledged transsexual girls. I expect some of these guys were not sleazy, but most seemed to be. Transgender "working girls" were in attendance too: usually Asian, sickeningly skinny, but never for free. As most of the male admirers in attendance seemed cheaper than the dismally ordinary house Chardonnay (which was as indifferent as the Merlot), I assumed that pickings for the prostitutes were equally slim. At the end of the night the DJ always played tracks by Bebel Gilberto; that was the signal to head home. Those lazy Brazilian rhythms also gave me notice that my own female persona was nearly set to go back in the box—until the next weekend.

I didn't resent that I was only female for one evening each week, as it seemed the norm. It became my little secret from everyone else in my life. I developed a routine for these Saturday evenings. I tried to paint my nails before going out—I didn't want the stick-on type—but as I rarely left enough time to do this, they usually ended up blotchy. I still had my man haircut so I had to don a wig to prove my femininity to the world at large. Thankfully there is no shortage of wig shops in New York and so the choice of weave was almost endless. I chose a style that was long and curly, one I imagined my hair would actually look like if it were allowed years of unbridled freedom. Then, to mask the join between wig and head I usually added a hair band. It was a kind of Janis Joplin look. That combination didn't look so bad, but there had to be lashings of foundation on my face to hide any 10pm shadow. I did have one make-up lesson back in Hong Kong (a hint of the future, perhaps?) so I had some basic ideas of how best to apply the camouflage, but the results were, at best, mixed. I enjoyed doing my eyes but I could never get the shape of my lips right with the bright red lip liner. I made do with clip-on earrings too, as I'd not had my ears pierced by then.

My fashion style was evolving but often embarrassing. In those early days I had not appreciated that squeezing into clothes one size too small makes you look at least two sizes bigger. But with a padded bra, sparkly top, knee-length skirt, curly wig, and flawed make-up, I was able to socialize in my own little way at that one little venue. I remember studying myself in the mirror before I left my apartment each time, and although I felt I didn't look *too* bad, I wasn't sure *who* I saw.

Disaster struck when the Silver Swan closed. My ragtag crowd of cross-dressers, transvestites, and whatever other trans-people we were, became homeless. I wanted to try a semi-swanky champagne bar further down 20th Street called Flute that had apparently expressed openness for us to go and play there—just as long as we didn't cause a nuisance. So after a lot of anxious text-messaging, a few of us plucked up our courage and headed there. The prospect became more daunting as it had a velvet rope outside; if they didn't like the cut of your jib, you were not coming in. But it took on a far greater level of intimidation for us, as this meant crossing the threshold into a *normal* venue, a prospect I found as terrifying as it was alluring.

I shouldn't have worried as we were made welcome, and Flute soon became the new place I gravitated towards on weekends. Again I would sit at the bar, but this time the quality of Cabernet was far better than the indifferent Merlot at the Silver Swan. I talked to *real* people—just as anyone does in any bar—but I was embracing deeper self-confidence. I expect others saw me as the transvestite at the bar, yet that wasn't how I considered myself. I was being a woman.

This became a key period in my transition. I started to go out on weeknights as the bars I liked weren't as busy then and the midweek crowd was more accepting. I didn't rely on my friends from the Silver Swan for these outings into the real world, either. In fact I began to *avoid* the transgender crowd that had previously been my crutch. I didn't need them anymore, and to be seen with them was cramping my style. There is boundless bigotry and prejudice directed at the LGBT world, and my actions showed that I was capable of it too.

I had started to grow my hair, but it was not long enough to lose that bloody wig. My circle of friends was also growing. These were people who obviously knew what I was not, but as they had never known me beforehand, I found their friendships warmer. They made no comparisons between *me-past* and *me-present* and so I didn't have to live up to any expectations or recollections of who I was. Even though they might have considered me transgendered, I still hadn't reached that conclusion about myself. I was merely going out dressed as, behaving like, and mixing as a woman. The frequency of these occasions was definitely increasing, but I didn't feel I was in any sort of transition from male to female. Yet I could sense something deeper that was advancing, even though I couldn't identify what it was. I wasn't living the rest of the week in a dress, but equally I knew that I wasn't just *playing* at being a woman, either. In fact these nighttime escapades in female mode were not just something I *wanted* to do, they became something I *had* to do.

Chapter 4
Nicky

After I started going out in female mode I needed to adopt a female name. There was no point going out in my finest wig, heavy-duty liquid foundation, heels, and padded bra if I still answered to a male name. I learned that the hard way on my first outing to the Silver Swan.

"Hi, what's your name?"

"Neil."

"Um, that's not very feminine…"

No, it definitely wasn't. I needed to find one that was.

I'm not exactly sure why I chose Nicky as a name, but it just sort of happened that way. There had been times in the past when I was with an ex and we used to play around with alternative identities when out socially in Hong Kong, so it may have stemmed from there. However, it often happens that cross-dressers, transgender folk, and others with both male and female sides pick a new name that resonates with the old one. Most usually start with the same initial, too. Thus there are plenty of *Stephanies* who were erstwhile *Steves*, *Daniels* who became *Danielle*, and so on. It might retain a link to the past, or sometimes it's done for more practical reasons; using the same initial helps ease the issue of identity on credit cards and bank accounts.

I should clear up confusion over my own name at this juncture too. My full name is on the front of this book, Nicola Jane Chase. But my friends and family call me Nicky. In fact 'Nicky' happened before 'Nicola'. The more formal-sounding Nicola came about when I was developing a new Facebook page for my new self, and Nicky Chase didn't quite resonate with me. Nicola was smoother and more elegant. Although it's a common name in Britain, here in the United States Nicola is an unfamiliar name and so is usually pronounced like Nicole-ah. And that drives me crazy. It should be said in a pacey three-syllable manner and not as an elongated version of Nicole. So in daily life (as opposed to passports, bank accounts and book jackets) I answer to Nicky. It comes equipped with a "cky" at the end, but I will not throw a temper tantrum if I see myself misspelled.

Several months after adopting Nicola I realized a middle name might be useful, and something quintessentially English might be nice. That is where Jane came from. Back then I never anticipated that Nicola Jane Chase would become my legal name. She was just a persona. I don't think I was in denial, but I certainly hadn't appreciated that my female self was moving forward at such a rate of knots. Nicky was developing a definite alter-ego aside from her male origins, with a distinct personality of her own—my own, that is.

It always made me happy when I was out and about with my newfound circle of *normal* friends and they referred to me as Nicky. It was validating, endorsing of my persona. Of course they had nothing to compare it with, but it still felt good.

Changing names at any stage of your life is tricky, but throwing in a different gender as well adds an extra layer of complication. Not only do existing friends have to get used to calling you something different, but there is also a long period of time that your own brain needs to accept that this new name is, in fact, you. For your whole life you have answered to one name and this has suddenly changed. Titles and prefixes cause similar pitfalls. You drop something when out shopping and the person behind you says, "Excuse me sir" or "Excuse me ma'am." It took me years of transitioning before I stopped looking back when I heard "sir," even when it wasn't being directed at me.

Pronouns are even harder. We use the pronouns him and her without thinking, and so to switch gender pronouns takes a lot of practice for everyone—me included. In the early stages of my transition most people tried very hard to get it right. If they knew me before as a man and they actively thought about the pronoun process then they'd usually be fine. But the more relaxed my old friends felt around the new me, the more likely they were to inadvertently include the old pronoun in the conversation. I reluctantly accepted that as part of *their* transition. Conversely, the occasions when I heard the correct pronoun, especially from people I didn't know, gave me deep satisfaction. It still does.

I consider May 2010 as the chronological start to my female life. I didn't plan it that way and it just seemed like a normal progression of the direction in which my life was heading. The trigger, however, was my hair. Finally it had grown enough so that I could lose that bloody wig. Freedom! Yes, I know that many genetic women have short hair, but disguising one's own history takes many forms. The first time I went out without my fake hair was on one of my frequent trips to Asia. I went to a shopping mall in Bangkok, in a dress, with only my own hair. It felt like there was a flashing neon sign above my head: *"Alert! Transgender person out for the first time without wig!"* Surely everyone would stare at me. But they didn't. Obviously they knew. Or perhaps not. I realized then that most people usually have far more interesting things to wonder about than whether the person standing next to them on the escalator is a man or a woman. Even if they did ponder that question for a few seconds, they would quickly return to the more pressing issues of the day—like what would be for dinner.

Perhaps the anonymity of being in a foreign land helped bolster my bravado, but that occasion in Thailand was my day #1. It was a moment of equal significance to the time I'd gone to the Silver Swan for the first time, two years earlier. I was finding my feet as the woman I was growing into. And so to celebrate, I bought a pair of shoes.

It was incredibly liberating, yet within the excitement of walking around as a woman, in broad daylight, was a layer of nervousness that I might be *found out*. That sensation was mirrored by the bathroom question. I used the women's bathrooms but I felt slightly fraudulent in the process. The first few times were distinctly harrowing, but that emotion was balanced by the sheer satisfaction of making it into the sanctuary of the ladies' room unnoticed.

When I returned to New York a few days later I wanted to continue this female status. It just felt right. It became natural and normal and I rarely thought anything of it. I still didn't consider myself *trans-this* or *trans-that*, I was just being me. This outwardly new condition confused my landlords and amused my neighbors for a while, but my default setting became female and any dressing up times were when I needed to revert to being a man. Life had almost turned full circle.

That summer, my dear friend Daisy came visiting from Europe. I have known Daisy for years, since the time we lived in Hong Kong and were both underappreciated stars of radio. We started work at the same radio station around the same time, and our program shifts followed on from each other. We touched base every day, even if the connection was just on either side of a news bulletin at the top of the hour. Often we'd chat on air during her program and debate the merits of some *topic du jour* on opposite sides of the mixing desk. One time I remember arguing the point that as transparent bra straps were still visible, their *raison d'être* was inherently flawed. Daisy disagreed. Never did I contemplate that one day I would be the wearer of such straps, and that indeed, they do serve a purpose.

Whenever I arrived in the studio I would see her dancing around, her golden curly hair unwilling to be confined by the obligatory headphones. Daisy is one of the warmest, most affable people you can hear on the airwaves. She smiles when talking and I'm sure that contributes to her singular ability to make listeners feel that they are the only person she is talking to when they are tuned in on the other side of the radio. Our opinions differ on her biggest claim to fame, but in my mind her interview with the Scottish chart-topping band Wet Wet Wet at the height of their career was a highlight. She was at a press conference ahead of the band's concert in Hong Kong and lead singer Marti Pellow allegedly told her to fuck off, right in front of the collected media and press gang. I dream of having such sparkling credentials on my broadcast résumé.

When Daisy came to New York that summer I hadn't yet achieved the required comfort level to present myself to her as a woman. It was one thing to live my day-to-day life around the city in this manner, as I was relatively anonymous, but to show myself like that to someone who had known me as a man for many years was just too daunting. Consequently, for the few days of Daisy's visit I slipped back into male mode. That felt weird. I had gotten so used to being female, and Nicky. This strange, alien, yet incredibly familiar male person wasn't welcome in my life anymore. He made me uncomfortable. So over morning coffee in Astoria that Sunday (though I had tea) I told her all about Nicky. She was unsurprisingly surprised but was wonderfully supportive both then and ever since. However, one thing that Daisy suggested was that I get some help from a therapist. Not that I *needed* help of course; I was just being me, a woman.

Chapter 5
Healing the Mind, Patching the Soul

Therapy is the favored method of soul-searching for countless Americans—essential for Hollywood celebs, and required practice for many others. I, however, am British. My race is renowned for keeping our thoughts and feelings locked up, believing that if you bottle up your confused, misunderstood or frustrated emotions long enough, then they will go away. It is a ridiculous premise, but a role that we Brits excel at—along with playing the stereotypical butler on network TV or the ubiquitous villain in American movies. On the American west coast, the view of analysis veers to the other extreme. In Hollywood, if you feel that you don't need a therapist, then you should really discuss that with a therapist so you can understand exactly why you think you don't need one in the first place.

But Daisy had a point. Maybe I did need to talk my situation through with someone else who had seen this before—whatever *this* was. So I searched around online and I found a gender therapist called Navi who seemed well-versed in people of my genre, whatever genre *that* was. I made an appointment and went to see her the following week. I also made sure I looked my best for the session, a tradition which probably goes back to my childhood. My sister and I always used to dress nicely when we went to see the dentist. Never the doctor, but always the dentist. It seemed perfectly reasonable at the time, but now the reason for looking good in order to have a tooth pulled escapes me. For my first visit to see Navi, I went with smart casual. It was vital that I looked feminine, even though there was no prospect at all of losing a wisdom tooth during the 45-minute session. Equally it would be terrible if she perceived me as a man. How ludicrous that was. The logic of wanting to look overtly female in order to see a gender therapist was, at the very least, self-defeating. Navi's area of expertise is the mind, and not whether some particular shade of purple makes my ass look fat.

I wish I could remember the specifics of what we talked about during that initial session, but I can't. However she apparently saw something in me that warranted further discussion, and so suggested that she see me on a regular basis, which I agreed to. I do recall arriving with some built-in unwillingness to bare my soul, but that kind of self-protection diminished with each subsequent visit. It didn't take long before I felt the ability to be completely open about anything that came to mind when on Navi's couch.

The anonymity of therapy is a strange bedfellow to the intimacy of it. Navi knows all my deepest secrets, many of which I probably don't even realize myself, and I know next to nothing about her. I am guessing that she is in her 40s, but I could be a decade out. I am aware that she is Jewish, that part we discussed, but she doesn't keep a kosher kitchen (I needed that info prior to baking her cookies one time). I think she wears a wedding ring but I could be wrong. She might be gay, straight, or from Mars, but it simply doesn't matter. She is an expert on gender, and specializes in helping those of us with gender confusion; her own back story is immaterial. For each of our sessions she greeted me at the door of her office near Union Square and I plunked down on the couch. She sat in a pretty comfortable semi-reclining chair (of seemingly better quality than the couch) and we started talking. She occasionally sipped tea through the session, which probably put me even more at ease. (I assume it was tea, though it could have been neat vodka for all I know. I'm kidding Navi, don't worry.) Sometimes I had an agenda of things I wanted to discuss with her, at other times we just went with the flow.

Navi is quietly spoken yet always friendly, if a tad serious. To that end I occasionally dropped a funny quip into our dialogue to elicit one of her richly rewarding deep chuckles. No therapist should be a comic (though vice versa is acceptable) but over the years I have come to appreciate her dry sense of humor. Above all I value her level-headed demeanor which makes the process of self-exploration far easier for me. Navi must have bad days—we all do—but I can't imagine what form they would take. She seems too gentle a soul to curse at telemarketers or swear if she trips over a manhole cover.

Life is often simpler than we give it credit for. But throw in curve-ball transgender issues and things become more confusing. So I accept therapy—I *welcome* therapy—and have definitely experienced its benefits. I appreciated having someone to discuss my feelings and emotions with, along with situations that I'd never anticipated. However, I do have frugal roots and so am always aware that we are talking "on the clock." Maybe one day I will be able to have a conversation with Navi without the mental image of shifting dollars of sand falling through a virtual egg-timer.

One of the earliest memories I have as a child is having a creamy yellow security blanket. It was called "Dunc." Maybe even "Dunk"— I don't think the name was ever spelled out, and I have no idea why a security blanket needed a name anyway. These days I suppose Navi is my intermittent security blanket. Her name crops up with regularity throughout this book and I am blessed to have had her help as I tried to make sense of the Tetris puzzle within my mind.

Chapter 6

A Question of Identity

I was starting to feel pretty good about my feminine status until I was reminded that others didn't always share my newly rejuvenated gender perspective. I was in my local post office. It is a tiny office with just two counters (one of them usually closed), along with the usual peeling paint on the walls, a shambles of boxes, labels, and stickers, and a work ethic that moves in slow motion. But it is convenient, just a block away from my apartment, and I was genuinely relieved when it survived fiscal cutbacks. It was the second time I'd been there that morning, as I'd screwed up sending a package of documents to Hong Kong before later realizing that I had forgotten to sign them. So I had to go back, cap in hand, and beg the postal workers to dig the package out of their black hole of bureaucracy before it sank into the deepest abyss of deliverance. Unsurprisingly, the wheels of progress were grinding along at their normally unhurried state. So mailman #1 spoke to mailman #2 about the conundrum, huffed and puffed at the wretched inconvenience, and then pointed to me and said that fateful word.

"Him."

Not "that drop dead gorgeous woman yonder," or even "the customer," but "him."

I admit I wasn't looking particularly glam that day but I felt like a woman, and thought I looked like one too. Hearing "him" felt like a slap on the face. What had I done wrong? Why had my female attire and blotched eyeliner failed to sway public opinion? Although hurt, I justified this mishap down to assumed familiarity. I had been to the same post office many times over the years as a man, and had usually seen the same guys behind the counter, too. So they recognized me as a man. Although I felt blissfully different, to others, much of my core appearance remained. They saw me as... well, what did they see me as? A man in a skirt? That concept made me feel worse. Back home, I consoled myself with a large pot of PG Tips.

A few days later, the question of identity hit me in a different way. There had been a change of legislation in New York. Consumers could now choose alternative energy suppliers to power their apartments, even though the electricity itself was still delivered down the same wires. I had often thought about trying to save a few bucks by switching to another source but had never been motivated enough. So whenever there was cold calling at my doorstep to try to persuade me to switch providers I just politely refused. However this day was different. I was about to say no to the latest person using the latest argument for using another electricity company but I had a change of heart. It was a drizzly, dreary day and the guy doing the selling was looking bedraggled. I figured he was a poor student trying to earn a few bucks for college, so the least I could do was to hear him out before saying no and slamming the door in his face. He was representing a green energy company that generated power solely from renewable sources. His argument seemed more equitable than just a bottom line and I found myself tempted by the greener option. As he had been a really civilized fellow who had patiently explained everything to me, in the rain, on my doorstep, I said yes. He started filling out the form using my latest utility bill from ConEd—which was still listed under my male name.

"I see the account is registered to Neil Chase," he noted.

"Yes," I confirmed, not quite wanting to explain the intricacies of it all.

"So you are the wife?"

Now that did take me by surprise. The slightly sexist slant to the question amused me, but put me in a quandary as how best to answer it. I paused momentarily.

"Yes, that's right." It seemed the simplest way to answer his question!

And that was that. He went away happy with a new account under his belt, and I developed a growing sense of satisfaction knowing that my lights would be powered by the wind. I suppose now, in the eyes of my electricity provider, I was married to myself. I didn't remember that ceremony. I wondered what I wore or what the cake was like.

These two events highlighted the conflict of recognition I was feeling. One person clearly saw me as a woman, the other did not. This raised another question that I hadn't anticipated: how much should I expect to be recognized? Unless you are an ax murderer or tax accountant, I'm guessing that most people like to be recognized. But in shedding my old skin did I want my past friends to recognize me when they saw version 2.0, or should I expect them to be blown away by such natural beauty that they didn't see the connection between old and new? I remember the satisfaction I felt the day my friend Gillian walked straight past me in a blissful state of nonrecognition when we had arranged to meet up for afternoon tea one day. She had known me *before*—that is, in my days as a man. She certainly didn't recognize me this time, the first occasion we were to meet with me in female mode. That felt good, and it seemed a positive step that someone who knew me in my past life failed to notice me in my current one.

The following week I went out to dinner with my dear Long Island friends Jon and Dill, in my recently reincarnated form. We get together every couple of months and take it in turns whether I head out east or they schlep into Queens. We eat, drink, and talk, and we've always gotten along like a house on fire. They used to own a company that supplied music to radio stations around the world, which was how I got to know them. That radio connection meant they knew me as the man I was, not the woman I had become. I'd told them of my change via email and—in common with everyone else—they had reacted with surprise, but with support too.

As I took the Long Island Railroad out to Floral Park for our scheduled get-together, the first as Nicky, I nervously mused that this was going to be another test of how others view my change. Although my inner evolution was gaining momentum, recognition stems from outer appearances. I was still viewing my newly-invigorated world from the same eyes out, while others saw something different in me. Or did they? When Jon collected me from the train station, I wasn't sure whether to be pleased or disappointed when he recognized me from afar as I walked down the steps towards his car.

"We weren't quite sure how to react," he said later, over salmon, brie, and copious glasses of red wine. "You're our first."

Their first transgender experience that is, and I was flying the flag for my adopted clan. In fact, they reacted better than I had expected, with Dill giving me a huge hug and then complementing me on my hair, nail color and shoes. Jon was a little more reserved and it took us a couple more dinners before he felt comfortable enough to give me a peck on the cheek. I tried to imagine it from their perspective; what does a woman who used to be a man look like? At that point I also decided that some protocol would be a good idea for when a familiar friend meets me for a renewed first time. I told people that there was no need for furtive glances. Please, get it over with, stare if you want—though few ever did.

With my own growing acceptance of self, and the frequency of meeting old friends as the new me increased, this became less of a concern. There was an occasional reference to my old name, or a wrong pronoun appeared, but these slip-ups I could tolerate. However, there was a bigger picture which I contemplated: to what extent did they truly consider me a woman? That tended to need time to mature; it wasn't an instant switch of gender recognition. Now, one of the most satisfying compliments I can get from an old friend is: "I can't remember how you were before. It seems like you've always been Nicky."

Chapter 7

Adam's Apple and the Burning Bush

My new life as Nicky was continuing apace. More friends were being brought into the gender loop and I was becoming increasingly confident as I walked around my neighborhood or to the subway station. I was shopping exclusively as a woman, and the balance of clothes in my wardrobe was shifting exponentially towards the female. However, since I'd not gone through female puberty, picking age-appropriate styles that weren't too trashy was a steep learning curve. Naturally there were bad decisions with skirts that were too short, or eye-popping tops beyond skimpy, but that was all part of finding my own style niche.

Although some transgender women don't strive for femininity, for me it was always top priority. The more I *felt* female, the further I wanted to *appear* that way, and part of that process was hair removal. Even back when I used to wear man-clothes I'd occasionally get my legs waxed, only to suffer pangs of guilt as this wasn't a process that men *did*. But I loved having smooth legs; they felt so good! Once I started living the female life this smoothness became legitimized. Over several years I invested in countless laser and IPL (Intense Pulsed Light) sessions that covered larger areas of real estate like arms, legs, and those pesky areas between waist and thighs. Each occasion was horribly painful and numbingly expensive. The comparison often used to describe the sensation of laser treatment is of a rubber band being snapped against the skin. For me it felt like a boatload of rubber bands simultaneously snapped for each zapping. I kept hearing the "no pain, no gain" expression in my head, and thinking that this extreme gain had better be worth it.

Thank goodness (or my parents' genes) I was never excessively hairy. How dreadful it would have been to have had a hairy back— surely one of the cruelest jokes that Mother Nature can play on the male of the species. I can only imagine the conversation when scripting the book of Genesis.

God: *"Whoa, slow down there Adam. Eat that apple and you'll get a hairy back."*

Man: *"That wouldn't be so bad would it? Besides, just think what Eve could do with such a delectable orchard fruit—baked, stewed, or just raw. It's all good."*

God: *"Up to you mate, but it's your choice between baked apple for dessert and some men looking like mountain gorillas for the rest of time."*

Man: *"Um, does the apple come with custard?"*

And so the deal was done and the fate of man-hair was sealed. Over custard.

I have been blessed in meeting some really wonderful health and hair experts, but have met some pretty dodgy ones too. Flick through any of the free papers around town and you'll see an endless array of ads for "permanent hair removal." I must have tried most of those places over the years, from ones verging on swanky, to others that seemed to be run by the Russian beauty mafia, with ice-cold receptionists to boot. Eventually I found the wonderful Chrissy, a sweet Filipina with whom I got on really well. So over the span of a year or two, every six weeks I had a laser-zapping with her. The results were large swathes of hair-free skin, which made me feel distinctly prettier.

There was one appointment I remember with great fondness. That day Chrissy was zapping around my genitals with her laser machine (and disarming gusto) when a question came to her about what my end point might be. She held up the tip of my penis with her latex glove and asked me in her finest accented Philippines English: "Are you going to take this out?"

Huh? Take it out? On a date? Me and my penis going on a fine-dining date together? A curious concept, but who picks up the bill? Then the penny dropped and of course this was simply my misinterpretation of language. She meant was I going to have SRS or not.

"Oh, I don't know," I replied. "I really haven't decided."

Even so, I still like the idea of going on a date with my genitals. Cheers and bon appétit!

While laser or IPL hair removal is good on some skin and on various body parts, it is rarely a good idea to do this on your face. The process can actually embolden the hair follicles that you are hoping to eradicate. Nevertheless, I went the fast, easy route and had multiple sessions on my face. Perhaps as a result, many pesky facial hairs seemed to develop a second life. Consequently there is only one permanent solution: electrolysis. This entails having a needle stuck into your skin while radio frequency waves, heat, or electric current is emitted causing the hair follicle to give up its will to live.

Kiki was my go-to person for electrolysis. I'd done considerable Internet research and she had received glowing reviews from the trans-community for accepting us as we are—which is all any of us ask. In fact, we got along so well that a few months later I started working for her as a part-time receptionist. Unfortunately electrolysis is a painfully slow process, as every hair needs to be treated individually. The "rubber band snap" I felt from laser treatment was intense and immediate yet with a vagueness of location, but I found electrolysis to be longer and drawn out, with pinpoint accuracy when it came to pain. In the later days when I was Kiki's receptionist, some clients would tell me how they almost slept through treatment sessions. This was such an alien concept to me that I wondered how desensitized they must have been in other areas of life. Would they have just said *"oh shucks"* if they stubbed their toe against a chair, or hit their thumb with a hammer? Four-letter expletives do it for me.

Chrissy had raised the question of a dinner date with my genitals, and although that made me consider my own endgame, I never dwelled on it too much. All I wanted was to continue the life as the woman I seemed to be, without overthinking where it might be taking me.

Chapter 8

In Visible Hong Kong

The times when I had to present myself as a male were becoming rarer. It stopped being strange clasping a padded bra in the morning, or wearing a skirt to go supermarket shopping. Even using female restrooms became the norm, something I'd previously thought would be a hurdle. My social life was strong, with past friends embracing the new me and new friends accepting me as a woman—albeit a transgender woman. There were still ugly instances when I was called names when walking down the street, or heard sniggers when riding the subway, but I had an enhanced confidence that helped numb that negativity. I was embracing New York with a brighter perspective, but might this outlook change when away from my adopted home? How would it be to visit other places that I had only known as a man? I was due for another trip to Asia, and so this would be a good test. I can't say this was entirely for business, though for accounting purposes, or if the IRS is curious, it most certainly was.

After living in Hong Kong for 12 years, Asia is coagulated in my blood. Maybe the frequent infusions of dim sum helped—especially as they were usually accompanied by lashings of green tea served in classic white Hong Kong teapots which never poured straight and always dripped from the spout.

It was wonderful to be in Hong Kong again, even just for a few days, especially as I was going to have a further few days in Bangkok. Stepping off the plane at Hong Kong International Airport made me feel at home, although experiencing *terra firma* anywhere after 15 hours in the air is welcome. The airport opened in 1998 and has all the bells and whistles of any custom-built modern airport, but it lacks the soul and excitement of the old airport at Kai Tak. That was renowned by locals, international travelers, and air crews alike as one of the most exciting airports to fly into. Planes flew so close to the rooftops of Kowloon on the final approach that you expected drying laundry to be accumulated on the wing tips after landing. There was also the unique late banking turn that pilots had to make in order to complete the landing. I remember talking to pilots at that time (back in the days when you could often visit the flight deck on request) and I would see their eyes light up when they thought of the more demanding approach that required some actual *flying* to be done, rather than just engaging the auto-pilot to place the jet on some anonymous landing strip.

I was living in Hong Kong in June 1997, the time of the handover back to China. That was a singular moment in history, and as such, raised many questions about how to mark the unique occasion. Beyond the politics of the event, was it a time to celebrate or one for collective mourning? In the end, many Hong Kong people chose the same resolution as they do at Halloween, Christmas, New Year, or most other calendar events: celebrate with a party! The authorities meanwhile did what they always do at key events—they had a fireworks display in Victoria Harbor. That led to a ridiculous competition of size and stature. The outgoing British-influenced regime organized a fireworks display on the closing evening of their reign, but then the incoming Mainland regime wanted an even bigger display the following night, once they were in power. Which was going to be the best display and who had the biggest rocket? It was like boys trying to be men while standing at the urinal. My resounding memories of that time, however, are of the rain. It rained for 40 days and 40 nights—or so it seemed. Former HK Governor Chris Patten sailed off on the Royal Yacht Britannia the night of June 30, 1997, but it really could have been an ark.

When I lived in Hong Kong I was in radio. I was a DJ, or as I'd prefer to call myself, a *radio presenter*. For more than a decade I presented a daily two-hour radio program on the main English channel of Radio Television Honk Kong (RTHK). I filled it with offbeat music that I felt passionate about, and although I had a following, I can't claim to have been famous. Even so, it was always gratifying to be called up for quotes by the main newspaper in the city or be asked to be a judge at 'Battle of the Bands' contests. I loved my job, as I lived for music.

The radio station was run as a branch of the HK government, and thus by overpaid, underworked civil servants. Radio is a marvelous medium that has the potential to be far more creative than TV, but when notionally managed by those who prefer the status quo to any change (lest change offend anyone) it doesn't make for a hotbed of originality zinging through the airwaves. On the flip side, it was a station that didn't have to pander to the whims of advertisers, which released it from the straightjacket of ratings. Sadly, promotion was an unfamiliar notion and to this day there must be thousands of people in Hong Kong who are completely unaware of a radio station there, broadcasting mostly in English, which produces some noteworthy programs.

Thankfully my long-term freelance association with RTHK allowed me to relocate to the United States in 2007. They sponsored my media visa which at least got me into New York. I made radio programs for the station from my home studio in Queens. I recorded numerous interviews with characters from the fabric of the five boroughs, but after budgets started tightening, I focused back on my love and my specialty: music. That was initially fine, but the more I embraced myself as Nicky (and female) the trickier it became. I was broadcasting as a man, and under my male name. I justified this concession as I was still broadcasting from home, so I didn't have to present to the outside world as a man. I could still feel and look female, just as long as I temporarily sounded and behaved like someone else. In a way, I considered myself an actress. At least I was an actress who had work. That was the bottom line: my radio persona was a financial necessity.

On this trip back to Hong Kong I needed to touch base with my radio overlords and that meant showing up as a man. I also wondered if this visit might be a gender finale for me; I couldn't remain outwardly male for much longer. I took the 13A minibus from Kowloon Tong up to Broadcast Drive and walked through the gates of Broadcast House again, just like I had done every day when I had been based there. Nothing had changed, apart from me. The building was probably chic in the 60s when it was built, but the concrete façade looks very dated now. I passed the huge banyan tree in the forecourt that had been reduced to half its full size following a battering from Typhoon York in 1999. Its stoic resistance to outside elements mirrored life inside the building, too.

Everything was so familiar and it was good to see people I had known well in my past. I suppose they were still workmates, though my status of working remotely from New York made that status less tangible. They asked me about life in the United States and I regaled them with tales, conveniently omitting the detail that I now viewed the place with female eyes.

That Saturday evening I presented my usual two-hour music program, just as I would have done from New York. However this time it wasn't pre-recorded but presented live from studio C1A in Kowloon Tong. It was good to return there, actually, and it brought happy memories of the many years I had broadcast from the same studio. Everything looked the same. The room still seemed disproportionately large for a radio studio and the same huge double glazed window separated this room from the production studio next door. People passed through that studio as they prepared their own features and programs for broadcast; some seemed familiar, others were new faces. There was the familiar gray tweed swivel chair which always squeaked, the exact same out-of-date posters in the studio, and the same shelves near the turntables and Studer tape players that hadn't seen a clean in years. Few presenters used the tape machines or played vinyl as the studio was now mostly digital, with music played off hard drives. Even CDs, which had seemed so modern a decade earlier, were being spurned. I still liked to play CDs when I could, not just as a rebellious throwback to the past but also because many of the rarer tracks I played were not available any other way. I smiled as I thought back to previous generations of broadcasters, working from the same studio, who must have thought the same about vinyl as I did about CDs.

As I had not worked there for a long time, that dusty familiarity was actually reassuring. I sat in front of the oversized mixing desk and absorbed the moment. There's a different sort of quiet in a radio studio, not just an absence of sound. Of course they are soundproofed, but it always felt to me that the quiet was almost tangible, like an invisible cushion. As the clock ticked (silently) to 6:10pm and the news bulletin finished, I opened the same microphone for the first time in years. I was nervous, but it was exhilarating and the buzz that I always got from live radio returned. I talked about life in New York and praised the bands that I had seen in concert; Richard Hawley at the Bowery Ballroom was incredible, and Springsteen at Madison Square Garden was an amazing experience too. It felt natural as I went off on musical tangents, or when unexpected memories sprang to mind. Live radio imbues the presenter with a unique edginess to whatever is said as the mind accesses recesses that are rarely plumbed—something that a pre-recorded program can never have. I'm sure the brain shifts to a different gear as fingers flick across the faders.

Not wanting to lose track of my adopted city, all the music I played that night was from NY artists or bands. There was the odd regional concession to New Jersey, and I kept my self-imposed "from NY" definition loose enough to include those who were from the state, not just the city, along with those—like me—who were not born there but had made it their home. The National ("Fake Empire"), Nada Surf ("See These Bones"), Rachael Sage ("Vertigo"), Brazilian Girls ("Good Time"), and Fountains Of Wayne ("Hey Julie") all got played, along with some vintage tracks from Television, Blondie, Public Enemy, Ramones, and Mink DeVille.

The two hours flew past and for that time, gender became unimportant. I forgot that I was doing all this in man-mode. It was good to be around creativity again, too. When I work from home in Queens there is no one to bounce ideas off, but in that building there are many people producing various programs in a multitude of ways, and in different languages. Just walking along the corridor past each studio, I could hear English, Cantonese, and Mandarin being spoken, along with music of every dialect too. I'd kind of missed that.

I joined my colleague Jack for a glass of wine at a local bar after we had both finished. Jack is one of those larger than life characters who will probably never exist again. He is the consummate Lothario who has banged and shagged his way through most of Hong Kong—and the rest of Asia too, I expect. He is the first to admit his 'dirty old man' status, but still manages to seduce wanton girls 40 years his junior. Jack was in Hong Kong in the early 70s when just being British in the colony was enough of a criterion to get you a job, regardless of qualifications. Jack's résumé is remarkable. He has been held at gunpoint, been featured in countless movies as the token Caucasian, and was taught by the best *mamasans* in the business. He claims to have lost count of the number of girls he has experienced on the horizontal (though it allegedly runs into four figures), and I doubt it was purely when horizontal, either.

But for all his history, faults and indiscretions, Jack remains one of the most amicable guys around. His shaggy locks and lean physique defy his age. His charismatic smile and twinkle of eye are quite beguiling too, features that I wondered if I was starting to appreciate from a new perspective. It is likely that Jack will keep on doing what he does until either his libido wanes or his penis drops off. However, talking to him did make me wonder why I was never the same. Of course not all men have a desire to copulate with everything that moves, but why hadn't I wanted to weave the same web of seduction back in the day? Wasn't my role as an erstwhile male of the species to have sex with women? The more I pondered that conundrum the less I could remember about the last time that happened, or even *who* it was with. It had certainly been several years, and selective recall enhanced that shade of amnesia. I was never the man that others are, and after the conversation with Jack, I felt more grateful than ever for that.

The following evening I headed out on the town. As every expatriate living in Hong Kong knows, the area of the city called Lan Kwai Fong is Party Central. Dozens of raucous sports bars are squeezed into an area half the size of a city block, and those who visit are drowned in enough alcohol to sink the whole of China. For the newbie white man in Asia it also sums up why this place can seem like Xanadu. Imagine the scenario: it is your first assignment out of Blighty, the kangaroo continent or Yankee-Doodle land, and this tight square block of bars has free-flowing booze till the early hours, combined with enough free-flowing wannabe girlfriends to keep you awake till tomorrow morning as well. It is a playpen of debauchery for the expatriate lawyers and bankers who make up most of the suit and tie population.

It has also been the starting point for many a divorce case. You've brought your Caucasian trouble-and-strife wife along with you as part of your remuneration package, but even though you got on well enough together back home, upon stepping foot on Asian soil you are surrounded by a vision of the exotic. Gaggles of giggling Chinese babes a decade your junior. Skinny-thin, dreamily doe-eyed, and all with an eye for the western catch of the day. Not an STD in this case, but that can happen too. What newly transplanted executive wouldn't be hypnotized by the sensual, beguiling, and Oriental world of Suzy Wong? What many of these ex-pat execs didn't realize was that to dip their toes in the local Chinese dating pool meant Prada was the minimum requirement at Christmas, and if you don't shell out for at least two dozen red roses on Valentine's Day, then you certainly won't be getting your weekly hump in the sack. Nothing comes cheap in Hong Kong (except McDonalds, but that doesn't count) and so the legacy of that first Asian romance can screw up many years of financial planning. Thousands of bewildered *gweilos* have fallen into that Venus flytrap of lust at the first hurdle. Many of them even find the exotic happiness they'd envisioned; the wives who came with them, not so much.

For me, retuning to Lan Kwai Fong in skirt and heels was going to be a curious experiment. I would be re-living familiarity, yet in a different gender. I wondered if I would experience what my white female friends had complained about before: as a white woman in Asia, you don't get noticed. So how invisible was *I* going to be? By default I knew I was way down the pecking order in the female desirability chart as I wasn't Asian; that is an inescapable fact of life in Hong Kong. This hardly mattered as I wasn't particularly attracted to men anyway. Even so, as the evening progressed I started to resent being imperceptible within the bowl of wantonness. It was about being seen as desirable by men; the invitation is what I craved, not the follow-through. In New York I welcomed the admiring glance, but here my looks counted for nothing. I was the wrong color, size, and shape for the Hong Kong market. I wasn't even last year's model, simply the unattractive one. The gluttonous scenes of bacchanalia all around irked me even more. I didn't like that party zone as a male, and I liked it even less as a female. I called it an early night.

The grimy proletariat that occupied Lan Kwai Fong hadn't inspired me, but maybe the upmarket hotel bars would. So the next evening I visited a swanky hotel bar in my glittering cocktail dress hoping for a different outcome. In my fantasy world I imagined sitting at a swanky bar in my stylish *cheongsam*, getting chatted up by numerous guys, and not paying a cent for drinks. In actuality I remained invisible there too, and picked up the check myself. But why did I want to flaunt my femininity in such a way? Did I see it as a challenge, a hope to contradict the principle of pale rejection that my *gwaimui* girlfriends had told me about? I should have known such expectations were unrealistic. The only solace that evening was the rhubarb martini served up at the Mandarin Oriental, which was as sumptuous as the view over Victoria Harbor was stunning.

Two days later I continued my journey to Bangkok.

Chapter 9

One Night in Bangkok

(It was actually 5 nights)

I never saw the *Chess* stage show, but the 1984 track featured on it was pure Eurocheese. Murray Head's musical picture of "One Night In Bangkok" did little to show this incredible metropolis at its best. It is a crazy, frantic, vibrant Asian city filled with incredible contrasts, where the smells of hypnotic green curries boil on the street, mingling with the wafting odors of sewage floating a few feet below.

There are many great things about the City of Angels, and I find myself deeply happy each time I visit. From the truly warm welcome that any visitor receives at any of the hotels to the cornucopia of products sold at the countless night markets, Bangkok is like a second home to me. In fact, I feel so at ease in Thailand I wonder if I was Thai in a past life—or will be in a future one.

Another fascinating aspect of Thailand, and Bangkok in particular, is that *kathoeys* are far more accepted within society. I hate the term *ladyboy*, as it feels both condescending and demeaning, but yes, that is what we are talking about. These are natal men who are, to a greater or lesser extent, women. Often referred to as the *third gender* they command an acceptance that is rarely present in other countries. Many are stunning in their beauty, but end up in the sex trade either to make ends meet or fund sex-change operations. It is equally depressing for many young genetic girls in Thailand too. The hideous prostitution trade here soaks up far too many souls. Some choose the oldest profession for themselves, but others get caught up in pimping scams or are even sold into the slave trade by their own relatives. The extremes of poverty pitted against easier money for sex is an unholy alliance. Buying into this darkness is something that every fun-seeking foreign male should weigh deeply on his conscience before heading out to the girly bars of Patpong.

This remarkable acceptance of transgenderism in Thailand made me question the issue further. Why does this country seem to have more transgender or gender-questioning people than any other? Is it the prevailing tolerance that makes it easier for latent trans people to be themselves, or is there is something deeper in Thailand's society or environment that actually *creates* a higher percentage of transgender women? I can't claim to know the answer, just as I don't know the *why* or the *how* of being transgendered myself. I just am.

This visit to Bangkok was going to be different. I was here for the first time as a Western crossover version of the Thai *kathoey*. That gave me a lot more latitude and freedom of expression. Whether or not I was clocked as such seemed less relevant. The linguistic differences in Thai also help demonstrate how you want to be seen. As a female, you end many sentences with a polite and very attractive *"kah"* sound. Men meanwhile use the rather less attractive *"kap."* So something as simple

52

as the way you end a sentence denotes to the listener what gender you are. I appreciated that absence of ambiguity even more.

Another great thing about this city is its diversity. There are humble noodle carts on the street where you can eat for just cents, while fancy high-end restaurants will charge more for Pad Thai than the servers by the noodle carts will earn in a week. One of the most opulent rooftop bars in Bangkok is the aptly named Vertigo at the Banyan Tree Hotel. On a clear day the views are stunning (above the pollution), and so what better place to try out my slinky cocktail dress again. I might not attract swarms of buzzing men (not that I had any idea what I'd do with them if I did), but I felt less social pressure in Bangkok than I did in Hong Kong. A cocktail or three at a rooftop bar seemed the ideal place to contemplate life.

I'd not been there for a couple of years but the view I remembered was still amazing, and the light breeze and perfect temperature 61 stories up made for a dreamy time. The dusty hubbub at street level was a world away from the white tablecloths and uniformed bar staff on top of the world. It hardly mattered that I was surrounded by couples, and whatever singles there were had little interest in the *farang* woman sitting alone at the bar. I wasn't looking for company this time and simply wanted to toast my gender liberation with a blissful libation.

I stayed until last orders around 1am, but on the taxi trip back to the hotel I was propositioned by the driver. Not in an improper way, but he suggested that I drop by another club. Of course he'd get a commission from taking me there, but this seemed a good plan. I was high from Vertigo and didn't want the evening to end. Besides I'd not heard some banging beats for a while and so a club vibe could be fun.

Club Bossy was the rank opposite of the opulence of the Banyan Tree rooftop. Here two floors of disappointing techno provided a backdrop for a panorama of hedonism. Smoke and sex curdled together, as the predominantly working girl crowd eyed up every man as a potential meal ticket. I wasn't wearing cut-off shorts trimmed up to my navel, nor sporting the latest in fake Dior string T-shirts, as seemed to be the uniform *de rigueur* for Bangkok ladies of the night. My heels were appropriate, my make-up understated, and in many ways I felt comfortingly immune in that house of predominantly ill repute. Besides, no white man in his right mind would go to that club in Bangkok looking to seduce a *farang* woman. Even so there were times I was approached by men with obvious lecherous intent. I was unsure how I felt about that. But as alcohol in the venue was notoriously cheap, the lustful advances I encountered were mostly from men barely sober enough to remain upright. The sweaty, drunk Dutch guy was a prime example. His optimal chat-up approach was a hairy arm wrapped around my shoulders, followed by breathing alcohol fumes in my ear so toxic to be a fire hazard.

I should have walked away there and then but I didn't. Sweaty Dutch guy started getting more physical. The principle of being groped as a measure of deemed attractiveness is beyond distasteful, I knew that, yet I tolerated it. Part of me even enjoyed it. I was curious to see how this experiment in the human condition could pan out. I was suddenly an object of desire (albeit by a drunken slob) and this was a new sensation for me. I had embraced my femininity as a woman, but in my past life I was attracted to women, not men. I put this nagging query about my new life on the mental back burner while I dealt with the Flying Dutchman. He groped, I squirmed, and when I didn't immediately drop my resistance at the promise of everlasting lust he went off looking for an easier option. I was admittedly three or four martinis worse off, but I'd kept up my guard. All the time his hands were wandering, I managed to keep the area between my waist and my thighs firmly pushed against the bar in a grope-free zone. Had I slipped up and he had discovered my Garden of Eden was more Adam than Eve, what would have been his reaction? Anger, embarrassment, a drunken punch? I have heard horrific tales of western men turning on Thai *kathoeys* when the truth was uncovered. This was an experiment in human behavior that I was stupid to pursue; my reckless trust had been downright foolish.

While many visitors to Bangkok are focused on frequenting the innumerable girlie bars of the city, I was always drawn to Bed. That's with a capital B and this amazing club was one of the best places for music in this city. Sadly no more, but then it was fresh (if a shade cliquish) and the high door prices kept out many of the working girls. It was Saturday night, two days after the Club Bossy debacle, and I really wanted to hit the dance floor and strut my funky stuff, sho'nuff.

As I was getting dressed, I recalled the era of my past life as a club DJ. That seemed like another person's lifetime away. I had ceased that club existence as I found the music increasingly dull and the radio world more appealing, but my rebirth as Nicky freed my spirit and returned me to the female youth I never had. I was inexorably drawn to clubbing again; this time as a girl. So going to Bed was ideal.

I really wanted to look my best for the occasion. Consequently there was a lot of pouting in front of the mirror when I applied the heavier than usual club make-up beforehand, and a true spring in my step when I left the hotel wearing my fave Express mini-dress and black 4-inch pumps. I was blistering with confidence. This was going to be far better than being the unseen girl in Hong Kong, or the subject of gross lechery at Club Bossy. This was going to be my night!

The club was a design masterpiece. Situated between the polluted canals and the crowded side streets it looked like a giant white space-age tube that had been left by Martians. It was incongruous in the extreme but also a structure of sheer beauty. You would walk up a long, inviting ramp, perhaps hoping for your own close encounter of whatever kind. Enter that club and you were in another universe. A continuous white sofa stretched on each side from one end of the main room to the other. There were two stories, and modelesque staff (naturally in white also) climbed ladders to serve food and drinks at the higher level. Ambient beats drifted over impeccably plated foie gras. I had eaten there once a few years before and the food had been as lavish as the surroundings. This time it was later in the evening, when the international DJs came out to play, and I had come solely for the music.

When I walked up the ramp and into Bed that evening, I felt like a million dollars. I found a spot at the end of the bar and equipped myself with a perfectly mixed peach martini. As the night progressed I soaked up the rhythms as I danced, and danced, and danced. The house anthems synced with my über-liberated self. I was the chick with vibe and attitude and I really did wave my hands in the air like I just didn't care. I was on fire! People wanted to be seen and be photographed with me. But wait... was this for being the cute 'n crazy dancing *farang* woman, or the misguided man in a dress? Those insecurities were never far below the surface but that evening they were forgotten as I was high on emotion. Someone who I'd been dancing with for the last hour passed me a line of white powder so I could take it into the bathroom and snort. I felt embarrassed to say "could someone give me a hand as I've never done it before." So Charlie and I became acquainted for the first and only time in my life. In hindsight it was the stupidest thing imaginable to accept drugs from a stranger in a club but this was a complete zinger of a night and I never wanted it to stop. I sprawled out on the white sofa like a tigress, sipping $20 cocktails, and feeling like a latter-day Queen of Siam.

It was one of the best days of my life, but it had to end. Somehow I managed to take a taxi back to my hotel, but even when I hit the pillow at 5am or 6am or whatever time it was, I couldn't sleep. The club demon that I had rarely embraced in my past life had come back to entice me. I had danced with the devil, and I loved it. Aptly, by then it was Halloween morning.

Chapter 10
Continental Switch

I left bangkok 48 hours later, after five days of being completely Nicky. It was the first time that I had been a broad abroad and completely living the female life. By the hotel pool one afternoon I also managed the unimaginable: my first bikini moment. It may not be comparable with manned space flight, round the world single-handed yachting, or discovering penicillin, but it was still a big deal for me. Those two strips of fabric barely cover the essentials while they accentuate all the flaws in between. Cosmopolitan gives us tips on how to be 'bikini ready' for the beach, but how many of us ever can be? For the transgendered woman it is even tougher. I had found a possibly passable little number in one of the Bangkok night markets but it was still an intimidating prospect actually wearing it by the pool. But it was the day after the Bed experience and my confidence remained sky high as the beats and rhythms dissipated in my head. I slipped it on in the hotel room and looked at myself in the mirror.

There was a Lycra skirt included as part of the bikini bottom and that managed to hide unwelcome bumps. My top half was not very curvy but the string bikini seemed to be quite flattering even so.

I walked down to the pool with a sarong wrapped around my waist and found a lounger just a few feet from the water. I unpeeled that wrap and nervously lay down, first on my front, and then with increasing confidence, on my back. The sun was baking and I needed to take a swim. Although I had to be very aware of where everything was positioned as I dipped in and out of the water, I managed the feat without undue embarrassment. For that blissful first time, I was the bikini babe by the pool. I loved it.

I am always sad to leave Thailand, but those five days had been the best yet—almost mythical in terms of my expansive enjoyment. The actual process of travel required far more practicality. For all my painted nails and increasingly shaggy locks my passport still stated 'M' and so I had to travel in broadly male mode. How broad that guise needed to be was debatable. Might my scarlet nails raise red flags to immigration officers, or could that simply classed as free spirit? And would it be a crime to travel in a skirt? Edgy pop stars and fashion models do, so shouldn't I be able to as well?

I discussed this conundrum with my photographer friend Phoebe before I left Bangkok. Phoebe is within the invaluable small circle of friends I have around the world who met me initially as a guy but our shared friendship as two women is far stronger. Phoebe and I had gone out for dinner that first time after connecting up from a local Craigslist posting on one of my past visits. In fact it was she who had introduced me to the Vertigo rooftop bar at the Banyan Tree Hotel. But just like most other times I'd tried going on a date with a woman, something was missing, or a part of me was holding back. Perhaps that makes more sense now. In the case of Phoebe, our embryonic male/female relationship was stillborn and didn't stand a chance, yet our connection since has been able to grow into a far stronger female/female friendship. It's a pleasure to see her whenever I return to Thailand.

As for the traveling poser, Phoebe's sentiment was that I should try pushing the boundaries a little more. So our consensus was *"nail polish OK, skirt probably not."* However, that raised some practical dilemmas. I wanted to leave the hotel in female mode but I knew that I couldn't be too feminine at airport check-in. The obvious solution was to use a toilet at the airport as a changing room: go in female, come out slightly less so. But to come out of a female toilet looking like a man might also have gotten me in trouble—and probably no better vice versa. So in a maneuver that would have made Superman proud (not that I remember him wearing skirts), I accomplished the gender switch during the 15-minute ride on the airport express train—which was conveniently larger than a phone booth too. I swapped my top with a T-shirt, removed my bra, and replaced my skirt with jeans. Heels away, sneakers on.

The record-breaking costume change at 70 miles per hour amused me, but then depression struck. I didn't like that I looked like a man again. Or had to behave like one, or use male phraseology in Thai. It seemed utterly out of place that I now had to adopt some sort of man persona. This was an out of synch U-turn from the natural state of female happiness that had prevailed over the previous days. Before I would have tried to hide my nail polish on the plane home, but this time I wanted to show it off. A display of defiance, or perhaps a cry from the heart.

The two and a half hours to Hong Kong, then subsequent sixteen to New York, dragged. As I sipped watery airplane tea I thought back to the boundaries I had discussed with Phoebe and how I could shift them forward. If I could establish better guidelines on what airlines and immigration authorities deemed gender definition, then future trips might lead to less internal conflict. I needed to check on the criteria from the horse's mouth.

It took me a long while to fully acknowledge that I am a transgender person, and at the time of this trip there were parts of that definition that I found hard to accept. I knew that when I was in female mode, everything was right in the world, but when that was taken away, my outlook was less bright. Yet still I felt strange calling myself *transgendered*. However to answer questions that I had about the practicalities of future travel, I would need to describe myself in that way to someone in authority.

Airport immigration officials are rarely blessed with a sense of humor (perhaps that's one of the job requirements) and regardless of gender complications, I routinely have a nervous edge when heading back into the United States through immigration lines laced with paranoia. After disembarking at JFK airport I made my way through the snaking line of edginess and migrated towards the next available counter at Immigration. Then it was my turn. I waited for the right moment. After the officer had gone through the rudimentary questions of what my work was, who I did it for, and how long I was staying, I took the plunge.

"I'm a transgender person," I said, following up that statement with questions on how my evolving appearance might affect the ease of passing through Immigration. The question was not even met with a raised eyebrow, and I'm not even sure if the official looked me in the eye when delivering the answer. The essence of his answer was that as long as the name and fingerprints matched, and the passport and visa were current of course, then the rest should be fine. Although that didn't give me carte blanche to jet around the world wearing a boob-tube and mini-skirt, I felt this clarification gave me a shade more latitude. It was also a landmark moment for me as this was the first time I had described myself aloud as "transgender." It was quite cathartic. Maybe I shouldn't have been so apprehensive about the scarlet nails after all. Next time I'd try eyeliner.

Chapter 11
A Hiccup in the Vocabulary

Reality can be such a downer. After two weeks in Asia, New York seemed terribly mundane. Not that this city is dull at any time, but I simply wanted to remain in vacation mode. It was mid-November and the city was on the cusp of transitioning into winter. To make matters worse, I got sick.

It's not that I don't value doctors, it's just that I'm always afraid that I'm wasting their time. Unless my leg is falling off from gangrene, I try to let my body cure itself. I suppose I only seek healthcare when the Grim Reaper has one foot jammed in the door. This theory is supported living in the United States, as most reasonable healthcare options are unreasonably out of my financial grasp. Growing up in the UK there was the National Health Service, which was largely free. Although that model is derided by many, free access to healthcare for all is surely the mark of a civilized society.

Healthcare is not a business and should never be run as that model; it is a societal necessity for any country not lingering in the Dark Ages.

After a good two weeks of hacking up a lung or two (occasionally it felt like three), the time was right to seek a second opinion. The bubonic plague had been such a hit in Europe during the Middle Ages, so perhaps it was making a comeback. As I didn't have health insurance I followed up a lead from Navi on the LGBT health clinic in Chelsea, Callen-Lorde, that offered treatment rates structured on the ability to pay. I was apprehensive about filling in the preliminary paperwork as I sat in the clinic's waiting area. This was a first visit and so I had to present proof of income, and legal documents of name and gender. That last qualifier made me the most uncomfortable. I felt female, but my documents said male. I know the "T" in LGBT should have given me reassurance that my situation was not unique, but I was still uneasy. Besides, when we are unwell, our souls are more exposed. I had already leapt over the officialdom barrier by announcing my transgender news to the immigration officer at JFK on my return to the United States, yet this was set to be a whole more personal affair. I would be talking to a real doctor about real health issues, and it was a good bet that possibly, just possibly, things transgender might be raised too.

Dr. Rose was surely born to be a doctor. She has such a relaxed attitude and calm demeanor that when I met her that first time, I felt I could tell her my life story. In fact, I probably did. On a subsequent visit I found out that she also has some British roots, so we were able to chat about English-ey things like PG Tips tea and Cadbury's chocolate and toasted crumpets. One time she even opened up to me about losing her mother, and that made us both cry. However, for this initial visit we discussed the sinuses and lungs and mucus of the moment, and ways to banish the marauding infections from the secondhand temple that is my body. She also put my mind at rest: no, I didn't have a case of bubonic plague. In the course of talking transgender matters I also brought up a possible Next Big Thing: hormone therapy.

I was already aware that many transgender women (and men) will take an appropriate hormone regimen to help closer align their mind and body, but I had never put any timetable on when that next stage might be right for me. I wasn't even sure if it should happen at all. I certainly didn't see hormones as a prerequisite to continuing living my life in full-time female mode, which I had been doing for quite some time already. Dr. Rose agreed, as she went through some of the pros and cons of hormone treatment. I was already aware of what this might do from a physical perspective (help the body shift from the less welcome masculine appearance to a perceptively more feminine one) but I had also gathered that there could be mental repercussions. Again, Dr. Rose patiently explained these downsides too. The concept of hormone therapy became alluring, but I wanted to mull over this possible action a lot more before I started a process that, in some ways, would be irrevocable. For that to happen, it would be a good idea if I could confirm to myself that I was indeed a transgender woman. As crazy as that seems now, and even though I had just declared myself as such to Immigration, I still had doubts. I couldn't see myself living as any other gender, but did that make me transgendered or had I just got caught up in the giddy excitement of ordering from the Victoria's Secret catalogue?

No. Each time I ran through those arguments and played my own devil's advocate, I always returned to one basic foundation: my sense of happiness, a feeling of something being *right*. Therapist Navi often refers to the term *authentic* and says that trans people usually feel more authentic in their acquired gender. However, that remains a hard emotion to substantiate.

It took a while, even with help from Dr. Rose's Medicine Show, but I did get better. The lungs that I had been hacking up miraculously grew back, and I started to feel normal again. But I needed to maintain my health better. I'd been vegetarian for several years already, but I still had to remind myself to eat more green veggies and ease up on making (and consuming) rhubarb crumbles for dessert. I figured I should update my vitamins and supplements too, so I visited the apothecary aisle at Whole Foods. Since living in the United States I have to remember to call vitamins *"vie-tah-mins"* as opposed to the quicker European way, which oftentimes won't be understood. It is the same for zebra. I once referred to a *"zeb-bra"* in a store (when trying to buy a print dress, as opposed to something that should be roaming the African savanna), and was met with blank stares. It needs to be pronounced *"zee-bra"* in American. Anyway, I wanted help finding the right multivitamin and so I asked the *team member*. (And that's another thing. When did it become socially demeaning to be an *assistant*? Do *assistants* really feel more sense of belonging to a store by being called *team members*? Maybe they do, but I was always happy to be an assistant when I worked in retail. However, my biggest bugbear these days is why we are now called *guests* within stores? Many stores insist that their *team members* ask for the next *guest* to come to the register, as opposed to the next *customer*. I'm not going to feel more communally bonded to the store just because you call me a guest! I am not going to stay there overnight, or have tea with you! I am not your *guest*, I am a *customer*, damn it! And don't even get me started on when used cars suddenly became more desirably and euphemistically re-christened as *pre-owned*.)

So I was in Whole Foods, in the *vie-tah-min* aisle, and I asked for help.

"You want the female one, right?"

I paused both mentally and physically. I felt reassured that he saw me as a woman, but I hadn't considered that part of my transition would involve purchasing the pink label vitamins. In fact, the team member in question was both friendly and empirically cute, and had a charming twinkle of eye. Unfortunately, like so many attractive men in New York City, I got the impression that he played for the other team. Such a shame, as I felt he would have been right up my shopping aisle. Wait... if that were the case, then it meant that I like men. That confused me again. I remembered the men of lecherous intent in Club Bossy in Bangkok, and other times when I definitely desired male attention, but I put that down to a confidence booster in order to prove my femininity. This was striking at another chord.

I paid for my vitamins and also left the store with an affirmed case of femininity. However, whenever confidence rises, always be prepared for the rug to be deftly pulled from under you.

I was at a club in Brooklyn. I wouldn't have considered this an entertainment option a year before, but my after-hours Asian experiences had bolstered my nocturnal self-belief. The Brooklyn event was in a warehouse dressed up to be a gallery. It should have been trendy but I couldn't see it that way. The crowd was ordinary (plaid shirts in a club, really?) and the house tracks were equally dreary. I'd dressed up for the occasion, but most people had dressed down or not bothered to change at all. They didn't seem to be enjoying themselves either, but maybe that was just Williamsburg cool.

I struck up a conversation with a Japanese girl called Suki who was there with a couple of gay friends. When she disappeared to the bar I chatted with the boys.

"You should get to know Suki," said gayman #1. "She's adorable."

I concurred, yes she was.

"Oh, and she loves trannies," added gayman #2.

And there it was: the T-word. Unleashed, exposed, and being directed at me. It felt like a right hook to my conscious self. The expression didn't seem to be spoken with malice by the gay men, but to them I was still *The Tranny*, with all the associations that went along with it. My heart sank; was I that transparent? Until that point I had considered myself quietly incognito, mixing within the female crowd, but no. I'd been made. It was the nomenclature that upset me the most. I was called a tranny by members of a discriminated group that really should have known better. Or did I overreact?

Trans people hold varying attitudes to the most obliquely offensive T-word, but I've never been comfortable with it. No, I hate it. It is an insult to who I am, and a term that can never be used in a positive manner. In the past I had I equated the T-word with the N-word, that it is OK to call *yourself* by that term but it is not a privilege that others get to call you. Now I feel that is just as wrong. I left the club soon afterwards. The music sucked, and by then I had a bad taste in my vocabulary.

Chapter 12

A Lonely Conversation

Ann chase is 80-something and the most amazing woman I know. Maybe everyone thinks that of their mothers, but I certainly do. She is nothing if not complex, however: open-minded yet set in her ways, feisty and fiercely independent. In addition to being partially deaf she also suffers horribly from tinnitus. She is gracefully gray, walks with a stoop (and a stick), and seems to shrink each time I see her. Yet still she swims 25 lengths of the local swimming pool twice per week. Mum lives in the UK and so we don't get to meet up as much as either of us would like, but we are constantly in touch. She is old, yes, but a fan of email and if I don't answer her mails promptly, then I'll get told off. Most people get on with her like a house on fire and appreciate the playful sparkle in her eye; others can feel intimidated by her directness of manner. She was widowed in her late 30s and never remarried.

I also have a sister, Sue, six years my senior, and Mum raised us both virtually single-handedly. Although we remain a close family, my sister and I have drifted apart over the years and I don't always meet up with her when I am back in Britain. However, the bond I have with my mother has always been strong and the thought of keeping a secret from her—especially one as singularly important as my gender reconfiguration—made me feel very uncomfortable. I had contemplated not telling her at all, but that was simply impractical; I had to let her into my world. Christmas 2010 was when that happened; I made a reluctant but essential trip back to England.

Up to this point she knew nothing of the woman I was becoming and like me, she wouldn't have picked up on any clues when I was growing up. I had played with train sets, brought girlfriends home, and often performed my own car maintenance. But gender is far more complex than toys and stereotypes. How on earth would she react when her beloved son suddenly became some unexpected kind-of daughter? How would any octogenarian process that sort of information?

My learning curve of self-acceptance had been drawn over a period of years, but when I tell someone from my past, their perception of me changes. In a way, it has to. It needn't be unfavorable but hearing those few words means that they have to reevaluate the person who used to be me. The announcement is normally greeted with surprise, and then, usually, with some measure of support. After that they tend to go away and gestate the facts a little more before advising me of further acceptance and bestowing a deeper level of blessing. However, there can be other questions that arise, ones which aren't always vocalized.

"What changed in you?"

"How did you become this way?"

"Maybe this is just a phase you are going through."

These sentiments are most likely to be raised by the people who know you the best. Family members share at least some of your DNA, have invested in your life, and that closeness of identity makes gender fluidity harder to accept.

I've shared almost everything with my mother over the years, asked her advice, and been there in times of need for her too. It would have been straightforward to ask, *"Hey Mum, how would you feel if I bought a new Mini Cooper,"* but there was no easy lead-in to the news I needed to break. It wasn't counsel that I was seeking, and in an instant, her perceptions of my long-established self would change. It's not like I could simply say, *"I'm thinking of becoming transgendered, what do you think?"*

Prior to making that trip I explored a number of options in therapy; what would be the least worst way to shatter Mum's world? Navi suggested a gradual process. So initially I told Mum that I was "doing therapy" but didn't add any further details. Then, before I left New York for England I advanced to Phase II and emailed her that I had a "gender situation—not sex, not sexuality, but gender" to discuss with her.

I had a brighter spring in my step as I walked onto the plane at JFK, even though those steps were taken wearing male footwear. (That was a downside of this trip; I had to revert to a male presence throughout.) I tried to think positively and hoped Mum might see a new happiness in me; perhaps that emotion could help her embrace who I was becoming. I knew her response would never be anything like *"Great, you're a woman now!"* but I didn't think it was going to be as bad as it turned out to be.

As I walked up the driveway, my past was right in front of me. Since 1977 Mum has lived in a beautiful 19th century sandstone house that feels like it is in the middle of nowhere, but civilization is still around, subtly, on all four sides. There is even a supermarket next door; trees in between hide its modernity. The house itself looks just like one a child would draw with wax crayons in kindergarten; one large window on each side of the front door, mirrored upstairs but with a smaller middle window where the door would be. There is a simple slate roof with a chimney stack at each end. A grassy lawn in front and colorful borders of plants around the edges complete the chocolate box appearance. It is located on a slight hill, just as most Crayola designs would suggest, and from the house there are magnificent views over the River Dee and to the Welsh hills beyond. I've seen pictures taken over many decades, and the images of immaculately dressed families having tea parties on the lawn in the 1930s further endorse a captivating sense of history. Nobody truly *owns* that house; we are all just temporary custodians.

My sister wouldn't be around for this visit, but that allowed me to focus on the required dialogue with Mum. It would be a conversation to change everything. I cast any possible fallout to the back of my mind as I welcomed the familiarity of history rather than the uncertainty of a new future. It was an unusually cold December, and as I glanced over the garden, most of it seemed to be sleeping for the winter; whatever colors remained were mostly monochrome. I continued my walk towards the back door. I could even see some smoke coming out of the chimney, which meant a fire was lit in the hearth; I really looked forward to warming my hands there. Chimney smoke is not as dramatic nowadays as local regulations require "low-emission" fuel to be burned, but in defiance of local bureaucracy, Mum often burns logs on the fire too. Their wispier smoke emits an imperfect quaintness out of the chimney, and they crackle much more on the hearth.

I opened the old pine door and walked into the kitchen, just as I had done countless times in the past. It was wonderful seeing Mum again, and she was just as I remembered her from a year or two before. (I am in denial of her age as much as I am my own.) We had a big hug, and over an essential cup of tea, chatted about the flight, and the weather, and how we both were.

Christmases in that house were always special. Mum doesn't decorate the place as much as she did when I was young, though many of my childhood memories were evident all around. A set of three gold trees that my sister had fashioned from cake boxes decades earlier was back on the mantelpiece; some strands of tinsel draped over the old clock gave those hands a festive spirit too. It had only been a couple of years before when we said a sad farewell to a snowman I built in kindergarten from cotton wool stuck on a yogurt container. The relentless progression of time had taken its toll on poor Snowy. In the box of Christmas tree decorations that Mum keeps in the cellar, there might still be a cardboard blackbird adorned with glitter that I made around the same time. In the years when I worked in the department store, I often came home on dark winter evenings and was greeted by the smell of hot mince pies just out of the oven, occasionally accompanied by the sound of festive carols on the radio. These days the Christmas tree is artificial, but there were still dozens of Christmas cards stuck on the doors and around the dining room that Mum had received, just like in all the previous years. I quietly reminisced about the friendly ghosts of Christmas past, but the spirit of Christmas future needed to be addressed.

I put off the event for a day or two, but my advance email regarding "not sex, not sexuality, but gender" had piqued her attention and she wanted to have 'The Conversation,' even if she didn't know what it was going to be about. I had no idea what she was expecting to hear and I don't think she did either. So one afternoon after lunch, with tea in front of us (PG Tips for me, Earl Grey for her), we sat down together in the dining room to talk. I pulled a chair over to sit opposite her so that I could look her straight in the eyes. Before I did, I gazed out the window for a moment, over the Dee Estuary and towards the snow-capped hills beyond. It was a cold, crisp day but warm and cozy indoors. That would soon change.

I took a very deep breath as I looked back at Mum.

Although I hadn't prepared a speech, I knew the essence of what I needed to deliver. I started off by saying that I'd been aware of my feminine side for a few years, and how, more recently, I had been expressing it. That turned into the bigger revelation that my everyday life was now spent in female mode. I went to work, to the movies, and shopped as a woman. This had become my normal routine. Friends had been understanding and supportive, and my life was feeling pretty good again. I told her how happy I was as a result and how it felt right for me. I had found a wonderful therapist who was helping me through something that I didn't fully understand myself, and a great doctor as well. I didn't want to go into too many details too soon; this wasn't the time to go into the science or theory of transgenderism. I don't know how long this monologue lasted but the tea in front of us grew cold. With each disclosure I felt release, as if a skin blister had been burst and the truth serum was now leaking out.

Mum had been listening intently, and I could see that she had absorbed what I said, even though it hadn't made sense to her. She paused for an instant that seemed like hours before she started to ask questions.

"Have you got breasts?"

"No."

"So you are changing gender?"

"Well, the term is transgender. I mean I feel that this is the way I am... Who I am... What I am."

"Well, these days many men and women look the same anyway—long hair on men, and women with skinny figures."

"Yes, that's true."

"Do you wear skirts?"

"Yes."

"Did you bring clothes with you?"

"I did bring a change of clothes yes—just in case."

"Do you wear make-up?"

"Yes."

"I don't think I want to see you wearing make-up."

"That's understandable."

"Many girls don't wear make-up these days anyway."

"Yes, true."

It had been fairly straightforward up until that point: a speech followed by a brief Q&A. But then the floodgates opened; she wept openly and couldn't stop. The cautious optimism I'd felt leaving New York now seemed foolhardy. Of course I had been naïve to think she could have any other reaction upon being presented with all this news all at once. I had bequeathed an ugly orphan on my mother's doorstep, hoping she could be taken in, but Mum couldn't identify with Olivia Twist. There was a blight in her being able to see me in any way female, and my brightness of spirit was clearly lost on her. The mental relief I had hoped for didn't materialize. Instead, I started blaming myself for what I had just done. This was all my fault; I had hurt the most precious person in my life. We were both in pain yet unable to comfort each other. An aching sadness overwhelmed me as I walked upstairs and lay on my bed. I too cried. I felt that nothing would ever be the same again.

"It's just such a waste," she'd said, "such a terrible waste."

Christmas Day came as a welcome respite. We subconsciously called an emotional truce, even if it was only peace on earth for a single day.

We managed to laugh about my childhood, and memories of all the fun things we'd done as a family over the years. How she never allowed us to hang decorations around the house until school had closed for the holidays. Or the fun times opening Christmas stockings, or the paroxysms of excitement I'd feel on Christmas Eve, seeing all the presents nestling under the tree. Beneath the wrapping paper one time there was a beautiful green locomotive for my train set, another occasion revealed a breathtaking steam-powered traction engine. But by Boxing Day that year, we had run out of fuel for it and, as the shops were closed, had to resort to using brandy to fire it up instead. That was the best Christmas ever.

The days passed and we struggled to find the happiness we knew before 'The Conversation.' There wasn't much joy to the world. We sidetracked the preoccupation of gender by reading or watching TV. One morning we reorganized the crockery cabinet, which we managed to achieve without bloodshed—something that probably surprised us both. Occasionally I attempted to explain my transgender perspective further and Mum would tentatively ask me questions, but we failed to find much common ground. These were raw, unappealing seeds of understanding which were going to be hard to germinate. A lingering disquiet prevailed, and however hard I tried to bite my tongue we'd occasionally slip into heated arguments about nothing in particular, and not even matters transgender. Things were just brittle between us and her mind was prickling with the shock that she couldn't absorb.

On the day I left we hugged awkwardly one last time before I walked down the driveway towards a waiting taxi which would take me to the airport. I wondered if I would ever return. My mother was bereaved; the son she knew had died.

Chapter 13
End of an Era

It wasn't just Mum that I had to deliver the gender revelation to that Christmas. Biker Bob has known me since school days, and we have rejoiced with many drinking binges over the years. I shouldn't say *binges*, but there have been nights over the last three decades when we imbibed more alcohol than was clinically advisable. It started back in the day when I hadn't even reached legal drinking age but we still went clubbing together. That was the post-Saturday Night Fever era when fat ties and polyester suits were flash—or so we considered them. He is a few inches taller than me and so a three-piece suit worked especially well on him. He had a biker look that made him stand out from the crowd. He preferred rock venues but he accepted that nightclubs where disco was played were more likely to involve available women. As I found Chic far more alluring than Motorhead, this suited me just fine. We'd usually head to a club in Chester called Tiffany's on a Thursday evening, a couple of hours after we'd completed the other musical ritual of the day: watching the British institution, "Top of the Pops" on TV. It was the early 80s and so the New Romantic movement was in force and synthesizer tracks were all over the charts. Soft Cell, OMD and Depeche Mode were at their height, but were being challenged in the charts by edgier styles from The Jam, Simple Minds and The Stranglers. It was a period of music like no other, and British music in particular. Mainstream American disco tracks from Kool & The Gang, Donna Summer, and Earth, Wind & Fire didn't chart as highly, but I'd always hope that they'd be shown on the program too, even if singers did lip sync along, as was usually the case with all artists that performed on that show.

Thursdays at Tiffany's found a far more accepting crowd (and less critical door staff) than when the glittery crowd attended on the weekend. The top floor was generally funkier with plenty of mirrors and sparkly dresses, while the ground floor and mezzanine were based around a massive, prefabricated plastic tree. This floor was more pop-centric. There were Space Invader machines at one side of the room so if it was a quiet night or if we got bored ogling the available women, we could waste time and money destroying electronic asteroids. It was all so hi-tech.

Bob remained my confidante over many years, long after Tiffany's was demolished to make room for a soulless apartment block. When I was considering quitting my stable retail management job for the uncertain life of a global jet-setting club DJ, he was supportive. He was around when I nearly married my mainland Chinese girlfriend, JJ, and was sympathetic when I sadly decided not to. When I quit Hong Kong and upped sticks to move to New York, he approved. He'd always been around, if not in person then via email. Biker Bob is the alpha male type and I've always considered him one of the people who knew me best. Even so, bringing up the issue of being inwardly female was not something I was looking forward to. We arranged to meet at a local pub; I went dressed as a man.

In the early days, our poison of choice was Bacardi rum, but over time we switched to vodka mixers, and then bottles of red wine. Regardless of the alcohol variety, the presence of it usually made our dialogue easier. The more it flowed, the more the conversation gushed. Of course it was good to see him again and the few years apart hadn't quelled our friendship. We were both older, but part of us remained the seventeen-year-olds that we were when we first started clubbing. His long black hair had put up little resistance to gray infusions and his drop-handlebar moustache seemed to have gotten longer. I think he had added a further Viking tattoo on his biceps (not that I understood the words underneath) but he was wearing the same old black leather jacket with the tassels off each arm that I always picture him in.

This time he was telling me of his ongoing Civil Service woes along with the pride of having a growing teenager, both of which I was interested to hear about even though I couldn't relate to either. All evening I was waiting to find a suitable time for the *"oh and by the way I'm transgender"* announcement, but I knew there wasn't going to be any perfect moment for that. It was getting late, past the time for last orders at the bar, and I still hadn't told him. Having reached the dregs of the red wine bottle, and as we were now at an optimum state of mental lubrication, there would be no better time. We started to walk home.

"Bob, I'm working through a transgender situation," I announced.

"Yes, well I'm not surprised," was the almost immediate response.

This answer stunned me. His stiff upper lip of not letting anything faze him is one of his trademarks, but even this news seemed to have been received far more smoothly than I had anticipated.

"So this is this not a shocker to you?"

"Well, I had my suspicions after you stopped telling me of your dating situations. I wouldn't pry, but it all adds up."

I was still flabbergasted at this ease of acceptance.

"And when you got both ears pierced, that was a big signpost too."

I mulled on this a bit more.

"Well, I certainly have some wonderful earrings now!"

We laughed some more but didn't talk about it further. Instead we continued our walk up Heswall's main street, just as we had always done in the past. We parted, and agreed to meet up again before I left England some days later. That had gone unexpectedly well; I had obviously stressed too much over this revelation.

The following day Biker Bob emailed me with a tirade. These were misunderstandings, bordering on abuse. His email was far removed from the friendly tone that had existed when we had parted the evening before. Having slept on it (or *not* been able to sleep, as he told me) it was clear that he had not taken the news with the good humor that I'd felt. He talked of me being swayed by a lunatic clique in New York, big bucks "mutilation," and being "pumped full of hormones." His was an intrinsic sense of disbelief.

"After all these years you've been hetero and enjoyed life. So what happened?"

I couldn't explain that either. His sentiment was that if I had still been living in the UK then I wouldn't be transgendered. It was obviously New York that had led me astray; otherwise he could have saved me from falling into this pit of femininity. Naturally (*unnaturally* as he said) it was something in the air, the water, or the company I kept.

It was a tough email to receive, and an even harder one to digest and diagnose. The thought of losing one of my longest-standing friends was more than saddening. I could understand his confusion at hearing this life-changing news but was I really a different person now? Was he right in thinking that my transgender self could have been restrained if I hadn't moved to the United States? Surely that wouldn't have been a good thing, even if it were true.

We had a further exchange of emails, though I felt my argument was already a lost cause. Once Bob has made his mind up, that course is set and the future is entrenched. When we met again a few days later I knew it was going to be difficult. Our defenses were up, the conversation was uncomfortable, and I felt awkward. I was drinking wine in a pub with one of my closest friends, dressed as a man, while trying to explain how I was actually a woman. We parted that night with a firm handshake but I knew our friendship had changed irrevocably.

Over the next few years we sent each other occasional emails and exchanged cards at birthdays and Christmas but a threshold had been crossed. He wouldn't discuss anything about my femininity and his only concession to my status was to refer to me as "N," as opposed to Nicky. I was hoping that our friendship would win through but our communication gradually waned. Eventually a final communiqué arrived. It was an email announcing that he wanted no further contact with me.

I have not seen Biker Bob since.

Chapter 14

Grace and Femininity

My time in Britain had been a *Christmas horribilis*. By contrast, New Year's was spent in New England and ended up being a joyous relief. I had returned to New York but my dear friend Grace had invited me (actually, I may have invited myself) to Providence, Rhode Island to spend New Year's there with her and her man. Grace is another from within my precious circle of friends who knew me in my male days but knows me better now. We had once even gone out on a date, man and woman, but surprise surprise, it didn't work out. I think we both sensed a mutual friendship and connection, but there was no relationship chemistry. Her unwavering support is another of the rocks on which my transition has been built. We are similar in many ways, though my blonde tresses have yet to catch up with her long auburn hair. We are of comparable height, we both love 80s disco tracks, and our shoe sizes are not too different either. But apart from a shared affinity for wearing boots, shoe swaps would never happen. I was still working through my feminine shoe puberty stage at the time. Grace had realized many years before that four-inch pumps are not practical for everyday wear; such heel sobriety had yet to dawn on me.

Grace never tells me what to do, but is always there for me if I need an alternative opinion. She is staunchly organic, though, and will review my refrigerator for offending foodstuffs whenever she visits. We are on the same page in that respect, but if she is due to visit I will double-check the contents of my fridge, just in case. She became involved in my feminine side a couple of years earlier, a time when cross-dressing had become vital for me but before Nicky was fully fledged and before I knew where I was heading with my gender. Back then I only ventured out on weekends and occasional weeknights. I had also just moved into a new apartment (as a man) and was showing Grace around. Even though my refrigerator contents were all green, I had not stowed away all the trappings of my part-time gender association when I displayed my closet space.

"Oh, you have a wig!" Grace exclaimed.

I fumbled for words and couldn't find any. So I took the easier (if more long-winded) option and filled her in on my then alter-ego. Ever since that wig discovery, our connection became even stronger.

I avoid going out on New Year's Eve. One of my DJ friends once called it 'amateur night' and that sentiment still rings true. Apart from the highlight occasion when I was the DJ for the Arab sheikh in Abu Dhabi, most other times when I worked that night were awful. I'd do it for the money, never the kudos. Fat, drunk buffoons would insult my musical judgment and ask whether I could "play anything good" (are you kidding, Curtis Mayfield's "Move on Up" is a true classic!) or if I had something that their "wife can dance to." (My assumption, therefore, was that aforementioned spouse was either too drunk to ask for this herself or lacked all notion of rhythm. So, no, she was a lost cause.) I know I am critical of other DJs' playlists, but I feel I have every right to be and will always make a point to congratulate someone on their technique or musical selection if I feel it is warranted. Besides, these days technology allows everyone to be a DJ, though very few actually achieve that. Bars are counted in time, and beats per minute come from experience not software programs. As a consequence of these bad memories, New Year's Eve is one night of the year when I am perfectly happy to be the homespun hermit. However, the thought of a house party with dear friends and a few days out of the city sounded like a good way to start a new year. It could also be a way to move beyond the ordeals of Christmas.

Snow storms and flight delays frustrated my return to New York from Britain. I had scant time to organize myself before taking the train to Providence, but there were some non-negotiable essentials to attend to first: a manicure was required and an eyebrow threading session was vital. Reasserting my own femininity was crucial after ten days of questioning and being questioned. Never was the pain of having my eyebrows threaded such a blissful relief.

Once in Providence there was just enough time to glam up before heading out to the house party Grace had been invited to. Perhaps I had overcompensated in bringing two strapless cocktail dresses to choose from while others relied on jeans and T-shirts to celebrate the moment, but I really, *really* needed to feel pretty. There was a splash too much makeup, the heels were an inch beyond sensible, but I felt like a woman again. That reassurance was far more comfortable than the boned structure of the dress I'd chosen, but it was glorious discomfort. For once I didn't care that the music at the party was predictably hopeless, that many of the people were in their own cliques, or even that the DJ got the time wrong at midnight; I was among accepting friends again.

I returned to New York City a few days later, but memories of that strained British Christmas lingered. I needed further endorsement of my feminine self. Reinforcement sometimes took the form of shoe purchases, but I also required something more enduring and without a rubber sole. The answer was photographs! My friend Daisy had suggested this a few months earlier. A few nice pictures might be a good way to feel better about myself, and who knows, maybe I could even look a tad sexy.

I trawled through Craigslist and found a Manhattan-based photographer called Elise. She had a helpful website, good price, and seemed understanding of my needs. She also suggested I get my make-up done prior to the shoot. Excellent idea! I'd been looking for a good excuse to get a professional makeover for a while. So having booked a spot at MAC for the make-up and fine-tuned my outfits to a mere five, I headed off to see Elise.

Her apartment on the Upper West Side doubled as a studio. That is a very acceptable norm in New York, where few self-employed people can afford an apartment *and* a workplace or studio. The biggest inconvenience stemmed from a particularly bouncy terrier that seemed to consider himself her assistant. Even after we'd decided that he would be better locked in the kitchen, the legacy of stray hairs and dubious aromas made me nervous whenever I changed outfits and left a dress over the arm of the sofa.

It ended up being a wonderful experience and I felt very special. Even with the tight limitations of a Manhattan apartment, Elise made the most of creative lighting, appealing windows, and my obvious enthusiasm. I enjoyed being seen by a critical photographic eye and loved the "turn this way" or "look into the camera, Nicky" requests. It wasn't Vogue, not even Marie Claire, but I loved being the model I was—if only for an hour.

Chapter 15

The Situation

One month after our *Christmas horribilis* things hadn't become much easier with Mum. She was still hurting and I remained deeply upset by the sadness I had bestowed upon her. It made me feel no better that I could appreciate why she felt the way she did. How could she embrace something that I barely understood myself? I knew the resentment I felt because of her lack of acceptance was illogical, but such awareness didn't make it go away. We were not completely estranged, but at times it felt like that. The orphan I had left on her doorstep at Christmas was growing but still homeless. Whenever we tried to talk about it on the phone, she would get upset, and as a result, I would too. So we resorted to using email to discuss the thing we both knew had to be talked about. She even gave it a name: 'The Situation.' It was a term that we both smiled over, even though the subject was not so funny.

Our ongoing email exchange was never easy but it did progress. We started discussing feelings and practicalities, such as the details of my day-to-day life and what I wore when I got up in the morning (skirt, sweater, and tights, usually). I explained how I told other people about The Situation and whether she might be able to say something similar to her friends.

"Stress that this isn't a choice, it's who I *am*."

She had an email conversation with one of her nieces which seemed to help. Mum forwarded the bulk of the message to me:

> "It must've been hell for Neil to come to terms with his situation and to realize that this was going to be right for him. THAT must have been very, very difficult. I send him tremendous support and love and will always be available as a cousin but also as a friend if I can be. He will always be welcome here. Prejudice is from people who do not care to understand what is going on. We all make life decisions with resulting consequences and this life decision of Neil's is a big one but also a necessary one for him. You know him well and he will not have taken any decision lightly. I know that much. No one plays around with something like this."

Regardless of names that I didn't like to see and pronouns that I felt awkward reading, I felt humbled by this show of love from a relative I barely knew. I felt even happier that Mum had chosen to share this with me. Did I start to see a glimmer of acceptance from her? I couldn't be sure. Here I was, looking forward to my future more than ever, but she, I expect, was still wishing it wouldn't happen at all.

There was another aspect of humor that we toyed with too. I hadn't disclosed what my adopted name was, but I had told her that it was the same as my birth initial. Over a few emails this became a sort of guessing game, as she asked me whether I was a Nina, Nora, or even a Neela. I eventually told her that it was Nicky.

"So I could call you Nick!"

That didn't seem like a helpful abbreviation.

Over our email exchanges, Mum and I discussed—regularly but awkwardly—my appearance. Then came the potential for a big step forward: she asked me for photographs. It seemed to be the manifestation of me as a woman that she was trying the hardest to process. That visual perspective appeared more important to her at that stage than the concept of me being transgendered. On the face of it, the request to see what I looked like was positive, but knowing how first impressions form the deepest memories, I needed to think long and hard before agreeing to this. Mum found my reticence difficult to understand, but a couple of days later I consented and sent her a few images from the photo shoot.

After I clicked send, I waited nervously for feedback. The next day I saw her reply in my inbox.

"THANK YOU, THANK YOU, THANK YOU for the pics. I'm not going to comment on them in detail just now, cos this is just to say a big THANKS for them. Suffice to say a) I'm not bawling my eyes out (not much anyway!) and b) I'm fascinated! Watch this space…!"

That boded well I thought. She followed up with another email two days later.

"The pics themselves, as I said when I thanked you for them, I found 'fascinating.' I was 'fascinated' by the means that brought abt. the change in yr. appearance, almost in an objective way. That's the

*only word I can think of to describe my feelings on looking at any
'trans-dressing' (I think that's the right word), and you in particular.
I'd also like to know more of what you imagined I would feel when I
saw the pics."*

I'd hoped that she'd be persuaded that I wasn't just a man in a
dress. Maybe she could be complimentary and perhaps even
surprised at how good I turned out.

*"I would like to discuss these feelings further but I'm afraid of
hurting you (c.f. emotional stress again), and I really don't want to do
that. Could you, please, let me know if you're ready / prepared /
whatever for me to do this?"*

We tried the following Sunday during our weekly phone call. It
wasn't a good idea. I knew my mother's honesty could be disarming,
but now I was being subjected to it. To paraphrase, she didn't like
what she saw, and didn't want to be seen with me like that on the
street or anywhere else. The outer self I had been gradually preening
had been rejected in an instant. My inner self felt the repercussions; I
recoiled. She was being honest but I was very hurt.

Sensing my feelings, she later elaborated that she'd prefer to see
how I looked when I woke up in the morning, and not when I went
out at night, or after I had professional portraits taken. I should have
predicted that; Mum always prefers natural scenery to posed people.
Look through her photo albums and there is a singular absence of
Mum herself featured in any of them. Nor is she a big fan of make-
up, so to see me in make-up, posed and set for a night on the town
was not what she wanted to see. It was still one of the hardest
conversations we've ever had. All I'd wanted to do was look nice for
her.

Chapter 16

Perception and Ms. Perception

One evening I was drinking with my friend Gina in Flute. It was only a year since I had been intimidated by its velvet rope, daunted by its normalcy. Now I felt comfortable walking in there as the bartenders knew me by name and they always welcomed me back—sometimes with a kiss on the cheek, too. Gina is blonde, leggy, and a bundle of fun. Her New Zealand accent is a charm and those roots make her beautifully down-to-earth. She always made me feel like a close girlfriend whenever she saw me at the bar if she stopped in on her way to work. She earns her crust at a certain place of male entertainment. She never called it a strip joint but that was the unspoken truth. Gina had often asked me to accompany her to the club after our tipple in Flute, but I'd steadfastly refused. I knew that I would feel ugly, out of place, and horribly conspicuous. One time, however, I agreed to go.

We walked out of Flute together and she said she'd drive us the few blocks to the club. I gawked at her vehicle. It was a huge Hummer and I couldn't decide if this was wonderfully apt or conspicuously inappropriate. But I climbed in and we listed to Beyoncé at full volume for the ten-block ride to the club. As soon as we arrived at this dubious joint of exotic entertainment Gina disappeared to undress into something more suitably revealing. I sat at the bar and looked around, taking in the view. I'd never been to a place like this before, not even as a man, and so there was a lot to absorb. It was clear that the many poles on the stage were not for the building's structural integrity. The lack of female clothing thicker than chiffon made it transparently obvious why men went there too. The music was ideal for gyration, the lighting deftly subdued, and the bouncers distinctly heavyweight. Having noticed the flotsam of discarded chewing gum on the carpet, I assumed that there would be the jetsam of unknown stains on the couches too. I tried to cast aside concerns of hygiene.

The venue certainly tried hard to be high class ($25 for a meager glass of indifferent house wine) but there are only so many ways to disguise a house of such indifferent repute. I noticed several employees wandering around in their lingerie, but I was surprised that I didn't feel as intimidated as I had feared. I did feel rather isolated sitting at the bar on my own, but I knew Gina would be back to keep me company before long. That was when Cardiovascular Surgeon Man (CSM) approached me. I thought I was looking pretty good, even feeling a tad foxy, in my Little Black Dress, but I knew I was completely outclassed by all the hot semi-naked bodies around me. Strippers might not be the best conversationalists, but they know how to wear lingerie. There were more G-strings in attendance than at the entire New York Philharmonic. I imagined the wearers were more plucked too.

I made it clear to CSM that I was not an employee of the establishment and had just tagged along with my friend. He was friendly enough and we chatted together as he observed the spectacle around him. After a while I figured he might actually be interested in me and there was a spot of flirting between us. I started to like it.

We ranked the various performers who were either hot or grinding or both, and then he asked me something I'd not anticipated in a million years. Would I like to have a dance with one? A lap dance, that is, which I would have with one of the strippers and he would charge to his credit card. I had no idea how I felt about that concept, but I knew that I was flattered by the offer. It probably meant that he was unaware of my transgender situation and that made me feel better still. I fudged his invitation by saying that it would be a bigger turn on for me if he had a lap dance with another girl instead. So he did and I watched. I kissed his fingers and looked him straight in the eye while Ms. G-string did her thing. It was a completely surreal experience.

"Have you ever been with a woman?" he asked me.

Good question. The answer was yes, but not at all in the way that he envisaged. But before I had time to answer, one of the bouncers from the joint called me over. Ever so politely he asked me if I knew the guy. I noted—far too honestly in retrospect—that I'd just met him that evening. Consequently the bouncer asked me to leave. Me? Why? Surely I was not competition with those adorned in G-strings? Apparently yes I was! If I never achieve anything else in life, I can be most proud of this one remarkable feat which will remain at the top of my life résumé: I had been ejected from a titty bar in Manhattan as a perceived threat to business.

So CSM and I left with our heads held high and my self-esteem on cloud nine. He also saw the funny side if not the irony, and apparently preferred my company to those more adept at pole dancing. We found a bar that was far less protective of itself where we made out some more. I could tell he was feeling pretty frisky but I wasn't putting up much resistance either.

"I really want to taste you," he whispered in my ear.

Wow, that was sexually forward.

No, you really, really do not, I wanted to reply. Instead I maintained my silence and just played coy. So he really didn't know.

This was a situation that I'd not been confronted by before. What should I do? I actually did like being with him, a man, and it would have been good to go on a date which didn't involve being around semi-naked women, but what was the right protocol for me as a transgender woman? He found me attractive but that was on the assumption that I was born with a vagina. At what stage should I update him to the contrary? I postponed resolving that quandary as it was getting late and I wanted to get home. I gave CSM my number and headed to the nearest subway station.

Although I never heard from CSM again, that evening had brought big issues to the fore. Not only might men find *me* attractive, but I may find *them* attractive too. I'd not been so bluntly confronted by this scenario of mutual appeal before. This forced me to re-examine the boundaries between gender and sexuality. For all the years I was a man, I always found women attractive. I dated women. I never found men attractive, and I felt no desire to be with them, sleep with them, or be half of a couple with them. I don't feel I was subliminally blocking anything out, as I was perfectly happy dating women. Those relationships never progressed to the point of getting married or even to living with anyone, but they did seem natural. I was a normal guy dating normal women. (Actually some of those women turned out to be psychopaths, but I don't think that was unique or pertinent to my subsequent gender flux.) However the abortive evening with CSM was different from all those occasions in my past. This time I was the woman, he was the man, and as the man, he liked the woman. But as the woman I also liked the man. Perhaps this was just me assuming the mantle of usual gender roles.

I recalled the more recent times when I was mostly living my life in male mode, yet occasionally cross-dressing and heading to the Silver Swan for the weekend trans parties. Then I had wanted the attention of men for the validation of my revised gender. That was the only reason—wasn't it? Bar hopping in Hong Kong and clubbing in Bangkok also served to reaffirm my femininity, but they were not occasions when I desired to ensnare a man. Or were they? I wanted to attract the opposite sex, but ironically hadn't felt attracted to them. The evening with CSM made me consider a confusing supposition: was my sexuality changing along with my gender?

Chapter 17
Finding My Voice

As time passed I became lulled into a tantalizing sense of almost assurance that I was universally perceived as female. I had ditched the wig months ago, my hair was getting longer and finding its own identity, and I was feeling increasingly at ease as a woman. Along with confidence, my style was also improving (two inches longer on the skirts, one inch shorter on the heels) and there were very few occasions when I didn't feel feminine. With increasing electrolysis treatments my facial hair was diminishing and so make-up could be applied more effectively. I still wasn't sure where I was heading, but it seemed that I was growing out of the first stage of my second puberty.

However, style and appearance is only one part of gender recognition. I recalled a time a few months earlier when a new neighbor was moving into the apartment below me. The cable guy was there too, but in the process of connecting her, he disconnected me. So I popped downstairs to have words with him. I explained what had happened.

"Oh, I'm sorry sir," he said.

Sir.

SIR!

What made him think I was a sir—I was wearing a skirt! In the months to that point I had worked on my external femininity in many ways: poise, posture, walk, appearance, hair, make-up, the whole shebang, and I thought the results had been pretty good. But this perceived bubble of assurance was burst with just one little *sir* from the cable guy. I talked this through with Navi in our next therapy session. She suggested that one of the factors that made him come to this conclusion could have been my voice. I thought I had addressed him with a feminine lilt, but even if I had, it still didn't tip the balance into perceived womanhood.

After the Cable Guy Incident I vowed to improve the way I sounded. There was no point looking gloriously femme if I sounded horribly masculine each time I opened my mouth. I accepted that many women have deeper voices but I felt frustrated at not having a pretty pink voice. I was a woman, so why couldn't I sound the same?

I subsequently went to a bunch of voice classes in Manhattan. These were held by a wonderful speech pathologist called Tina who held sessions in her Wall Street office. They were scheduled after the office building closed and so visitors had to sign in with the security guy at the front desk. To prevent any awkward ambiguity, I had prepared a Xerox copy of my passport for such instances, which I'd suitably photoshopped to update my name and gender. (I knocked a few years off my age while I was at it.) This British passport was an unfamiliar form of identification and, perhaps as a result, never raised any eyebrows when I presented it. I used the same fake ID for the odd occasions that was needed when entering bars in the city. I'd like to think those checks were to prove I was barely over 21, but were usually just a mandatory requirement to abide by New York liquor laws.

The group voice sessions in Tina's downtown office were usually held around a large meeting table and although there was often a topic to work around, there was also enough flexibility to go off tangentially if the group was heading that way. We would discuss topics like the best way to cough, sneeze, and giggle.

"Try and be breathy!" Tina said. "Bring out your inner Marilyn Monroe!"

I later tried singing "Happy Birthday Mr. President" but I knew Tina's suggestion wasn't meant to be taken too literally. Just as well, as my impersonation was dreadful.

The voice sessions were enjoyable but I still felt frustrated at not sounding as feminine on the outside as I felt within. And even though it was helpful being around other transgender women at these sessions, I found scant consolation in knowing I was not alone. I also met some trans men at these workshops and had to sympathize with their situation too; they wanted to sound deep and manly, but instead were too light and fluffy.

Raising volume was just as relevant as raising pitch, and that comes from diaphragmatic breathing and not straining the vocal folds. Never let the throat get too dry, either. In several sessions we also addressed one of the biggest problems for any transgender woman: how to talk on the phone and always be perceived as female. I remember one of those sessions in particular when one of us left the room to make a mock phone call to Tina (on speakerphone) on the pretense of ordering take-out. The conversation was recorded and then Tina and the rest of the group offered advice on further feminization as we dissected the dialogue.

Over time I felt my voice was improving (especially when ordering spring rolls) but still I had phone identity problems and I simply didn't sound as feminine as I wanted to. Then I received a tip from another trans woman who suggested I contact a speech pathologist at NYU who was looking for transgendered individuals as part of her student teaching program. I did, and meeting Dr. K was another key moment in my transition. She reminded me of Yoda: a slight frame with large, expressive eyes and wisdom that seemed disproportionate to her diminutive size. She directed students who were in the latter stages of their speech pathology degrees and needed actual subjects to help them relate classroom theories to practical dilemmas. Individual sessions were structured at the Department of Communicative Sciences and Disorders at NYU Steinhardt. I sat in a small room with a microphone, video camera, and student while Dr. K observed remotely from across the hallway. It was an interactive experience as she would often pop into the individual clinic room to enhance the advice given by the student. It amazed me how Dr. K picked up on the tiniest variations of tone and delivery and then suggested ways to make them shift further towards the feminine. Just a tiny difference (such as not letting the voice drop at the end of a sentence) could make all the difference.

These one-to-one sessions continued on a weekly basis over more than one year, and even though Dr. K was replaced by Dr. M it remained a wonderfully symbiotic relationship for me. I was the lab rat for students at the dawn of their careers. They got firsthand teaching experience while I learned new ways of shifting vocal perceptions. Back at home, I developed a daily routine for vocal exercises (stretching, gargling, relaxing, humming, and making buzzing noises that sounded like an angry hornet) and never lost sight of the way I wanted to sound. Many changes were incremental but made an appreciable difference. Bigger than that, they made me feel appreciably more feminine. A year later I was asked back to speak to students at the clinic; I started to feel proud of my voice.

My own vocal situation was laced with a complexity that many other transgender women would not have experienced. I had been a DJ, first in clubs and then on the radio. I had earned a living from playing music or criticizing it, or expounding on its virtues as something exciting, fresh, or different—and most importantly, I used my speaking voice to do so. In Hong Kong my voice became familiar over the airwaves and I was associated as the person with that voice. I had done voice-overs for TV documentaries and commercials for events, concerts, and CDs. For many years my voice was my job; I earned money from it, and used it to my best advantage. Ironically, as a transgender woman, it had become a liability.

Chapter 18

Hormonally Yours

I t had been ten months since that momentous day at a Bangkok shopping mall when I went out as Nicky for the first time in daylight, and without a wig. Before that day I had switched between genders and personalities, but from that point on I stayed in female mode virtually all the time. I was just being me. I'm not sure I even thought of myself as *transitioning,* but that was effectively what I was doing. My femininity was becoming increasingly self-evident and I was embracing those changes, even if I still didn't quite understand them or know where they were taking me. Had I reached a point of presumption that I was inherently female? I didn't feel it in such straightforward terms but I did know that my maleness was becoming less relevant. In fact, I started seeing it beyond those terms and as an unwelcome distraction. Having given myself almost a year as a woman, I felt more alienated than ever from my former self. Further femininity was calling.

Usually called hormone therapy or sometimes HRT (hormone replacement therapy), this was the next logical option for me to consider. But why should I want to have this discussion with myself? I had been living quite happily as a woman without these additives, and I knew that if I started down hormone boulevard, there would be limited scope for turning back.

I read up on the pros and cons of hormone therapy, along with all the different ways of administering the components. This process would be the start of a progression to bring the outside of my body more in sync with the inside—an inequality that, until not long before, I didn't realize I had. The benefits of hormones would include gaining a possibly more feminine shape, nicer skin, and perhaps a better frame of mind. The downsides were possible weight gain, mood swings, and having to continue the process in some form for the rest of my life. If I chose to start hormones but then not continue, some changes would be reversible (skin, mood), but others (breast formation in particular) would not. So this was not a step to be taken lightly: it had the potential to change my life.

It is rare that any of us has the power to modify ourselves in such a profound way and that notion added further gravitas to my decision. I have seen transgender women who rushed into hormone therapy without completely appreciating the life-long consequences; the results were rarely good and such a premature decision can lead to greater emotional issues further down the track. With that in mind, one thing was clear to me: any changes to my physical self would only happen on *my* schedule. Only when I was ready would I consider moving forward. Somehow, for reasons I couldn't quite identify, I felt that I had now reached that point.

It was an exciting prospect heading into the great hormonal unknown, but part of me wondered what the heck I was doing. That protective maleness still questioned whether I was transgendered at all, but I considered that perspective was like a turkey threatened by the prospect of Thanksgiving. I knew my female side was in the ascendancy and she was steering me forward.

Using the organic logic that I feel most proud of, I discussed my decision with Dr. Rose and she agreed. In order to start the process I needed a letter of approval from Navi and another assessment from an in-house mental health professional at Callen-Lorde. A blood test was also required, presumably to ascertain that I didn't have a spare X gene lurking around that I wasn't aware of.

It is possible to have estrogen administered through pills, patches, or as a self-administered jab. However, in order for estrogen to most efficiently work its charm, it is ideally served with a side dish of an androgen blocker, so the testosterone still being produced can take a back seat. You don't want the testosterone to get into a fight with the estrogen. That fighting spirit is, after all, what testosterone does best. One of the questions I was asked in order to be given a clean bill of mental health was what expectations I had for starting hormone therapy. That was easy: if I didn't grow my own vagina in two weeks, I'd be most disappointed.

My hormonal dawn was actually an anticlimax. I had lunch with Grace at Chelsea Market and then headed to Callen-Lorde for the hormonal showdown. I was already fairly psyched with anticipation, though not giddy with excitement. Dr. Rose confirmed that the blood tests were good (damn it, there was only one X gene), and the paperwork and other reports were fine too. Then, almost glibly, she added that "*if I wanted*" I could start the hormone regimen that day. The next stage in my new life could begin there and then. It was an easy affirmative to answer. So Dr. Rose went through the printed disclaimer line by line, got me to sign it, and processed the pre-scription for the pharmacy downstairs. I returned from the pharmacy with a vial of the angel estrogen (which I would shoot up myself every two weeks) accompanied by a container of an androgen blocker called Spironolactone (or Spiro Gyra as I nicknamed it, being a fan of 80s music) to ward off the devil testosterone. It all looked so unassuming; my life-changing formula was contained in a small white paper bag. Nurse Joss talked me through what he was doing and instructed me how to continue the process at home. I presume he also needed to establish that I wasn't going to faint at the sight of a hypodermic syringe. Then, after a quick jab in my thigh, it was all over. I'm not sure if I had expected to hear choirs of heavenly angels or cheers from a thousand stadiums to ring in my ears, but neither happened. I went home feeling no different, except that I had taken a big, big step into a brave new tomorrow.

I gathered that it would take several months for my new hormonal equilibrium to be found, but some effects made themselves known much quicker. I stopped having erections, conscious or otherwise. Feeling feminine yet still having erections had been very confusing to say the least, so it was a welcome feeling to be unburdened from that legacy of manhood. The other aspect I quickly appreciated was gaining a whole new erogenous zone. In the past, girlfriends had done the nipple-licking thing on me, but I'd never quite got it. It felt like sucking my own elbow, and thus was not a turn-on at all. But within a week of estrogen working its way into my body, my nipples grew and became incredibly sensitive. It was the next part of my second puberty—in my 40s.

In subsequent weeks I started to appreciate the softening of my skin, though having super-sore nipples was no bowl of cherries. But hormones are deceptively powerful and although I welcomed some of the physical attributes, mental ones crept up on me with pure stealth. I became aware of a darkening mood. It was not a gloom-ridden, throw myself under a bus sort of depression, but a nagging, subversive sense of unease. It was not present all the time either, and that made its effect worse. I was getting severe mood swings and they were disarming.

"Welcome to the club!" many of my female friends said.

But what was I feeling? I knew something was different but I couldn't quite identify what it was. I definitely felt less self-assurance, plus a lack of wanting to go out, and even reticence to write more notes for this book. I just didn't *feel* like it. And with that meandering melancholy came questions of self-doubt. I knew I was doing the right thing, and following the correct path, but… well, actually, was I? I had sometimes considered myself on the cusp of the male/female equation and so had this hormonal effect increased that self-doubt? The fact that the gloom wasn't consistent only added to my sense of confusion.

A question kept peering through the fog of self-doubt: did the hormone therapy mask what I *should* be feeling (that I was actually a man after all) or did it *enable* me to feel more authentic (I really was a woman)?

It was sobering to experience firsthand how the balance of estrogen and testosterone so intensely affects the way we think. Testosterone is a multi-faceted hormone that makes men who they are on countless levels. Remove it and not just the wish to copulate goes away (yes that also went down to zero), but a whole set of intangible reference points vanish too. They had been like virtual goalposts that I knew existed in my male life, yet I couldn't see where they were on the pitch. Even though these tracts of maleness were invisible, their presence had given my life foundation and structure.

Now they were gone. As a result I found that my outlook, perception, and self-belief had all been compromised. This hormonal confidence gap didn't seem to be replaced by anything more reassuring on the estrogen side either. My gender equation was in disarming flux, and confusion was never far away. I accepted that my body was in a state of unrest from the hormones I'd induced, but where was the real me in this equation? Was I still there?

Chapter 19

The Love Match

As time passed I found myself becoming better acquainted with my hormonally revised self. I was still amazed that these two little chemical messengers could affect every single way that I viewed the world, but I started to see beyond that. My balance of normalcy was still swaying on the kitchen scales of life but there were fewer dark patches weighing me down and more days when I had a lighter mood. I wasn't ready to gaily dance through fields of poppies, as TV commercials for antidepressants would have us believe is the norm, but I was starting to feel less confused.

Physically I was also changing. My boobs were becoming increasingly visible and the rest of my body was re-evolving too. I felt my skin was better than ever, the weight on my torso seemed to have shifted slightly southward, and what little body hair I had left was reducing. I was becoming appreciably more feminine. Finally, these were effects that I could enjoy!

Regardless of the hormone equation, I was still puzzled by other emotions. I thought back to the time with CSM in the Manhattan strip club. I had been surrounded by beautiful women in notional underwear but I was more interested in the guy by my side. It was hard to believe that I was now attracted to men, especially as this balance seemed to have shifted once I had assumed Nicky's life yet before any hormonal influences had filtered through. I needed to put this to the test: how would it be if I dated another woman? So I put a profile on one of the free online dating websites in the hope of satisfying my curiosity. I wanted to be open and honest—a rarity for Internet dating—and so on my profile page I stated that I was looking for both men *and* women, and also specifically noted that I was transgendered. I knew that such information would likely cut down the level of interest from potential suitors, but it could also give a litmus test of who was out there and how I felt about them, whatever gender they were.

I was not only surprised by the level of interest (I received a lot of mail) but also at the number of men who simply couldn't read. Or maybe they were too lazy to look up what transgendered meant. I did go out for brunch with one fellow I met through that site (who did acknowledge my status), and although it was a cordial enough occasion it never led anywhere, nor was there any follow-up. Perhaps he just wanted to see what a transgender woman looked like in person and if we ate French toast.

One of the few women on the site that had any appeal to me was Willow. She was blonde, interesting, and with a coy, captivating smile. Her profile showed that she clearly had a brain, and was not afraid to use it either. Perhaps this could be someone I might be interested in. We struck up an email correspondence, and after a few weeks of unsynchronized scheduling we finally met up at a restaurant in Chelsea. It wasn't a date per se, but was a nice dinner over a glass or two of wine. Her story was also fascinating. She had considered herself straight for most of her life, but then a few years ago embraced her gay side—or realized that she was gay. So there were obvious parallels to my life, except for "gay" read "transgender." I still felt slightly weird though, as I was now on a kind of *gay* almost-date. Not that I was suddenly lesbian by going to dinner with someone I found both interesting and attractive, but what *sort* of attractiveness was it? Back in my male days I would definitely have found her sexually attractive, so was that still the case? I tried to analyze my thoughts as I peered over her spaghetti. She was certainly very cute, but would I have wanted to make out with her or see her naked? Was that a parameter of date-worthy attractiveness?

It ended up being a delightful evening and we talked at ease and at length. She also made me further address the dynamics of transgender dating that had already been bobbling around in my own head. How might the dating process be for me at this stage of my life? I found the question bewildering in itself, and the answer even more so. It had been years since I had had any meaningful relationship with anyone, and so throwing the transgender card into the pack was an impractical joker. I didn't feel comfortable with the concept of dating someone who liked me *because* I was transgendered. I thought back to times at the Silver Swan, and that type of man was unappealing. No, if I were to date someone, it would have to be because they considered me a woman, not a transgender woman. However, too much was changing in my life and so I decided that I should focus on my own agenda before I even considered letting others into my life. That was an ethic that would be severely tested later.

My cordial pseudo-date with Willow drew to a close and we agreed to stay in touch, though I knew we probably wouldn't. And no, I didn't want to see her naked. Maybe that was the answer I was looking for.

Later that summer I made my yearly pilgrimage to Flushing Meadow. I am no great sports aficionado, but I do like tennis. Being blessed by living in Queens, NY, the biggest stars of tennis come visiting my borough once per year for the US Open Tennis Championships. The event is just a 25-minute bike ride from my apartment (I really do chain up my bike outside one of the biggest tennis arenas in the world) and I usually make it there at least once during the championships. My favorite spot to watch the passing stars is at the smaller, more intimate Louis Armstrong Stadium, and this time I was watching Juan Martín del Potro being given a severe test by Gilles Simon. I'd actually seen Delpo play the mighty Roger Federer in the US Open final two years earlier—and win—which was one of those crazy upsets that nobody saw coming. This time it was more fun for me, if not for del Potro.

The match was engrossing, but I was getting sidetracked on the sidelines. There were a couple of guys sitting in the row in front of me and we exchanged the odd tennis quip when a break in the game allowed. They seemed friendly enough and I always welcome talking to strangers like this. As the games progressed, there seemed to be an additional tactical undercurrent with the man on the right.

He was a good looking 40s guy, maybe even early 50s, but he clearly kept himself fit. I could see that after he took his shirt off. I thought there were restrictions about bare torsos for spectators but I wasn't going to call the stewards. His nutmeg brown hair was thinning, but that seemed to enhance his charm. He was tanned without being an Adonis and his voice was warm and rich. We chatted between sets, then between points, and then most other times when there was a break in play. His confidence was evident without it teetering on arrogance. I was probably wrong about perceived chemistry. Then there was the odd brush of the hand. That was surely accidental, wasn't it? Then it happened again. That one wasn't! Ooh, I rather enjoyed that. Then some transfixing eye contact; just near the end of the third set. Then he became even more touchy feely. This was fun! We started to hold hands, sneakily, surreptitiously, so that the guy he was with didn't notice. We seemed to be getting away with it too as his friend remained seemingly unaware of this deuce tryst. Time was pressing, however, and I had to leave the grounds soon, but there was something between us that remained unresolved. I went for a walk to the top of the stands, ostensibly for some air, but hoping he would follow. He did. There was more flirting and more contact, and then a shared ice cream to normalize the exchange. Even though there was something in the air—that was now blatantly obvious—there was no apparent way to quench it. But he tried, and in doing so, went way beyond love-thirty innuendo and into full-on sexual advantage break point. He suggested that I should remove my panties before leaving. I felt a 70s-era John McEnroe outburst brewing.

You can't be serious! I wanted to exclaim, but I kept my cool. I didn't even call in the match referee. I was never going to do such a change of strip for an almost-stranger. Even if I had the lady-bits that he *imagined* I did, I still wouldn't have opted for those ground strokes. It had been a hot day's tennis, and so maybe we both had sunstroke. He didn't even tell me his name, though I knew he was married. So if you are reading this Mr. Realtor Guy from the 2011 US Open Tennis Championships, then perhaps this will make sense. Or perhaps it will make anything but sense.

That tennis incident had been game, set and match Ms. Chase, but it underlined a deeper realization: I could—and did—find men attractive. I wasn't just playing the traditional role of my gender and I was genuinely turned on by the man and the occasion. I compared that with the extremely pleasant but sexually lacking dinner I'd had with Willow, and there was no similarity. Of course I don't find all men attractive (it seems to be a minute percentage), nor are all women out of play, but these two events signaled a significant moment in my shifting sands of attraction.

Chapter 20
One Word That Changed Everything

Time is said to heal all wounds. Or perhaps it just lessens fractures. The end of 2010 was when I broke my life-changing news to Mum. She felt loss, I felt estranged, and our deeper friendship was on the rocks.

But nobody should underestimate the bond between a den mother and her cub. The months after that *Christmas horribilis* were never easy. Whenever we talked on the phone, we rarely managed to discuss any part of The Situation without Mum breaking down in tears. That made me feel worse, and I couldn't see how either of us would be able to move forward. Yet we didn't give up.

We resolved that phone conversations would be reserved for regular items on the agenda (what she'd been doing, how her local cricket team had scored, whether she'd done 20 or 25 lengths of the swimming pool that Tuesday), but we'd use email if something regarding The Situation needed to be addressed. Those virtual discussions were often painful, yet we both accepted the unspoken truth that they had to happen. Whenever I saw a new email in my inbox with The Situation in the subject line, I felt nervous before I opened it. Would it be one step forward or two steps back? Occasionally things seemed to be less toxic between us, though there was always the potential for an emotional breakdown. Occasionally I'd take offense to something she'd said but when I told her, she couldn't understand why. Or I'd suggest that she should speak to a therapist, yet she was reluctant to follow that course. Still we kept talking.

There were times when I sent her more photos, hoping that by increasingly seeing me as a woman, she might be better able to accept me as one. That rarely worked. In the ones where I considered myself pretty, she thought I looked fake. In the more natural ones, I thought I looked too male. Yet throughout this communicative ordeal (and it often seemed an ordeal) we kept our dialogue going. We knew we had to get beyond this.

Then one Sunday, we went one stage further: we Skyped. I felt incredibly tense before I clicked the Video Call option. How I should dress? Was make-up a good idea? (I went with subtle options on both.) That first Skype conversation was a groundbreaking moment. Seeing me as a real person on a video chat gave her imagination less opportunity to run riot. I think we even laughed together, and we'd not done that for a long while. The more times we Skyped, the more frequently she saw me as the woman I was. I don't think she saw me clearly belonging within the feminine frame, but at least she was thinking of me less as a man. Just like the phone calls and the emails, it wasn't always a success but we maintained that contact. Throughout everything, we kept talking.

Then came the biggest step forward of all, and it came at her instigation. She wanted to see me in person, in New York. Had we moved that far, that fast? Was I ready for something that I might never be fully prepared for? Of course there was only one way to find out. In September, just nine short months after that miserable Christmas, she made the trip.

I went to the airport to meet her. As I took the subway I was consumed with nerves. I am always excited to see Mum, and have never once been nervous at the prospect, but this time there was so much riding on it. In a way I felt I was meeting someone else's mother, a potential mother-in-law perhaps, but this was *my* Mum. I wore a simple denim skirt and T-shirt but I had no idea how it would be perceived. Was I wearing too much make-up? No, I thought the balance of femininity was just about right. Still I felt on parade.

Waiting in the arrivals lounge was the most nerve-wracking of all. I arrived before the plane did and the extra time I'd allowed made my anticipation even worse. How much longer? I couldn't sit down but I couldn't stand still either. Surely the bags must be off the belt by now. My palms became sweaty the longer I wandered around. Did Immigration take longer than expected? I gazed fixatedly at the door into the arrivals area. Where could she be? Then I saw her. She needs a wheelchair these days as she can't walk airport terminal distances but there she was, being wheeled towards me. She saw me and waved, smiling that great big smile she has. It was directed at me. I cried.

We took a taxi back to my apartment. All the time we held hands while she told me all the things that she felt were important, like what she had eaten on the plane and what sights she saw en route. I think she said I looked nice, but I was so overwhelmed by the occasion that I couldn't think straight. Back at my apartment we talked and talked. Although she had been to New York twice before, this was the first time she had seen my current apartment and looked out over the garden. The American robins courteously popped by. I made some tea (one pot, two china cups) and mused how this time was so different than the last occasion we had shared an emotional cuppa. We were together again. Gender, in that moment, was irrelevant.

The next few days were remarkably normal. This routine was putting our relationship—our *friendship*—back on track. We didn't argue (an event in itself) and we didn't seem to be walking on eggshells either. I was amazed at the utter contrast when I had shattered her world of normalcy nine months earlier. I remembered what she had said when I sent her the first pictures, that she wouldn't want to be seen on the street with me looking like that. That sentiment had stung, but when we stepped out of the apartment together, those words were forgotten. These were not the baby steps I had anticipated, but giant strides.

We pottered around the neighborhood, went shopping, and did some of the sights that she'd not seen before. There were occasional trips into Manhattan and a walk along the High Line. Wherever we went, we talked. Sometimes this was about transgender issues, but mostly it was just about everything else. Ultimately this was about spending time together.

There were still limits to her acceptance and I wondered how deep her understanding of The Situation really was. This was echoed when we had a mutual session with Navi. Although the 45 minutes was remarkably relaxed, she struggled to either refer to me as Nicky or use the right pronoun. Her recognition went beyond seeing me as her son in a dress, but how far beyond that I wasn't sure. She tried hard, though. One time we were shopping in Whole Foods and someone asked her if she needed assistance.

"No, I'm with my daughter" she replied. She then beamed broadly and whispered to me, "I said it! I said you were my daughter!" Those buds of acceptance meant the world to me.

One evening she said something that I will never forget. There was an event in the city I had to attend. I couldn't get out of it and so

Mum stayed at home. I hadn't made much of an effort to look like a princess, and was just wearing a simple black top and pencil skirt. My hair was down and the heels were subdued. Minimal jewelry. That was when she said it, just before I left the apartment.

"You look stunning."

My mother said I looked stunning.

I was so taken aback that I couldn't even cry. I just stood there, overwhelmed.

"Go on, hurry up, you're going to be late!"

My ego had been shattered when I sent her those first pictures of me as a woman. I had been really hurt. But all that pain had been banished by one little word.

I gave her a huge hug, but knowing that my tearful reaction would soon catch up, I took her advice and headed out the door. I felt disoriented on my walk to the subway, almost ashamed of the immense pride I was feeling. But this was not about looks, it was about acceptance. We had bridged the gap that once seemed immeasurably vast.

Chapter 21
Rhapsody in Blue

Having decided that I wasn't averse to men and might even like to try dating one, a whole bunch of potential complications cropped up. The biggest issue was disclosure. If someone is coming on to me, or if I take a shine to somebody and envision even a possibility that I'd like to develop something with that person, when is the right time to say '*Oh, and by the way...*'? I wondered if there would *ever* be a good time to have that conversation.

I discussed this question of etiquette with Navi several times. She couldn't offer any magic solutions but I already knew that there were none. She encouraged patience and suggested that things would likely become clearer over time. Patience seems to be something that every transgender person needs in abundance.

I tried to put that emotional tussle to the back of my mind. If I bury my head in the sand, then of course the problem goes away; I am British after all. I concentrated instead on feeling pretty and flaunting my femininity, regardless of what complications might then occur. My moody hormonal times had mostly gone, I had a new endorsement from Mum, and my confidence was back on top. Apart from the dreary club experience in Williamsburg, and the strip club experience with CSM in Manhattan, I'd hardly been out in a posh frock since my last trip to Asia. I needed to retest my desirability quotient on home turf. So one Saturday night I glammed up, put on a hot dress (mostly pink for prettiness, but with enough black to qualify as a New Yorker) and headed out for a martini. I felt very Carrie Bradshaw.

I found my way to Whiskey Blue in Manhattan. This upmarket hotel venue seemed a perfect solution: a nice long bar to sit against, some half decent 80s music, and a few admiring fellows to bolster my ego. I felt classy and desirable. I spurned Carrie's requisite Cosmopolitan (few New Yorkers will drink them now after they became ubiquitous on *Sex and the City*) and instead ordered a black raspberry martini. At $15 per glass, plus tax, plus tip, I wasn't about to run up a big tab; thankfully, fate was on my side. Sometime between the glass being half-full (it was never half-empty) and me nibbling the accompanying raspberry that signified I was nearly at the bottom, I attracted some welcome attention. He was actually rather handsome, albeit far too young for me, and his compliment of me being "the most beautiful girl at the bar" boosted my half-full attitude even further. It hardly mattered that he probably said the same chat-up line to every girl there; I was admired, and thus sought after. He went off and chatted with his friends (which allowed me to survey the rest of the field as well), but returned to find me again whenever my drink was ready to refill. At the end of the third martini we even made out a little at the bar. I French kissed a strange guy at a strange bar that I had known for barely two drinks! How delightfully wicked I felt! I was completely caught up in the moment and also seemed to be the object of desire for more than just one man. When I returned from the restroom one time, someone else stopped me en route hoping to converse. I wanted to say, *"Well, I'm busy with another man, take a number, and wait in line!"* I was in full-on flirtatious mode, and felt sexy as hell.

Three-quarters of the way down my fourth martini, I felt an alcoholic haze descending. A look at my watch confirmed that it was well past my bedtime. I bade a brief farewell to my drinks sponsor (no tongues this time) and took the subway back to Queens. The fun of that evening didn't negate the issue that had been niggling me: if any of the proposals from any of the bar fellows had developed beyond alcohol-infused flirting, what would have happened? What *could* have happened? At what point would I have needed to have the "oh, and by the way" conversation? Once again I chose to ignore that issue. The large pink elephant in the room was still there, but that night it was swimming in a martini glass.

It wasn't long before I returned to Whiskey Blue. I had felt extremely comfortable as the single lady at the bar and wanted to try my luck again, though I don't know what outcome I was hoping for. The next time was weirder, as it was Halloween weekend. When I was growing up, Halloween (which was spelled *Hallowe'en* back then) meant bobbing for apples in a bucket, eating candy apples, or drinking apple cider. (Apples were apparently very popular in England at that time.) Here in New York the event is monstrously huge. It is an excuse for freakishness to become mainstream, women to dress up as hookers, and everyone to believe they are from either Sodom or Gomorrah in the pre-fire and brimstone era. It was actually the evening before Halloween when I returned to Whiskey Blue, so nobody was wearing scary costumes or had applied over-the-top make-up. (Except for the New Jersey girls, who do this by default for every night out.) I plumped for a black raspberry martini once again and talked to a very civilized gentleman who admitted to me from the get-go that he was married. Immediately that took the pressure off our conversation, though ironically his admission might have made him more attractive. He started asking me about my past relationships. I hadn't had any since relocating to New York some five years earlier, and before that I was picking up the dregs from past relationship missteps. Rather significantly, those had also been with women when I was a man. So for the purposes of stimulating conversation, I decided to fabricate a few fictitious friendships. I mentioned that during my time in New York I'd had a few 'serious relationships' but none had lasted more than four months. I elaborated on my inability to hold onto a non-existent relationship by saying that I was too picky, very independent, and besides, I didn't actively need a man in my life. An essence of that sounded plausible, though I hoped that I wasn't writing my own future in such a single way. As we talked, I could almost visualize the imaginary partners I'd been with for those short-lived serious relationships I'd mentioned. I couldn't see specifics of his appearance but the tiffs we'd had and the trips we'd made were almost lifelike, such was the authenticity of my false memories.

The weekend trend of heading to Whiskey Blue continued. I didn't admire myself on the *modus operandi,* but it was financially scrupulous if not morally so. I'd buy one drink on arrival, and then lusty men with an eye to a sexual fling would supply them after that—not that it ever became physical. It couldn't, after all. Occasionally it crossed my mind whether men wondered why this single girl was going to an obvious pick-up bar on her own. Surely they didn't think I was a hooker? But if they did, that would have served as a further endorsement of my femininity, wouldn't it?

One evening my routine didn't go according to plan. I was sitting in my now-regular spot at the bar but the first guy (who bought me my second drink) was a major disappointment. His conversation was self-centered, his looks were barely ordinary, and his manner far too touchy-feely for my liking. As he droned on about his corporate successes, I found myself tuning out, pondering my own past while he talked incessantly about his. I rarely had the confidence to chat up a girl in my guy days and I usually saw this process as an imposition from the girl's perspective. Perhaps I was right.

"Nicky, am I boring you?"

His words cut through my retrospections; my glazed expression was jolted back to the present.

"Huh? No, sorry, I was just thinking about something else."

"Some*body* else?"

I smiled inwardly and awkwardly.

"Actually, yes."

I excused myself as I went to the bathroom, and by the time I returned he had gone. Now I had a clean slate to start again. It didn't take long for someone far more interesting to swarm to the honey pot. This time it was a visiting architect from Texas. Or it could have been Arkansas. And he might have been an engineer; those martinis suddenly seemed quite strong. I remember a full head of hair and an engaging smile, but other specifics were vague. We were getting on wonderfully, and I was hot and truly desirable again. I leaned into the conversation when talking to him and smiled a coy smile whenever he said anything remotely funny. I realized that I had become a prize flirt. But I felt entertained by him and I was enjoying his company. Then, of course, came the inappropriate suggestions. No, I was not going up to his room, and no, I was not going to fly back with him to Houston or Little Rock or wherever he was from. But in fending off his advances I realized that he was a fun guy, and maybe I might like to have dinner with him sometime. However, his intentions were firmly in the realm of the here and now. The more I looked at him, the increasingly open I found myself to that idea too. Other girls have one-night stands, and so why couldn't I be the same?

Up to that point I had felt thoroughly feminine. Not transgender feminine, but *female* feminine. But as soon as the impractical practicalities of a potential one-night stand sunk in, I was instantly brought back to reality with a lump. I was not born with the right equipment. He was a very persuasive guy and I felt drawn to his swagger, but this was neither the time nor the place to have the *"oh, and by the way"* conversation. In fact, there was no way to pitch this quandary in any form that he might appreciate. I couldn't do what he wanted—probably what *I* wanted too. That physicality of who I was jarred me as never before. My license to flirt had been revoked and I had been unmasked, even if only in my own head. With this self-revelation I couldn't even look him in the eye anymore. Instead I put up various protestations about how "I couldn't," quickly took my coat from the back of the seat, and fled out of the bar, tears dribbling down my cheeks as I ran to the subway.

Chapter 22

Innervisions

The next few weeks I didn't go out much. My confidence bubble had been deflated by truth. I was constantly reminded of what I was and what I didn't have. I *wasn't* like all the other girls that I had seen at Whiskey Blue, however much I had thought I was. I stayed in and cemented my status as community hermit while making frequent friends with Mr. Cabernet. I even tried changing my tea of choice from PG Tips to Typhoo to see if that helped my mood. It didn't. This became an intensely isolating time for me.

I tried to forget my thwarted social life and concentrated on work instead. At that time I was dividing my time and income in two ways: I was presenting radio segments for Hong Kong in man mode yet female guise from my home studio, and also working as a receptionist, assistant manager, and Girl Friday for my electrologist, Kiki. These two aspects of work mirrored my own gender-divided life. I had once loved working in radio but this pleasure was now muted as it involved assuming the personality of a man. I accepted the financial requirement of it, though I knew that my days on the radio in this format had to be numbered. Conversely, the times working as a receptionist in midtown Manhattan were blissfully happy for me. I could be who I was and who others saw. It didn't matter that I was genetically different from the other women in the office. Even if they knew or suspected my past, it was never an issue.

The office was a stone's throw away from the Flatiron Building on 23rd Street. It was nine floors up in a classic Manhattan 1930s building, with a uniformed doorman and two elevators each barely large enough for six people. (When it was built, obesity hadn't reached the same level it has now.) The elevators had another disturbing quirk too: they occasionally stuttered and stalled, accompanied by the sound of clanking chains when ascending. These were the perfect elevators for Halloween, but for the other 364 days of the year they bordered on scary.

Ours was a shared office. In addition to my electrologist boss Kiki, there were herbalists, acupuncturists, and other natural healthcare providers. Not all of these practitioners were in the office every day, but they added an extra layer of activity which I liked to keep an eye on, while guiding the right clients to the appropriate practitioner from the front desk. Our thoroughly international gang was composed of Lila (Chinese acupuncturist with whom I practiced my rusty Cantonese), Charmane (American of Philippines descent, also known to stick acupuncture needles in me), and DeeDee (an outwardly bossy but inwardly warm Korean herbalist). Also playing a key part in the office environment was the totally Brooklyn KC, who specialized in facial treatments. I tended to be the collective router for their individual lives. Lila was looking to buy an apartment and so was always showing me pictures of potential places to ask my opinion. KC, meanwhile, had been trying to hit it off with her regular bus driver on her way home and so would give me reports on what had happened on the bus the night before. The most daunting task was helping co-workers decide what they wanted for lunch, if only to gain a quorum. But by and large it was a happy office and one where egos rarely got in the way.

My responsibilities were to Kiki, though. She had initially offered me a part-time job there for Saturday afternoons but then it grew to several days per week. Of course she knew of my past but she respected me as a transgender person and thought no differently of me for that fact. I took payments, attended to emails, and booked appointments. Routine as it was, there was never a dull moment and I felt validated being able to do this successfully as Nicky.

It was still only a part-time job though, and so I looked for other ways to supplement my female income which might then enable a move away from male radio. I took a bartending course and became a fully qualified New York bartender. I answered an ad for a job in a SoHo gallery and even went for an interview there. It felt greatly empowering being able to present a résumé entirely in the feminine, even if much was fabricated. I also looked into other types of office receptionist work or even shifts as a restaurant hostess. I felt I was ideal for all these jobs but nothing ever worked out, mostly because of my complicated non-resident visa status. However much I noted that I have a cute English accent, doors of opportunity remained closed. I felt sure that one day this would change, but in the meantime, I couldn't press eject on my radio lifeline. That led to further frustration.

However, something uplifting happened in my bed around that time. Like everyone else I believe I dream a lot more than I remember, but knowing that dreams fade quicker than the morning dew, I started to keep a dream diary by my bed. It's actually a notebook in the shape of a camel that a friend brought back from a business trip to the Middle East many years ago; Humpy is now my dream log. Navi is a great believer in dreams as a route for our subconscious to communicate with reality (that is my paraphrasing rather than something from the Acme Therapy Handbook), and it was at her suggestion that the camel found a job. As a result I had been monitoring dreams to try to determine *who* was featured in those dreams. Of course it was me looking out at the world (can we dream any other way?) but was it *male-me* or *female-me*? I'd never been able to pinpoint my own gender in my own dreams—until I did. In a jumbled-up nocturnal voyage that ventured back over 20 years, I was working in the old department store in Birkenhead and senior management was looking over me. There was nothing unusual in that, but this time I was most certainly in heels. The store was different (more supermarket than haute couture) but the same players were there, and they definitely perceived me as a woman. That journey into my surreally adjusted past raised my spirits: I had dreamed myself female.

That was a small but welcome endorsement, yet gender frustration imbued itself in other ways. It was early December and I was writing Christmas cards to old friends, but this year it seemed trickier than ever. I mentioned my trip to Asia, visiting the tennis championships at Flushing Meadow, and even how Mum had been to see me in New York. These were all things I had done as a woman, yet the name at the bottom of the card was male. I was able to sign off a few cards as Nicky but practicalities dictated that most had to be from *him*. Those cards were the hardest to write and I felt deceitful letting others assume that a man was enjoying these experiences. I vowed that this would be the last time I'd switch personas; that next year would be different—which it certainly ended up being. This hint of future positivity gave me an encouraging sense of closure. Consequently I headed towards the holiday season with some confidence renewed. That would all be wiped out again in one crazy, unexpected night.

Chapter 23
The Crying Game

I t all started when my lawyer friend, Portia, asked me to go to a cheese and wine mixer at a swanky art gallery in Chelsea. Like her Shakespearean namesake, Portia knows how to strain her qualities of mercy, or at least negotiate trust funds or family endowments or whatever she does. We met many years ago when I was working in Hong Kong and she was living there. We had found each other through personal ads, and formed a friendship through our creative responses. I always looked forward to her missives as they were smart, witty, and fun. At that time she was notionally married and I was somewhat male but we started a friendship that has rarely waned since. She is a proud New Yorker and returned home from Hong Kong a couple of years later, and once I relocated here some years after that, we resumed our friendship. In common with all my female friends who knew me *before*, we get along far better now that we are of the same gender.

As for the mixer: the theory was that if singles mingle over cheese, wine, and art then they might meet their life partners. I doubt there are many couples who have headed down the aisle due to a catalyst between Brie, Chardonnay and Matisse but this seemed like an interesting way to spend an evening, especially as I had been keeping a low social profile since that teary exit from Whiskey Blue. I still found it hard to gloss over being unlike other women, but I tried to relegate this unwelcome truth to the background of my own self-portrait.

I felt pressure heading to the event. Would I be as pretty, interesting or desirable as the other girls there? I wanted to look my best for the occasion so I wore a flattering black cocktail dress which I matched with black knee-high boots. I looked at myself in the mirror when I was getting ready and I felt attractive. That reassurance helped boost my confidence. Portia had forewarned me about this type of mixers: they have the propensity to be extremely female-centric, a plethora of ring-craving, baby-desperate females, all chasing a handful of distinctly indifferent males. When I arrived at the gallery with Portia, I observed that this event didn't seem quite that extreme but it did appear to follow the same protocol. Even so, I enjoyed talking to some of the other girls, and browsing artwork that was interesting if not gripping. There were no instances when I wanted to grab a man to debate the merits of impressionism over cubism, but that was due to the watercolor shades of masculinity present. Those men generally interpreted the 'dress to impress' advisory as matching an ill-fitting suit with ten-year-old loafers. As neither Michelangelo nor David was in attendance, Portia and I made the most of our $35 event ticket by cleaning up on the cheap wine and pre-packed cheeseboard.

At the end of the three hours, both of us were in the mood for something stronger (alcohol ideally, but men would have sufficed) so we headed to Whiskey Blue for consolation martinis. I hadn't been back since I had left the bar in a weepy state of dejection a couple of months before. Perhaps now I would be able to put those tearful ghosts to rest.

It was two weeks before Christmas and the place was packed with dinner jackets and out-of-towners in New York for the holidays. Portia and I jostled for a place at the bar and, once seated, a ringleader from one of the dinner jacket brigades promptly bought us drinks. That felt reassuring after the disappointing gallery event filled with dreary wine, dry cheese, and dull men. But this fellow seemed quite pleasant, and whether it was the support of Portia by my side or the strength of the martinis I was sipping, I found myself being attracted to him. *Superflirt* was back. The emotional downers of my last visit were forgotten and I was back in my element.

His name was Leo. He chatted with us, then returned to his friends, then came back to us again. It was a very easy and non-intrusive time, aided by the fact that he never once let our glasses run dry. Whether I asked him, or he asked me, I really can't remember, but he offered to take Portia and me out for dinner one evening. I took his cell number and said I'd text him the following week. As Portia and I left the bar that evening, a newfound hope came with me.

A few days later I consulted with Portia and we agreed that it would be less confusing if Leo's attentions were focused on just one of us. I wondered if we should toss a coin for the privilege but Portia deferred: he was going to be all mine! I texted Leo with a tame version of that consensus, and after some mild text-flirting (I am not restricted to flirting in person), he offered to take me out to dinner the following Saturday. I had an *almost-date* to almost look forward to! Or worry about. The more I considered it, the more I stressed over whether he really would want to see me again. Had I press-ganged him into a dinner promise under duress? Then a bigger anxiety hit: when he next saw me, might he not see me as the woman I was? My transgender shroud was the biggest concern and I needed to resolve it. I came up with the idea of a relaxed coffee with him first. If that went well then we could have dinner together later that same evening. Leo seemed confused by this proviso but went along with it anyway.

We met at a tiny coffee shop off 59th Street and shared a couple of espressos. (I needed the kind of encouragement that tea doesn't give.) I was anxious heading there but he put me at ease as we talked about nothing in particular. He also seemed very happy to see me again, which my previous insecurities hadn't let me expect. So dinner was on. I had a few hours to dart back home, find the most appropriate dress, and wonder how long I could get by without having The Conversation—aware that once I did, it would invariably change everything.

I got back home sometime before dawn. The evening had been a mind-blowing amalgam of the amazing, bizarre, confusing, and revealing. After our afternoon coffee chat Leo had showed me where to meet. He would be waiting at the bar in the restaurant he pointed out across the street. As I headed home to change I felt some rare optimism; maybe this could be the evening when dinner evolves into more than just one date. In my apartment I showered and changed, then picked a shimmering dark blue satin dress which I matched with understated black heels. I kept make-up simple but classy and felt unusually confident as I returned to the city to meet Leo again.

When I arrived at the appointed dinner venue, I realized this was the exclusive Le Cirque restaurant—one of the finest in the city. My eyes popped as I entered; I'd not been to a place as fancy as this in years, and never before as a woman. The ambience was opulent without being stuffy, moneyed but not ostentatiously so. The presence of a coat-check larger than my whole apartment highlighted that I was somewhere special. Leo met me at the reception desk, having noticed me, my outfit, and my bewilderment. We sat at the bar and talked over velvety red wine and delectable appetizers. I was able to look at him closer now. He was probably an inch or two shorter than me, but as the tall woman I am, I've learned to accept the realities of mismatched height. His short, mousy hair was brushed back, and his skin was weathered but not craggy. I'd somehow not noticed his moustache before. I wasn't sure if that was attractive; didn't they go out with 1970s porn flicks? However, his voice was easy and he was a total gentleman, chivalrous and well turned out. A well-tailored blazer over a smart button-down shirt disguised a slight paunch that comes from excesses of beer and fine dining. He was the head of a construction firm and his Italian tailoring demonstrated the abundance of cash in construction. It also underlined why Manhattan's mythical 2nd Avenue subway line will not be completed: budgets flow far more easily into wallets than into tunnels. However this evening I was the beneficiary of seeping contractor run-off so I didn't care that the T line will never reach the Lower East Side.

The conversation continued to flow as easily as the wine. We shared pleasantries and some life histories, but I was uneasy talking too much about my past, imaginary or otherwise. After an hour or two of sumptuous food on gorgeous plates (and even nicer wine in crystal glasses) we moved on to another bar; promising the barman at Le Cirque that we'd be back later for dessert. The next venue was a downbeat Irish dive bar. This was a good contrast to the preceding affluence, even if their Cabernet was not a patch on the previous three glasses. Our dialogue remained relaxed, though he sensed I was holding back. I was becoming defensive over a secret that I couldn't tell him. I knew my difficult truth would have to come out at some time, but not now. I loved living the euphoria of the present, regardless of its foundation being flawed.

We returned to Le Cirque for a sensational Grande Marnier-soaked soufflé, one of the finest desserts I'd ever had. Still, he couldn't give up probing about my hidden secret. Perhaps I too wanted to unburden. We left and I held hands with him as we walked to his apartment block close by. He asked me to come up. This felt right and I wanted the evening to continue. I said yes.

Naturally it was a gorgeous apartment with sensational views. We talked, and kissed, and I felt at ease. Once again came his question of what was troubling me. Was my transparency that apparent? I hedged but he persisted.

"Please tell me what's on your mind," he said. "I can see there's been something troubling you all evening."

I still had grave doubts about sharing the inevitable but we seemed to be approaching a point of no return. We were like lemmings, about to seek the abyss. I could at least hold hands with him while we jumped.

"Honestly, you can tell me."

Then wanting to lighten the situation, he added, "… just so long as you weren't a man before!"

Had he a subliminal hunch? Maybe this was the best lead-in to breaking the news. I paused before adding my own question.

"And if I was?"

He turned white as a sheet while his jaw dropped the whole 11 stories.

There was silence.

"Oh…"

More silence.

"And do you still… have…?"

My eyes fell to the floor; there was no need to fill in the unspoken blanks.

What happened in the next half hour is hard to remember. My emotions were topsy-turvy, and the excesses of that classiest of wine were clouding my perspective. How did he feel? Betrayed? Hurt? Cheated? All I felt was loss.

I had played out this scenario in my mind before, but when it happened I wasn't prepared. I had been far too trusting as well; different outcomes could easily have led to violence. Had I made a mental judgment that Leo would not turn to abuse if I went to his apartment? No, I had blacked out those possibilities, instead being giddy on the emotion of the moment. Alcohol had blurred my ethical compass as I'd taken the elevator up.

Minutes passed awkwardly. I couldn't look at him and silence was more comforting. My head still rested on his chest but he made no effort to move. I think he mentioned that he had "been with" someone like me before. I assumed I knew what "like me" meant, but I found no solace in that admission. Our stilted conversation continued, but his next query stunned me. What intimacy options might be available if I were with him? In retrospect, my own response shocked me even more. Letting the last drop of judgment evaporate faster than the alcohol from the earlier flambé, I explored one intimacy option on him. There and then.

Of course that didn't help at all. It made me feel oddly wanted, though even more confused. He suggested I stayed the night in his or another bedroom, but I needed my zone of familiarity back. I left his apartment via the walk of shame past the security guard on duty in the building lobby, and jumped in a taxi back to Queens. Back home I slept restlessly, unable to digest what had just happened.

I was surprised to receive his text a few hours later. "Sex and breakfast" could be scheduled at 11am, but after that he would be returning upstate. I had no idea what form the sex or the breakfast would take but I needed more time alone to contemplate this surreal series of events. I declined, hoping that this might be a temporary postponement but fearing that it might be terminal.

Chapter 24

The Most Wonderful Time of the Year

The more I looked back on those events with Leo, the more extraordinary, unbelievable, and contradictory that experience became. It was just one night, but I was the trophy girlfriend to a successful man. For all its inherent complications, this scene became hypnotic. I had peered through the blinds of achievement and loved what my imagination saw. How would it be to be the wife of someone like Tony Soprano? To live the life of a glittery partner with all the trappings that prestige bestowed, only to wonder if gifts were guilt-edged to counterbalance late hours or office dalliances. I thought back to the immediacies of the evening before. All the elements had been there: fine dining, fancy frock, and good company. It was all that an ideal date should have been, apart from a happy ending. Not for me anyway.

The sex and breakfast message was the last I heard from Leo and subsequent texts I sent him went unanswered. I tried to rationalize the outcome: it wouldn't have worked out anyway. Regardless, part of me wanted to try. Instead, I had been knocked back at the first hurdle, and that incident left me with a dark feeling of despondency and a deeper sensation of rejection. I also wondered if Leo had left me with more than just a memory from our brief oral adventure. A few days later my throat was scratchy and my imagination was in panic-strewn overdrive. Those fears were allayed the following week with negative results from throat swabs, but it was another reminder that I had been recklessly foolish.

Portia tried to comfort me, and suggested that the best way to get over this disappointment would be to get back right on the horse. She devised a plan to get me out of this mental funk: speed dating.

Speed dating is another of the assorted methods that New Yorkers (female ones in particular) use in the desperate attempt to secure a mate. Of course it is not just New Yorkers who desire to find *the one*, but living in this city bestows extra pressure on single women as they attempt to find single men. As most of the *Sex and the City* episodes proved, good men here are either taken or gay.

The process of speed dating is actually quite fun. Women sit at individual tables with a first name stuck on their top. Then a procession of men (also with names on their lapels) visits each table for a pre-determined length of time, usually three to six minutes. A brief conversation ensues (hopefully), before a bell rings and the man moves on to the next table. Then at the end of the night you enter your *"yes, there was possibility—I'd like to see him again"* or *"no, God no, never again—five minutes felt like five hours"* choices on a secure website. If both Ms. A and Mr. B feel a connection (or at least think that a second meeting might not be a thorough waste of time), then their respective email addresses become visible to each other. It is quite a simple system, and although there are multiple versions run by different companies, this was the format used this evening.

I had been speed dating some years before, but with one crucial difference: I was a man. This time the tables were turned, quite literally. How would it be to see things from the opposite perspective? Not only that, but I had my insecurities to consider. It is one thing to meet a guy at a bar and for him to *assume* that I am genetically female, but for speed dating I would be putting on a big label across my chest stating "I'M A CHICK!" Metaphorically anyway; my sticker just said *Nicky C.*

The evening was fun and I forgot the pain of the previous weekend. Portia was the ideal collaborator too; in the intervals between 'dates' we mocked the collection of social misfits that had been placed in front of us and mulled over the desirability quotient of the others. There was a tall, bespectacled guy from the Upper East Side who piqued my attention as a potential mate, but then he started droning on about American football, or baseball, or some team sport, and so I mentally turned off. There was also a science teacher with bug eyes and overlarge spectacles who had a lot to say. In fact, too much to say and I couldn't get a word in edgeways. So, along with most others, I crossed him off my list once he moved on to the next table. But there was an astronomer-turned-banker who seemed particularly interesting. However my stargazing interest was unrequited as he didn't pick me on the website later, and so our quasi-quasar connection headed into a black hole. Overall there seemed to be far too many beer bellies, too few success stories, and remarkably little self-confidence.

It was interesting to see the other ladies at the event too. I was in their camp now, but I wasn't sure how close I felt to them. Most seemed to be as bad as the men, having sunk to new levels of desperation and lingering over guys who clearly had no interest in them. I tried to remember how I had behaved as a man at speed dating events. I considered myself fun and polite, but recall finding it hard to find anyone who sparked my interest. That sentiment seemed to be echoed from my updated gender perspective. As I wondered what impression I gave as a man, I contemplated an impossible meeting: if *me-the-man* met *me-the-woman*. That conundrum seemed as baffling as the three-dimensional puzzler image of stairs that go up and down in an infinite spiral circle. I hope that I'd at least have found myself interesting, one way or another.

I felt emboldened by the speed dating and so I signed up for another one the following week. This one was even less of a success. Not only did there seem to be a higher percentage of oddball basket cases, but many of them had also attended the event the previous week! That shouldn't have surprised me as I know organizers will often throw out complimentary spots to daters from past events to balance up the gender equation. Yet I felt gypped. There was minimal fresh meat, and the available cuts were more gristly (or grizzly) than lean. Then it degenerated from bad to worse. One of the social misfits from the previous event came to my table for his allotted five minutes. His first question was innocuous enough.

"Where's your friend from last week?"

"Not here tonight."

"Is she with a date from last week?"

"Huh? I've no idea."

"So are you pre-op or post-op?"

"Excuse me?"

"Are you pre-op or post-op?"

"If you mean what I think you mean, then we are done here."

I believe he left the event soon afterwards. I survived the rest of that speed dating evening but I felt really hurt. Angry and saddened that someone had made me out for what I actually was. I knew that I shouldn't be bruised by the truth, but the manner of his affront was off the scale. It shook me up and made me feel even more self-conscious. I had no idea if anyone else in the room questioned my gender status, but if they had, then they had the grace, tact and diplomacy to keep that question to themselves.

In a couple of days it would be Christmas. I resigned myself to being alone again for another holiday season. This would not have bothered me normally, but there was something about this year that made it seem worse. I had a reinvigorated desire to socialize, but these efforts kept being stymied by actuality. Depressing times at Whiskey Blue, the abortive incident with Leo, and now the speed dating debacle. I was developing a deeper sense of femininity and conflicted by a wish not to be seen as transgendered. I wanted to be out there, but not out here.

Still I was determined to celebrate the holiday season in my own little festive way. I bought a tree and lugged it back to my apartment. I spent Christmas Eve adding lights and decorations and when finished, it looked a picture. Just like at Mum's house 12 months before, I was reminded by trinkets and ornaments that I had bought over the years and were displayed on the tree like a collage of history. Baubles from Hong Kong, a wooden bird from the Middle East, and a Swarovski crystal star I was given by an old flame. This year I had also found a new tree ornament in Macy's that seemed newly appropriate: a sparkly black high-heeled shoe. I gave it pride of place on the tree even though Cinderella was right here.

Christmas stockings have always been a tradition in our family. Our custom is to give each other ten little things, all minimally wrapped, and fit them into a Santa stocking, though we actually used huge woolly socks when I was young. These little gifts can be anything from chocolate bars to cheap pens, to a Satsuma tangerine or a bag of nuts. The gift—or value of the gift—is less important than the surprise on opening it. When I was growing up, my sister, Mum, and I all used to sit on my Mum's big double bed on Christmas morning and take turns opening our stockings, which had been left hanging on our bedroom doors overnight. Mum would prepare one each for my sis and me, while Sue and I would prepare a joint one for her. It was a precursor to opening bigger presents downstairs later in the day, but stockings on Christmas morning were always very special.

Mum and I still maintain that tradition even though we are mindful to avoid heavy items to keep the postage down between New York and the UK. These days the postage often costs more than the ten items combined, but we overlook that, as maintaining the tradition trumps all. That sense of occasion was particularly poignant this time after such an emotional divide with Mum the previous year—our *Christmas horribilis*. Since her visit to New York, our friendship (yes, friendship) was back on track. So just like every other year, when we were not together, she sent me a Christmas stocking in the mail which I opened on Christmas morning. I smiled, as it was like nothing had changed between us. There were fun, silly things that meant the world to me: a bell for my bike, chocolate coins, packets of instant hot chocolate, a tin tea caddy with pictures of birds, and a pair of gardening gloves to use in my back yard. But also included was something that would have been unthinkable just 12 months before: a small bottle of bright blue nail varnish. I burst out crying when I saw it. Not the tears of upset from one year ago, but tears of unabashed happiness: my mother had given me something for a girl.

Chapter 25

Is This The Future?

Every so often in therapy, Navi and I would talk about SRS—
Sexual Reassignment Surgery. For some transgender women it
is an ideal to strive for: a final piece of the transition jigsaw. Others
don't feel the need for that surgical ordeal to feel complete. But I
expect every trans woman will weigh up the pros and cons of SRS at
some time in her life, whatever decision she comes to in the end.
This assessment is filled with countless physical and emotional issues,
along with the stark reality of cost. Nor is it a choice that, once made,
can then be forgotten. Invest in a new vagina and it needs a lot of
upkeep for many years. So this is an extremely complex, emotive and
obviously life-changing decision to make. Although Navi and I
touched on it a few times, I never felt it high on the priority list.
There were usually more pressing issues to discuss: jobs, money,
hormones, self-esteem, acceptance, and goodness knows whatever
else cropped up in our weekly soul-cleansing dialogue. The SRS topic

was there, but it was pending, on the back burner; a topic to revisit if necessary. However, after the holiday season something changed and it was like a light inside my head was suddenly switched on. I started to obsess about SRS.

As I thought about the complexities of the subject, myriad practicalities came to mind. Where to have the procedure. The pros and cons of each surgeon. Costs, recovery, and time off work. The many complications that could happen. These are mind-boggling issues that few outside transgender circles can appreciate. I hadn't dwelled on them much before, but now I did. Would surgery enable me to make a new start in life or might it be too drastic? If I considered myself in gender limbo-land (which I oftentimes did) then could this be the defining way forward? Ultimately, would this extreme of surgery confirm my femininity or highlight its absence?

I spent countless hours online checking out the various methods used by different surgeons, and followed up with several emails to inquire about costs and waiting lists. A bottle of effervescent emotions had been shaken up and I started bubbling over just thinking about this prospect. I became a woman possessed in my relentless research: it was the Vagina Epiphany.

Every day I was reminded of my inability to comply with even basic standards of femaleness; with SRS, perhaps this could change. I would have the ability to wear proper underwear, or a nice bathing suit, or jeans that actually fitted. And, I supposed, sex. I started to become aware of a far huger concept that could fill my future reality: I had the potential to become the woman that I really was, and not the person that I nearly was.

The more I thought about it, the more I found myself in favor of the procedure. Perversely though, that newfound clarity of emotion was tainted by a conflicting confusion: why hadn't I felt the same desire before? I mentioned this to Dr. Rose on my next visit but she didn't seem surprised that this realization had evolved along a progressive timeline. She noted that my process of change had happened very organically; whenever a logical next stage became apparent, I had moved on in that direction. That had happened when I voted to venture down hormone boulevard so why should SRS be any different?

There is a tendency by some transgender women to suppose that after surgery, you become 100% passable all the time. Of course it doesn't work that way. Vaginas, whether formed in the womb or created by scalpel, are obviously (and thankfully) invisible to the man on the street. Consequently, for anyone not seeing you in the boudoir, nothing has changed. Thus SRS is only a partial equalizer: A solution for the soul (and perhaps the bedroom) but for everyone else it remains the big invisible.

While I appreciated that SRS wouldn't make me instantly or universally seen as an all-natural-woman, I was developing a much deeper desire for it. I continued my research into surgeons and the places I could go for the procedure. The obvious place was Thailand, partly because the SRS surgeons there are renowned, but also because the country is so familiar to me. I had visited Thailand countless times over the years, especially when I was living in Hong Kong, when a jaunt to Thai beaches was just a long weekend away. So I started to contemplate making a brief trip to Thailand to meet the surgeon who was fast rising to the top of my provisional short-list, should I go ahead with SRS. I needed to meet the person who might be changing my life forever. I still had not made a firm decision, but the more I considered the surgery option, the more it became paramount to where my life was heading. It started to become a *need*. Before I could make a trip to Asia, a journey to the motherland was needed: a visit back to Britain.

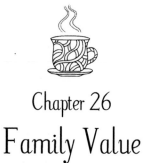

Chapter 26
Family Value

It was the first time I'd been back to Britain in 15 months, since that emotionally scarred Christmas with Mum. This time I knew it was going to be different. Then it had been an unusually cold winter; now it was April and signs of spring were evident. As I walked up the driveway I could see crocuses and daffodils starting to flower where before had seemed barren ground. I smiled at the metaphor. I walked in through the back door and nothing had changed. The clock on the mantelpiece was quietly ticking, though it was running a few minutes fast—a sign that it needed winding again. Mum was sitting at the same table, a mug of tea in front of her, the same mug with the red cardinal that I had given to her the Christmas before. When she saw me enter, she quickly got up (or as quick as she is able to these days) and we had another huge hug. Better times were back again.

I would also be meeting my sister, Sue, for a renewed first time. Although we didn't actively dislike each other when we were growing up, we were polar opposites and so rarely saw eye-to-eye about anything. There were parts of our childhood when we enjoyed experiences together, but those were mostly times when we were decorating the house for Christmas or playing with our loveable English sheepdog. Perhaps that alienation seems stranger as we are a one-parent family; Mum took care of everything after my father died when I was three. In some families that tragedy brings siblings together, but in our case I don't think it did. Sue is the scientist of the family just as my father was, and has more letters after her name than I have combined in mine. She has post-doctorates but I called the education process a day after leaving school at 18. We think differently, and with her dark hair and fairer skin we don't even look alike. I've joked with Mum before that surely one of us was due to a fling with the milkman.

I had emailed Sue a month or so after I dropped the transgender bombshell on Mum, but after an initial email of qualified support from her, I didn't sense a wave of understanding. I consequently assumed that Sue was not an enthusiastic member within my camp of supporters. But she is my only sibling and thus an inescapable part of the relationship we both have with our mother, so one of the agreed responsibilities on this trip home was a family reunion. I had no idea how this would go and it had the capacity to be at least awkward, and maybe even to develop into a verbal slanging match. Both situations had happened before and this time I felt highly protective of my new self.

It was good that I was now able to be a woman around the house as well as all the places in the area that I knew so well when I was growing up. I felt more relaxed than ever, but I still wasn't sure how the meeting with Sue would go. I was out shopping when she arrived at Mum's house and as I turned into the lane, I saw her car parked at the bottom of the driveway. She was upstairs with Mum, doing some work on the computer as I climbed the stairs. I wondered what her reaction would be. I said hi and greeted her as "your new sister." She laughed and any tension I felt quickly dissipated. We even had a brief hug—something we'd not done for years.

What followed in the subsequent hours ended up being the most deeply surreal soul-baring dialogue that I've had with anyone about my whole transitioning process. I felt completely at home (well, I suppose I *was* at home) and able to discuss everything that I'd been through with both my mother and sister. They were treated to the whole story, from my early days prior to identifying who I am, to my first steps cross-dressing, and then the most recent two years when I had lived my life in female mode. Not only was Sue remarkably understanding, she was also extremely interested in knowing everything about why and how I became who I am. Perhaps that was the analytical scientist in her. But it was still a huge surprise to me, as neither of us had ever been especially interested in the deep and personal goings-on of the other. But the ease of talking about my past, along with her acceptance of the female me was a total revelation—probably to us both.

I was amazed that I felt so at ease talking to Mum and Sue about hair removal, hormones, and even my strange exploits into the New York City dating world. Good heavens, I even gave them the lowdown on my date with Leo a few months before (though I conveniently forgot any mention of oral sex). Telling of that time was cathartic for me, though they had differing thoughts on that Crying Game incident.

"I think you deceived him," said Mum.

"You should have gone Dutch with the bill," said Sue with disarming honesty.

I disagreed with both comments but that wasn't important: this was about a bigger picture of them accepting me as I was. There we were, the three of us sitting by the cozy hearth in Mum's sitting room. The logs on the fire were crackling away and the conversation around it was burning preconceptions. Our past unease was the ash left behind.

One of the topics that I wanted to broach was the intricate and intimate subject of my possible sexual reassignment surgery. I knew this part of the conversation had the potential to stall their gender acceptance, or even shift it into reverse. I wanted to get the point across that I, as a genetic male, couldn't envisage having sex with a woman ever again. In fact, the more I considered being the man in that sexual act the more it repulsed me.

It was in the middle of this remarkable family heart-to-heart when I realized a key fact which became another marker point in my transition: I didn't consider myself male anymore. Of course I had been living as a woman for a couple of years already, embraced femininity and wanted to date men. But regardless of the signposts I'd seen, feelings that I'd had and happiness I'd experienced as a woman, there was always a lingering element of doubt in my mind. I wasn't sure exactly when that uncertainty left me but during this fireside chat, I realized that it had. Men were now *them* and women were *us*. I was transgendered. That term described me.

This fundamental realization also made it easier for me to explain to Mum and Sue that surgery was becoming increasingly relevant and progressively more imperative.

I considered myself the public advocate arguing my case before the unconvinced jury. What I saw between my legs every day simply didn't correspond with the woman I was. Yet however much Mum and Sue saw me as a woman (the court was yet unclear on that aspect), both considered such personal refurbishment more trouble than it would be worth.

"You can't direct where you pee you know," my sis explained helpfully. And while I accepted this inconvenience, I considered SRS to be more than replacing a hosepipe with a slighter faucet.

Another point I tried to emphasize was that both my sister and my mother had already had sex before as women, obviously. I meanwhile had not. And in my anatomically male state, I never could. But I wanted to be able to try this whole sex thing out, as a woman, and before I became too old to stand up afterwards. The jury mulled over the evidence. I was living my life as a woman; now I wanted to advance to being a sexual woman. Did I have one final point to help sway my two closest relatives? I chose to close my familial argument with succinct simplicity.

"You," I explained, "have both done that. Now I want to have a go!"

They paused, considered the situation further, and seemed to agree on the verdict. Consent to surgery had not been given, but at least from this point on, they could see things more from my perspective.

By the middle of the evening Sue had already expressed the sentiment that she enjoyed me more as a woman than as a man, and that I was a lot 'softer' this way. Not in a chocolate mousse kind of way, but that my inner self seemed more at peace—which although it undoubtedly was, I hadn't realized it was so apparent. When she left that evening, she said something previously unimaginable.

"It's been a real pleasure meeting you."

I felt the same. Things had changed between the two of us as she sensed someone new in me. I knew we wouldn't be going clothes shopping together or heading out for sisterly spa treatments, but there was a much deeper understanding of who we are—who we both are. An obdurate family rift had been bridged; our paths to both past and future were opening up.

In subsequent days my mother and I continued an occasional discussion around the issue of SRS. The acceptance she had shown me already had been incredible, but SRS was a much more prickly topic. Still, just like we had done at the time of my first revelation, we kept the conversation going. Another important evolution this time was that we both achieved it without crying. On more than one occasion she mentioned the word 'mutilation.' In fact she always referred to it negatively. However, while the notion of surgery was wedged somewhere between uncomfortable and abhorrent, part of her understood my reasons for contemplating it. Maybe, at this stage, such a baby step forward was all I could expect from a life-changing dialogue so close to home. Like so many matters transgender, conflicting emotions blur perspectives, and reality often doesn't seem very real at all.

Chapter 27
Old Friends, New Me

A nother reason for this trip back to Blighty was to do the rounds and visit some old family friends. My past *re-introductions* had been in New York and Asia, and although they had all gone well, Brits are renowned as a more reserved bunch. Now it was time to start spreading the word on home turf. I would not be doing this alone as I had my special ally who would be holding my hand throughout: Mum.

For more years than I can remember, our family used to head up to the English Lake District for summer holidays. My mother was always a part, sometimes my sister, and occasionally extended family or close friends. It was a place of sanctuary that Mum, Sue and I found ourselves drawn to after my father died. It has never lost that touchstone significance, and in fact Sue now lives there. The holidays comprised a week, or two, or occasionally three, usually in June or

July, back in the untroubled days of youth when all summers were long, hot, and forever sunny. This was the Lake District, however, so they were usually cold and wet—*especially* in the middle of summer. Right through my late 20s, a summer would never go by that didn't involve some time up there. The valley has always been a special place, the valley dwellers even more so. And now it was time that old friends there were brought into my new loop.

In the same way that she guided me from crawling to walking, from a baby to a boy, Mum would be there for me again. We were going to do this together. She had pre-warned people by email to say that we were coming for a visit and that I was now Nicky. So they knew what to anticipate, even if they didn't know what to expect.

First there was the baker, then the engine driver's wife. Just like I had told friends in New York, I stated that it was OK to stare at me for the first time; there was a lot to take in, after all. I noticed a few inquisitive glances from the baker as we sat around her kitchen table, but both seemed to accept me without much issue. Tea was also consumed in both homes, though one brew was definitely on the weak side.

"There's actually a transgender person in the village," the engine driver's wife noted, "so it's not so strange a concept, even here."

Even here was a pertinent point. These are small rural communities where word travels fast, and gossip even faster. I had imagined that the jungle drums would be beating as soon as the latch on the first farm door dropped, but maybe my revelations weren't as eye-opening as I had expected. It was remarkable to think that in these most traditional of farming villages, being transgendered wasn't so strange after all.

Those first two meetings had gone well, but the couple that I was most nervous about re-meeting was the former garage owners. I suppose it was a gas station, but with just two pumps and a main car repair area, we called it a garage. I have always felt very close to Tom and Nancy as their straightforward, no-nonsense approach to life is as solid as the granite that the valley was forged from. When they owned the garage (and I was a man), I had the hots for one of their daughters who was usually on petrol pump duty in tiny cut-off shorts. I always seemed to use far more petrol than was normal back then. No idea why.

I had agonized over the best way to introduce myself again to Tom and Nancy, but the most obvious way was the most familiar: pop round to their place for a chat and a cuppa. There must have been countless awkward conversations in Britain throughout the ages, but more often than not, these will have been discussed over tea. I was following this trend too. I parked at the side of their cottage and cast an admiring look at their always-blooming garden, a verdant oasis under the rugged fells. It made my Queens yard seem like an imperfect postage stamp. Mum rang their doorbell and I waited hesitantly behind her, fidgeting in my skirt and sweater. Nancy opened the door and her welcome was as affectionate as ever. She looked the same as ever too, as did Tom, though he might have lost a few hairs and gained a pound or two. I occasionally felt the subject of curious glances but I shouldn't have worried; their warm Cumbrian lilt reminded me that I was among friends. In fact, we got on as well as ever and their acceptance was almost overwhelming. I struggled not to cry while we were sitting at their kitchen table nibbling some excellent scones Nancy had made, but at the end of the first cup of tea I had to excuse myself for a few minutes. I wandered round their garden while my tears of release flowed. The biggest block on their understanding had nothing to do with gender. Rather, it was me trying to explain what a vegetarian was and why I didn't eat meat anymore; that notion was far more befuddling to Tom than me now being a woman. And that blissful normality is exactly why they will always be special people.

Unless you are French, men don't kiss other men. So one of the greatest tests of whether men can truly accept me as a woman is whether they are willing to give me a peck on the cheek. The kiss or the handshake? For Tom, it was straightforward.

"You look like a woman, you sound like a woman; I'll give you a kiss on the cheek!" And he did.

I have always felt so utterly at home in that valley, which these days is much too seldom. But that occasion was filled with a far deeper sense of contentment: I was rededicating myself to my past. This was so much more than just being able to wear a skirt when walking along the path down to the river by the church (and avoiding stinging nettles on my bare legs); it was all about me being profoundly me in my uniquely special home away from home.

Back at Mum's house, I reflected on the remarkable acceptance others had shown me. Friends who had known me for many years suddenly had to get used to me as someone else. Or was there enough of the old me apparent in who I now was? That familiarity had shown itself in me being called sir at my local post office a long time before, but the same essence of me also helped re-bond old friendships. I also needed to remember that for some, my change was too much. Biker Bob had been like a protecting big brother but he could not accept me as Nicky. As Robin to his Batman, there was no place for Catwoman.

My actor friend, Corelli, was a completely different story. He is an artsy man of the thespian underworld, but our shared love of music enhances our connection. I've known him from schooldays and we've always gotten along famously, but it had been many years since we'd met up. Last time that had happened, I'd been a man. I was surprisingly anxious about meeting up this time, even though I had advised him of my new self some months earlier and he had been very supportive. I checked for wardrobe advice from Mum before heading out. Was the skirt too casual? Did my hair look OK? I felt like I was going out on a date (though Corelli is already taken) and needed Mum's blessing on my appearance. That reminded me again of how much had changed. She may never perceive me as her daughter but Mum was appreciating my femininity and giving me style tips as a woman. And yes, the denim skirt was fine.

"You look great!" Corelli said as I opened the back door and saw my old friend again. I breathed a huge sigh of relief; my nerves dispersed as we walked down the drive to his car. He opened the car door for me (a nice touch) then we drove to a local pub for dinner and a glass of wine. We reminisced about listless times at the hopeless school where neither of us blossomed. Then of musical memories and 80s one-hit wonders, quizzing each other on obscure music tracks and Number One's from decades past. Each of us would try to outfox the other. (*"Yes, but what was the year?"*) At the end of the evening he came back to Mum's house for a cuppa just as he must have done 20 years earlier. Maybe there was now the additional shared wrinkle between us, but we both had new aspects of life to be thankful for: he'd beaten cancer, I'd overcome being a man.

I returned to New York a few days later with a renewed sense of deep satisfaction. The trip back to my birthplace had gone far better than I had hoped. Old friendships had been renewed and I had bonded with my sister. I had discussed surgery options with Mum, and through that conversation, its necessity had been further distilled in my mind's eye. We even touched on the possibility of her helping me with the finances of the operation. She remained torn by the bigger picture and unpleasant imagery. So we agreed on a compromise: if I did go ahead with surgery, then I would let her know when it had been done and not before. That plan was conceptually sound but flawed by the practical. Should I decide to have surgery in Bangkok, then I would be away from New York for several weeks and so our weekly phone conversations would turn into radio silence. But this was a divide that could be addressed later.

My future seemed clearer than ever and I started consolidating choices of a potential surgeon. There are at least three world-class SRS surgeons in Thailand, but also several options closer to home. A clinic in Montreal has many fans, and there are highly regarded surgeons in Arizona, Pennsylvania, and California. There are many more besides that, but those were the ones I was the most interested in.

"But which is the best one?"

That is a query that most trans women will ask if they consider going down the avenue of surgery, but a question to which there is no definitive answer. With at least half a dozen top-notch practitioners who have rave reviews, choosing one over another comes down to factors beyond the surgeon's credentials. Location, price, and availability are important, but an instinctive gut feeling is vital. A *feel* for the person who would change my life forever was my biggest consideration. I emailed most of the surgical candidates, and the ones that replied with helpful comments beyond a form letter interested me the most. There are commonalities to the procedure, whoever performs it, but differences too. I researched information online and read countless reviews from those who had been through the process. Price was an obvious concern, and one of the Thai surgeons seemed particularly expensive. Of course nobody can put a price on life-changing surgery, but I still have to pay rent every month. Practicalities can betray dreams.

Having digested replies from prospective clinics, and reexamined my own mental compass, I felt I was close to making a decision. However before I did, I wanted to meet the prime candidate. My direction was heading east, so I booked a ticket to Bangkok. I was about 90% in favor of surgery at this point. I don't know what the other 10% was telling me but I brushed those concerns aside. Little did I realize how they would later rise to overwhelm me.

Chapter 28
To Travel Hopefully

*"T*o *travel hopefully"* wrote Robert Louis Stevenson *"is a better thing than to arrive."* My own love of travel is both a blessing and a curse. Journeying to far away exotic places has definitely broadened my mind—experiences in Egypt, China, and the U.A.E. all impacted who I am now—but it's also a drain on my finances, even in cattle class. As a transgender woman, apart from lackluster food plonked down on my tray table, there was another unappetizing aspect of flying: my passport stated male but my inner compass said not. Security paranoia peaks in New York, and so when traveling out of the airports here, the pragmatism of identity becomes even more arduous. To give the impression that you might not be who your passport claims is tempting fate, or tempting a body cavity search, neither being an attractive option. Even though I had broached the subject of being transgendered to Immigration last time, I still didn't want to push my feminine luck. So in practical

terms that meant no make-up (lest I appear to be a terrorist), no overtly female clothing (lest I appear to be a terrorist), and no heels, lest, well, you get the idea. (Though I am unsure how many Al Qaeda operatives wear 6-inch heels.) When I walked out of my apartment on my way to Thailand that evening, and wheeled my case along the sidewalk to the subway, I resorted to my standard flying outfit: black unisex trousers, black unisex sweater, simple stud earrings, and a pair of rather funky sneakers which were arguably more femme than not, but at least didn't scream *vagina*. This time the look was topped off with a loosely wrapped black and gold patterned pashmina to hide my improving curves.

Taking the E train to JFK, I wondered if I was behaving differently with a male passport inside my asexual carry-on bag. I had a seat on the subway train but should I have given it up for *another* woman? I was traveling in unisex style, but how did the other subway passengers perceive me? This faded from being a concern when I remembered that, after all, this was the New York City subway system, where any overt eye contact is greeted with either suspicion or disdain.

At the airport, the check-in process went without a hitch, though passing through security I did perceive a hint of a double-take from the official on duty. Or was that my own reading of paranoia? Thankfully my frequent flyer status granted me access to the business class lounge in Terminal 7 so at least I didn't have to mix with the hoi polloi before I slunk off to the back of the plane after boarding. It was a late night flight out of JFK and I was enjoying some savory nibbles and a glass or two of red wine—if only to aid the sleep process on the plane. (Yes, I know the folly of this faux logic.)

I found myself an area to sit in but then noticed a far classier set of three armchairs which looked better than anything that rightly belonged in an airport departure lounge, business class or not. I wanted to sit in one of those. The problem was that in one sat a man. Quite a nice looking chap from what I could see, too. But if I approached him in order to sit in one of the two vacant chairs, might it be construed as overt friendliness, or even a pick-up? One into three chairs goes, two into three doesn't.

I was still scarred by the fateful Leo incident several months before, and also remembered something else he had said after I had revealed all during that pre-Christmas debacle.

"I should have known," he said. "You kiss like a man." Though the more I pondered that comment, the more it raised questions about him rather than me. Here, all I wanted to do was sit in a comfy armchair!

I moved over to the chair threesome and said to the single fellow in question that I just had to sit in one of them, as they were the sexiest in the lounge. I think I really did refer to the chairs as sexy. Perhaps that was my flirtatious side coming out to play again. He said it was fine if I sat down there. So I sat. And I snacked. But out of the corner of my eye I could see him checking me out. Should I take the initiative or maintain demure? Time was pressing.

"You're drinking cocoa!" I exclaimed. It was an improbable way to start a conversation, but he confirmed that yes, he was indeed drinking cocoa. It also transpired that he was Danish, worked for the United Nations, and lived in Copenhagen. Fair, clean-shaven, with blue eyes (those things I figured out myself without him telling me), and with two daughters aged 15 and 19 who he saw every other weekend. Aha, a divorced man with a ready-made family! I liked the sound of this scenario! Two mostly grown kids could be ideal for inheriting, as they probably wouldn't be overbearing or require much maintenance from me. I envisioned being the perfect stepmother. Not the evil Disney-esque type, but the big sister variety who could assist them with wardrobe decisions—or perhaps they could help me in mine. I started contemplating birthdays and Christmas, and Thanksgiving, or whatever the equivalent is in Denmark. Not only was he European, but he was exceptionally well-traveled (an aphrodisiac in itself), and seemingly quite fit, having mentioned that he ran in Central Park every day.

"Have you got any kids?" he asked me.

"Um, no." I hedged. "Long story."

I had been to Copenhagen with my mum and sister when I was 13, so I told him that I vaguely remembered the Tivoli Gardens and the Little Mermaid.

"She's still there!" he noted which, if nothing else, was reassuring.

In these types of scenarios it can be remarkably easy for me to say *"when I was a little boy,"* which although technically accurate, would be confusing for everybody. So I try to check my words and keep it to non-specific gender terms like *"kid"* or *"when I was young."*

Our conversation was rolling along nicely. But then I heard the boarding announcement for my flight. I was heading off to Asia, and he was going in another direction altogether, back to Copenhagen. Thankfully he took the lead.

"I think I have a business card somewhere, if you're ever passing through Copenhagen."

It is not exactly a place one passes through, but I definitely liked the idea of maintaining contact. I too gave him my card, asking him when he would be back in New York again.

"Before the end of this month, actually."

"Oh!" I said, somewhat startled. "Then maybe…"

Did I say *"maybe we'll meet again"* or *"maybe we could meet up"* or *"maybe we could have dinner"* or *"maybe I can rip your clothes off then?"* I don't remember, as in my mind I was already picking out the wedding china.

I boarded the plane with a wonderful glow, not just originating from the glass and a half of lounge-standard Cabernet Sauvignon. I envisioned my future life accompanying a UN jetsetter, splitting time between New York and Copenhagen, while being the belle of the ball at high-powered black tie functions with Pel—that was his name. We sounded such a perfect match but maybe I had misinterpreted the smoke signals. Perhaps he was blissfully married and only saw his undoubtedly gorgeous daughters every two weeks because they were on UN missions in Africa. Probably they were ending world hunger, alleviating poverty, or helping disadvantaged children. Or some other sickeningly worthy cause. I never spotted a wedding ring, but he could have been wearing one of those invisible ones that men often wear when traveling. Or maybe he was a recovering alcoholic (thus the cocoa). Or was only 5'2" and had a wooden leg; I don't think he ever stood up, not even when I was leaving. Maybe that lack of chivalry was due to prosthetics and not the natural diplomacy I imagined he excelled at.

For the rest of the flight I mulled over my game plan. I certainly wanted to see him again, there was no doubt about that. How long should I wait before I emailed him? Or did I have to play the damsel card and wait for him to contact me? I guessed that was how gender roles and dating rules would have it, but as a self-proclaimed New Yorker was I not permitted to be more proactive? I also tried to imagine how I would have followed up if I were the man in that situation. That didn't help as I couldn't remember even one instance from my past when anything similar had happened.

Ah, but there would be an unavoidable topic that would need to be raised before he marched me down the aisle. I knew that such a fact-finding conversation didn't have to happen immediately and so maybe I could just forewarn him that I had "woman problems" that needed to be dealt with. That was such an understatement. The daunting fear of rejection and the looming inevitability of reality dampened my exuberant hopes, but I vowed to keep checking my inbox when I was away, just in case he wanted me as his own Little Mermaid.

Even having planned out my future life between New York and Copenhagen, there was still a lot of leftover time to kill on the flight between JFK and Bangkok. Pel had obviously seen me as a woman, hadn't he? Whenever we see anyone for the first time, our brains have already made a subconscious decision about gender, rather than us actively looking at someone and pondering *"hmm, I wonder what gender that person is?"* Yes that happens in a few cases, but usually the brain has instantaneously weighed up myriad factors before dividing the population into two convenient options: male or female. What they are wearing, how tall they are and how their hair is styled are aspects. Facial features, skin type, deportment, and what the person is doing at the time are also tossed into our internal gender computer. The brain is an outstandingly intelligent piece of hardware with almost perfect facial recognition software, and most of the time it makes these gender decisions flawlessly without us even realizing it. The main exception is when the brain meets someone transgendered. Then it can be flummoxed. My hope is that, in time, our brains can be coaxed into appreciating that gender is not simply black or white, but multiple shades of gray.

I landed in Thailand and was greeted by a stark reality check. The experience with Pel before boarding, and contemplating the gender equation mid-flight, had lulled me into a deep sense of personal femininity. I approached the immigration desk in Bangkok and beamed carelessly as I handed over my passport and documents to the immigration officer. He examined the picture in the passport and looked back at me. And then again. He picked up the passport with the picture of my male self in it, and shook it at me alarmingly.

"Who is this?" he asked with a distinctly aggressive tone.

"Um... me," I confirmed nervously, recoiling and pulling my hair away from my face in a vain attempt to look more masculine.

"Ah..." he added, his hostility reduced a fraction. Another pause.

"What is your name?"

I recited the name in my passport while feeling increasingly anxious about what was happening right in front of me. More checking by the official who was seemingly going through all the databases on his computer to see if I was actually a threat or simply an oddity.

What felt like far too many minutes passed before he eventually stamped my passport and I was on my way. I smiled broadly to myself all the way through baggage claim and onwards into the city via the airport express train. It was only after my semi-euphoric state eased off that I realized that the consequences at Immigration could have been a lot worse. I recalled movie scenes of drug runners being thrown into the slammer at the so-called "Bangkok Hilton." Mine was only a case of perceived mis-identity and nothing illegal, but even though I love that country dearly, Thai officialdom is neither bureaucratic nor corruption-free and I had no desire to be on the wrong end of it.

Robert Louis Stevenson had got it mostly right: I had traveled hopefully but it was still wonderful to arrive.

Chapter 29

The Rhinoceros Factor

Bangkok in May is oppressively hot but I loved being back again. I would have barely 10 days in the city this time, though I had high hopes that I'd accomplish everything I'd planned. I had come to see a surgeon. Actually, I had come to see a brace of surgeons. (Or whatever the collective noun is: a scalpel of surgeons perhaps.) I wanted to meet the man who I felt increasingly certain was the one to perform my SRS. However it seemed churlish to come half way around the world for just a 30-minute consultation so I had a nose job too.

Rhi.no.plas.ty: noun—the process of applying a Band-Aid to a rhinoceros

As I mentioned at the start of this book, I don't know exactly when I realized that I was transgendered. I progressively embraced a process of inner acceptance that the body I arrived in was not the one I felt most at home with. The more I progressed along the

165

transitional path, the clearer those indications became. Once I reached the conclusion that I was female (or *probably* female at least) the process of adapting my current body to my revised gender became very important. I wanted to be as outwardly feminine as my inner self (and my outer pocketbook) would allow. That vain subjectivity of attractiveness also meant being open to surgical tweaks.

I don't think I disliked my nose as a guy, but as a woman I grew to see it as anything but femme. It was not as extreme as a hook, beak, or character from a vintage Punch & Judy puppet show, but its lack of self-synchronicity was evident whenever I looked in the mirror. Consequently, a nose tweak had been on my surgical to-do list for a while. When I had my Vagina Epiphany earlier that year, I started to contemplate a time when I could actually be complete. There really might be a time in future when all my past-gender physical characteristics would have been changed, snipped, or reconstructed. A boob job would be the icing on the cake but it is best not to do that until the effects of taking estrogen have run their course and breast tissue has developed—usually around two years after starting hormone therapy. Having a Designer Vagina would be the biggest step but a new nose was not to be sneezed at either.

Many transgender people have long wish lists when considering plastic surgery options, from relative subtleties like reduction rhinoplasties and trachea shaves (reducing the Adam's apple), to breast augmentation and more adventurous feminization procedures. Some will elect to have their forehead skin peeled back and then have crushed-up bone inserted to give their foreheads a nicer contour. That procedure really does get done by many transgender women, and I've seen before, during, and after photographs to prove it. While some trans people are blessed with androgynous looks, others are not, and those are the people who feel the most need for Facial Feminization Surgery (FFS).

Dr. N is pretty old school. He is a renowned professor of plastic surgery and is invited to lecture on his craft around the world. He doesn't have a website and relies on word of mouth rather than advertising his skills. It was almost by accident that I found him a couple of years earlier when he was consulting at a local hospital in Bangkok. For this visit, I had emailed him from New York to check on his schedule and arrange the details. It was going to be good to see him again.

His clinic is down a quiet side street off the main Sukhumvit Road and is more 80s quaint than hi-tech gloss. Inside there is a large waiting area equipped with slightly incongruous easy chairs that I feel rightly belong in a royal palace. In fact there is a picture of Dr. N being received by the Thai royal family with the doctor himself reverentially prostrate on the floor in front of the Queen. There are magazines (all in Thai) on the large coffee table, and the articles highlighted inside seem to show universal acclaim for his work. I always notice a small, ornate fountain near the front door that has a glass ball on top that is rotated by the flow of water. I presume it has to do with *feng shui*, or perhaps the Thai equivalent. Dr. N also seems remarkably balanced and performs gratis facial reconstructive surgery for disadvantaged patients in Thailand. I appreciate his humanity as much as his obvious scalpel skills. He doesn't do SRS but rhinoplasties are right up his septum.

I was led into his office by one of the smiling receptionists (everyone smiles in Thailand) and Dr. N also welcomed me with a thoroughly genuine smile. Of course his English is impeccable and so we discussed what designs I had for my new nose. I'd brought some pictures and sketches, but he suggested a lower key profile and not going with too much of a "ski slope." I agreed, and bowed to his clear sense of aesthetics. The next day I returned to the clinic for the operation, which would involve an overnight stay. I wasn't nervous at all and knew I would be in good hands.

His nursing team was wonderfully caring, although I didn't like the recovery period immediately after the rhinoplasty. I had an ugly plaster cast over my supposedly reduced schnoz, along with multiple strips of sticking plaster to keep it in place. That had to stay on for one week and I had to resist any temptation to scratch it, and certainly not remove the sticking plasters. The days after saw a rainbow array of purple and yellow bruising around my cheeks, the stuff of nightmares for small children—and probably bigger ones too. I tried to hold my head up high when popping out for daily supplies from my rented apartment (fresh milk for my morning tea was a must) but I found myself doing this under cover of darkness so as not to attract undue attention. I started to appreciate the self-esteem issues the Phantom of the Opera had to endure.

The seven days under the cast dragged. I couldn't imagine how people coped with having casts on broken legs for many weeks, as just one week in this state almost drove me insane. I was relieved as I headed back to the clinic for the unveiling ceremony. Excited too, as soon I would be able to see the results. I returned to Dr. N's consulting room with high anticipation. The moment came… the plaster came off… the strapping too… and then… my new nose didn't seem that much different than the old one! Had I suffered a week of looking like Cyrano de Bergerac in plaster for this? However, as Dr. N showed me the before and after pictures, I realized that there was a significant difference, it did look more feminine, and yes, it was definitely worth it. Besides it would take many more weeks for the post-operative swelling to disappear completely. I suppose it would have been worse to take off the cast and exclaim, *"Wow, that's an awesome new nose!"* as then it would likely have been too different from the one before. The point is—and this is the strength of Dr. N's work—that a natural appearance is paramount. That is where many surgeons (or people's expectations of surgeons) fail. Except with new boobs of course: those need to stand out more than a bartender at "Hooters" on wet T-shirt night.

Chapter 30

The Second Doctor

T hey say that the road to hell is paved with good intentions, but my road to hell was a notorious Bangkok traffic jam. My intentions were clear though: I was going to meet Dr. S, the front-runner to be my SRS surgeon.

It was a Wednesday morning and the appointment was for 9.30am. I'd mapped out the journey online and the Google God suggested it would take 18 minutes. I figured that I knew Bangkok traffic better than any website, so I doubled that trip time and added an extra half hour for good measure. I had been impressed by the lack of spectacular traffic jams on the trip so far—Bangkok is famous for them—but this was not the day to be caught up in one.

Oh, but it was! I felt overwhelmingly helpless, trapped in a taxi in the middle of a three-lane highway with solid lines of traffic on both sides. Didn't move one inch. Ten, fifteen, twenty minutes. The meter was ticking over, the radio was still blaring out Thai favorites, but the taxi remained stationary. All the while my scheduled appointment time was creeping ever closer. My options were minimal, but when my anxiety touched the boiling point I decided that Plan B was the only way forward, even if it might mean going backward. So I paid the cabbie, jumped out into the heat and fumes of the gridlocked highway, and headed for one of the thousands of price-negotiable motorbike taxis. The word 'taxi' when it follows 'motorbike' is a complete misnomer. These are freelance bikers, usually identifiable by green or yellow nylon jackets, who will take you on the back of their bikes for an agreed fee, negotiated in advance. They always wear helmets but those are strictly optional for the passenger, unless there is word of police checkpoints, in which case the driver will reluctantly proffer one. I don't often find the headgear effective anyway, as my *farang*-sized head rarely fits inside, and so the helmet looks like an oversized plastic pimple on my pate, further exaggerating its disparity.

Whether it is the thrill, creative dynamism, or a death wish, taking a motorbike taxi is still one of the most mind-blowing things to do in Bangkok. These two-wheeler entrepreneurs assume the rules of the road are conceptual guidelines and deem red lights as annoyances rather than directives. I found a clutch of bikers by the nearest 7-Eleven convenience store (usually a good staging area) and showed one of them the map of where I wanted to go. He promptly turned it the right way round and looked at it closer. He hummed and hawed and debated the options with his colleagues, a process which seemed to be happening in slow motion as the minutes ticked away. Through Thai fractured with minimal English and a lot of sign language, he eventually accepted the job and we agreed on a price (about $6 for a ride that might last half an hour), and we were on our way.

The process involved me losing all concept of dignity as I straddled his motorbike, skirt flying in the wind, and holding on for grim death (or avoidance of grim death). Most of the local girls will ride, as my mother would say, 'side saddle,' certainly if they are wearing skirts or dresses, but I figured that lack of poise was favorable to loss of life. There were a few startled looks from fellow riders as they noticed this unlikely *farang* woman clinging to the back of a motorbike, pink skirt wedged up around her thighs, sandals slipping off the broken foot holds, and blonde hair billowing in the wind. Some smiled at me and I smiled back; I felt in my element again. I loved the adrenalin rush of dusty air blowing in my face after the air conditioned frustration of a stationary car. But then… even more traffic! As we pulled up behind a solid line of vehicles that seemed to stretch beyond the future, my heart sank. I had come all this way, halfway around the world, only to be blocked by a totally typical Bangkok traffic jam. Surely this logjam would stymie even the most creative of motorbike impresarios. I could only try one last push. Figuring that cash might be the biggest incentive for invention, I upped the biker's fee to $10 if he could make it to the destination in the next 10 minutes.

The effect was like adding super-octane fuel to the tank. A quick U-turn and we were off like the wind. I felt that my adopted suicide jockey was waiting for this sort of incentive to show off his abilities, as he relished weaving through gaps barely inches wider than his trusty, rusty steed—and at breakneck speed. (Though again, I was hoping that breakneck injuries would not be a consequence.) I felt a huge buzz on the back of this supercharged 100cc Yamaha, and not just as a result of the thinly padded seat, but one errant pothole and it would all be over. We were really flying! Zooming around bends, whipping past buses, always going for pole position at traffic lights. And he did it! He pulled up abruptly outside the address I had given him. Yes, this was the place; I recognized it from the website photograph. So along with effusive congratulations he also got a rare tip too, which made his eyes pop out from behind his cracked visor. I don't think I fell off the bike as I dismounted, but my legs wobbled as if they had been astride a shire horse for a week. The supreme irony, however, was that beating the insufferable Bangkok rush hour traffic was all in vain; Dr. S was running late, and I had to wait a further 30 minutes to see him.

I must have looked a windswept, grimy mess when I walked into the clinic, so the waiting time allowed me to freshen up. But I also chuckled to myself that I was probably the only foreign woman who arrived for a consultation on a motorbike taxi. I caught my breath, smiled some more, and enjoyed the cool calm of the waiting area while I looked through the window outside. I could now take more of it in.

There was a mix of old and new low-rise buildings, but the odd half-baked concrete monolith was there to further break up the asymmetrical panorama. I suppose it was like most other streets in Bangkok: two lanes of snaking, dusty traffic, with taxis and private cars bumper-to-bumper, and an array of smart new motorbikes or decrepit mopeds plaited in between. There were pedestrians ambling along the sidewalks, occasionally stopping at one of the many stalls by the side of the road. Fruit, noodles, and more often these days, coffee, are always available at these places, and undoubtedly served with a smile by vendors earning just a few dollars per day. Taxis in Bangkok are nondescript vehicles in blue, red, or green, depending on the owning company, and operate on meters that the drivers actually do use. Gone are the days of negotiating a fare, and the once-common *tuk tuk* has mostly been consigned to tourist areas. Yes they were hugely fun, but the two-stroke motorbike rickshaws were no match for air conditioned taxis. Noise and pollution has been reduced with their endangered status, but so has Bangkok's soul. As I gazed outside the clinic, life in the City of Angels was trundling along as normal, and I wondered if those passing by knew how lives were being changed within these four walls.

"Nicky?" It was Sam, the business manager from the clinic, whose voice brought me back to the reception area inside. I had exchanged several emails with her over the preceding weeks and so it was good to hear the voice behind those messages. We shook hands and she apologized for the delay. I told her that I was grateful for that extra time and I elaborated on my journey there. She seemed quite impressed and we joked together easily. A native of the city, but with plenty of experience overseas, I imagined that she'd be perfect at her job. I filled out some details while she answered most of my general questions; the more specific ones would be addressed later by Dr. S.

Shortly afterwards I was ushered into his consulting room and met the man himself, a very calm and quietly spoken person, slightly shorter than me and with a kind, squarish face and, of course, a friendly smile. I felt immediately at ease with him as I asked him more of the specifics of his technique, along with the recuperation period, and any other practicalities of such a big operation. Some of this information was on his website, but the main point of my visit was because I wanted to get a gauge of the man himself. It struck me how intently he listened and then responded to points I made. Of course all doctors need to listen, but the intensity of his concentration was apparent. After that I needed to show him what I had between my legs. Since accepting my transgender status it had been a constant source of embarrassment, but equally, it was the very reason for this consultation. I didn't like standing in front of him with my underwear around my ankles but it was a necessary state.

Another reason I'd felt so optimistic about Dr. S was that I didn't want to be part of an SRS production line. Some surgeons will race through this procedure in three hours, or will do more than one per day. But Dr. S never performs more than one SRS per day, and I got the impression that he had the endless patience needed to achieve the best results that he—and the patient—could hope for. Of course there is a huge amount of skill involved, but I wondered about artistry too; surely that must play a part in using the raw materials wisely. I wanted my SRS surgeon to be something special. I wasn't sure how, exactly, but I needed to sense something, likely intangible, to tell me that I had met the right person.

I probably should have had consultations with other surgeons, but there was no need. My instinct was that Dr. S had those qualities. In barely half an hour my mind was made up: this was the man to change my life and reshape my future.

Chapter 31
Equation of Outcome

I returned to New York the next day, still with a few questions but with far more answers than I had two weeks before. And I had a new nose too. However after the identity glitch I suffered entering into Thailand at the start of the trip, I had heightened trepidation about passing through Immigration in order to be allowed back into the United States. Even though an immigration officer had assured me previously that it was the paperwork and fingerprint match that mattered most, I was nervous as I stood in line waiting to pass through the immigration counters again at JFK. When I reached the counter the first question the officer asked was whether I had any press credentials. That question stumped me, as even though my visa was specifically a journalist "I" category one, I'd rarely been asked for any supporting documentation. So I fumbled around in my bag and found a business card which seemed to pacify him as he continued the validation process. Then he asked me something even more surprising.

"How do you prefer to be addressed? Mr.? Ms.?"

I immediately relaxed.

"Ms, preferably." I smiled, adding that I was a transitioning transgender person.

"Yes," he continued with a more welcoming tone, "I gathered that."

Not only did he just gather it, but it seemed glaringly obvious to him. With my anxiety gone I added that I hoped this would be one of the last times my paperwork didn't match my own image of self. He seemed supportive and I felt relieved.

Meanwhile it had been two weeks since I had the rhinoplasty, and although there was still a little bruising around my eyes and cheeks, this was nothing that a little concealer couldn't, well, conceal. One of the downsides of any surgery is that surgeons have to be particularly careful about what medications you are taking lest they complicate the anesthetic effect or subsequent recovery. My hormone regime at the time was twofold. I took one Spiro Gyra testosterone blocker pill twice daily to prevent me from turning back into a werewolf, and then every two weeks I would shoot up with neat estrogen into one of my thighs. I didn't find the injections too onerous and the biweekly event reaffirmed my femininity. Even so, I couldn't imagine doing it for fun. How do junkies cope? I suppose, by definition, they don't.

As a precaution, Dr. N wanted me to stop taking the testosterone blocker for a couple of weeks both before and after the nose job. That seemed fair enough, but I wondered what the effects might be. Part of me (the most cynical third) questioned the effects of hormones again: did I feel female *because* of the hormone therapy, or were the hormones giving me greater clarity about who I truly was?

I felt that this time *sans* hormones could be a good test. By removing the anti-testosterone drug for a few weeks, would I then want to have sex with everything in sight, or want to punch everyone in bars who disagreed with me? Thankfully this didn't happen, and I was the same feminine person with the same feminine feelings (and highlighted insecurities) throughout. I appreciated that reassurance.

I was very busy after coming back from Thailand. I was working progressively more days as receptionist and Girl Friday at Kiki's. One of her most admirable qualities is that she likes to help transgender clients as much as possible; however, one aspect of that dedication took me by surprise. I was having a treatment session from her one day when she asked me something completely out of the blue. And I should point out that trying to have a conversation while having electrolysis needles poked in your face is as about as easy as reciting Shakespeare with a dentist's drill in your mouth.

"So if you do go ahead with SRS…"

"Yes?"

"Can I watch?"

"Huh?"

"I mean would you mind if I observed the procedure."

"Well, it is likely to be in Thailand."

"Yes, I know, but I have wanted to watch this operation so that I know how I can help my transgender patients more."

I thought about this request over the following days. Her motives were clearly altruistic, but they also seemed weirdly voyeuristic. I imagined that surgeons would be unlikely to consent to such a request but it allowed me to consider the operation from a different perspective. In my research about the SRS procedure I had seen some very graphic details about what the surgeon does and they seemed nauseatingly gory. If I were to go ahead with SRS, I didn't want to be too aware of the step-by-step process. I would rather be *avec penis* when the anesthetic kicked in, and then magically *with vagina* when I woke up; what happened in between was something I preferred not to think about.

However the biggest issue I needed to resolve from the Thailand trip was not regarding the operation itself, but the subsequent maintenance required. In an ideal world, one where I could have my Designa Vagina (DV) functioning in exactly the same way as a natal one, the decision to go ahead with surgery would have been far easier. Sadly though, a DV does not work in the same way as a genetically formed one. On the outside it is possible for the DV to be somewhat indistinguishable from one assigned by the gene genie at conception. However on the inside it is a very different matter. The body perceives it as an open wound, and therefore wants to heal the gash: a result far from the one intended.

To counter this, there is a required process of dilation. This is the mantra (*"womantra"* perhaps) for any post-op transsexual woman. Different surgeons apply different regimens and this was one of the big questions I had for Dr. S, even though I suspected that I wouldn't like what he told me. His answer? Two hours per day for at least the next year. That meant I would need to insert a range of different sized stents (essentially dildos) for two hours, each and every day for at least the next 12 months, and probably two years. After that the repetition can decrease, but maintaining that routine for the first year is critical. Use it or lose it. And don't forget about your responsibilities to self when you grow old and senile, either. There still needs to be some degree of ongoing dilation after that two-year honeymoon period for the rest of your natural days. Only in the afterlife do you get time off for good behavior.

When Dr. S advised me of this regimen during my consultation in his office, my heart sank. Yes I wanted to go ahead with surgery, but how could I possibly keep up this maintenance regimen? The logistics of such a total commitment seemed so utterly overwhelming. I wondered how other post-op trans women coped, and so I checked out many online blogs for guidance. I was probably looking for magical short cuts too, though I knew there probably wouldn't be any. The consensus seemed to be that it was just something you *had to do*. I wasn't sure if I had the strength of mind to do that.

I knew that I was being inexorably drawn to this operation, even if I couldn't grasp exactly why. I would be one step closer to completion, that seemed certain. I needed to focus on the practical upsides too. If I had surgery then I would be able to wear nice clothes that fitted. Proper swimwear and more attractive underwear would also become available. I would have the future option of sex. That notion seemed incomprehensible: It was difficult enough envisioning my new genitalia but even harder to conceptualize someone else being there at the same time.

The equation was clear: If I wanted to have SRS (which I did) then I would need to dilate for two hours per day for at least the next year (which I didn't want to do) and possibly up to two years (which I wanted to do even less). I frowned at the irony that natal women often strive to have vaginas that are tighter as the years go by, but for the transsexual woman it becomes an ongoing process to keep the neo-vagina as flexible and elastic as possible. Differences in genetic anatomy disguised as another unkind twist of fate.

I spent ages weighing up the pros and cons, and tried to balance how I wanted to be physically with what that entailed practically. The pre-conditions were daunting but my resolve was clear. I emailed Dr. S's clinic and asked about his availability.

Chapter 32
Let's Get It On

The next day some unexpected good news arrived on my laptop. It was an email from Pel, the Danish fellow I'd met at JFK on my way to Thailand. He was in town and asked me out for dinner. I liked that idea. Although I'd only met him for a few minutes in a business class lounge, I had gotten a nice vibe at the time. So I promptly replied yes and we arranged to meet at a cozy Italian restaurant I suggested on the Upper East Side. It was the sort of place that could be intimate without being suggestive, yet it was casual enough not to be intimidating.

I was excited as I was getting ready to head out. I chose to wear my hair down; others seemed to like it this way though I was never sure. From my closet I selected a simple white skirt (it was after Memorial Day so the style police would have no problem with me wearing white, as is the unspoken rule exemplified by New Yorkers not in a permanent shade of black) which I topped off with a light plum-colored sweater. A casual black purse and some beige Clarks sandals with enough heel to be flattering, not so much to be slutty, and I was good to go—physically, anyway. I didn't consider that conversing over dinner would be a problem, but going out with a man did raise the same huge issue again: although I never categorically stated that I was a genetic woman, would I need to have The Conversation with him?

I was afraid of history repeating itself. There had been the disconcerting non-affair with Leo and then my aborted speed dating efforts a few weeks later. Maybe this time would be different, as there did seem to be extenuating circumstances that might push the balance towards a more positive outcome. For a start, I was naturally androgynous when I saw him last time at the airport; I wasn't actively trying to be female. Who knows, he might even have had a sixth sense about me. Besides, he was from Denmark, and so perhaps an open-minded European sensibility might prevail over the Neanderthal attitudes on this side of the pond.

Anyway, I would keep my mouth shut about matters transgender and try to avoid revealing too much about myself on the first date. Gosh, a date. That was daunting vocabulary but I was looking forward to it. I felt butterflies as I fumbled for the tiny holes that my earrings slipped into. I also giggled to myself when I remembered one of the wittiest things my friend Portia had ever said.

"Our ability to accessorize is what separates us from the animals!"

For this evening I went with ornate silver rings on three fingers and dangly earrings with little red hearts—as Pel would obviously desire mine. I sprayed a dash of Coco Mademoiselle on my neck and resolved that the ideal scenario for the evening would be one where we both had a relaxing and entertaining time, yet also one where everybody's underwear stayed in place. After that we would disappear our separate ways before I turned into a pumpkin at midnight. Then on the morrow, when he would *obviously* email me to plead for another date, I'd let him into my little transgender secret. Gently, via email, rather than sobbing over a bowl of gelato at the Italian restaurant. As I left my apartment to walk to the subway I could see storm clouds brewing over the skies of Manhattan. I wondered if that was an omen.

He was perfectly on time when we met at the restaurant and seemed agreeably surprised at the way I looked. The sentiment was mutual. I loved seeing those clear blue eyes again and I was relieved to see that he was a good few inches taller than me, too. I never want to give up the option of wearing heels under my 5'9" frame, and so dating Tom Cruise would never be an option for me. (Sorry Tom, but I have standards.) Pel wore an open-necked white collared shirt, unbuttoned just enough for hints to be visible from his clean chest, and beige trousers that were casual but still denoted style. I tried not to stare but I was drawn to him; besides I wanted to take in my future husband so I could plan his wardrobe for the honeymoon.

The ominous storm clouds eased so we were able to sit outside on the terrace sipping a refreshing Sauvignon Blanc and nibbling antipasti. We got on tremendously, even better than I'd hoped, and talked of everything under the sun. There was his work as a global mediator, travel (he'd been everywhere), vacations (why he should come here), and New York (ditto). His Danish accent was delectable and I watched his lips as he spoke of some or other project he had been assigned which dealt with toxic oceans, or mercury in fish, or the pension plans of retired whales, and even though I empathized with the cause, it was the man who spoke of these good deeds who intrigued me more.

I welcomed that the conversation revolved around him and I was content to keep nudging it in that direction lest I develop any sudden impulse to prematurely disclose my past. By the end of the appetizers there had been the occasional electric touch. My pulse fluttered and I felt desirable. Even so, I kept myself in check, delicately maneuvering away from his advances yet lingering just enough for these moves not to be perceived as rejection. By the end of the main course I wanted the evening to continue; I was feeling positively sexy.

We skipped dessert, keeping that as an option for elsewhere. Leaving the restaurant I felt like a giddy teenager in love. We took a taxi downtown and I was tempted to make out with him, but I kept my composure and restricted myself to just holding hands; I knew I had to play it at least slightly cool. We jumped out at 42nd Street and walked through Grand Central Terminal. As an adoptive New Yorker I felt some responsibility to show him the sights, if not my underwear. It was there, walking through the Whispering Gallery, when (in his own hushed tones) he asked me if he could be direct. While I respect straight talking, his question was not one I'd expected: Would I like to come straight back to his hotel room, in preference to hitting another bar? Wow! That laid his intentions bare and put hanky-panky right up there instead of the cheesecake I had been anticipating. Showing remarkable restraint, though with a cursory thought about my unaccommodating anatomy, I politely declined his kind offer of an immediate romp and instead we went for another drink at a little Irish pub I knew close by. My delicate refusal to advance straight to the carnal stifled the conversation for a while, but it clarified his intentions: my Perceived Desirability Quotient (PDQ) had shifted from 'unknown' to Marvin Gaye-inspired "Let's Get It On."

The Irish bar was a good change of scenery, and an equitable way to procrastinate having The Conversation that I didn't wish to have. There continued to be some flirting, a bit of discussing options for the following weekend—I had a party to go to at Portia's and he would be an ideal 'plus one'—and a fair bit of spilling red wine on my pristine white skirt too, which seemed indicative of the dither he'd put me in. When I looked around the bar later it seemed we were the last ones left, so it was clearly time for us to leave as well. I walked him back to his hotel on 42nd Street; surely that was harmless enough. As we sauntered hand in hand, I mulled over my options, although there was only one: I must return home alone. We dawdled at the entrance to his hotel, his arms now around my waist, my hands pushed against his chest. It felt so perfect. He kissed me, delicately at first, and then more probing. My body arched and my mind flirted with options while he tried to re-convince me about his bed linen. I felt his body more under that crisp seersucker shirt; he certainly kept fit. There was no denying it: I wanted to get naked with him. But the baggage of reality that travels with me dislocated that high; this was neither the time nor the place for the intimate disclosure that was becoming inevitable.

"Come up."

"I can't."

"Please…"

"I'm not that kind of girl."

In hindsight that was probably one of the funniest things I've ever said.

As I took the subway home I drifted off into a land of dreamy possibilities. A casual meeting at an airport departure lounge had evolved into, potentially, something a lot more. Maybe a life flitting between Copenhagen and New York wasn't so far-fetched after all. But the stuttering train car also jolted me back to reality. I was not the woman he thought I was. My optimism faded with each subway stop. As I peered through the train car's rear window my future was leaving faster than the tracks behind me.

The train paused and I wondered how different it might have been if I'd had a Designa Vagina? Would I have kept the same stoic line of Victorian defense, or might I have succumbed to the allure of hotel linen? It was a question that I simply couldn't answer. Or perhaps I didn't want to.

The following morning dawned bright with a gorgeous early summer day. My garden was verdant but inside the apartment, things were not so rosy. The previous evening had been almost perfect; I had felt attractive and sexy, and was desired by someone with whom I felt a real connection that was beyond just physical. However, for us to move on he had to be brought into my secular world. I started to compose an email. I stared into my oversized mug of tea in the vain hope of finding inspiration.

"I had such a good time with you last night! You are very easy to be around."

That was the simple part.

"It would be good to see you before you disappear from the city again, and if you can make it to my friend's terrace party on Saturday evening, then that would be wonderful. However there is kind of a factor I need to discuss with you first."

As I typed the next words, tears welled up inside me; these would be the deal breakers.

"I am a transitioning transgender woman, and so things are somewhat different with me on many levels. It can make a difference with some people, it doesn't at all to others."

I tried not to make a big deal of the issue, make the facts seem more casual, tried to help him appreciate that I could see things from his perspective, but there are only so many ways to downplay my situation.

"I would like to get to know you more, but before that becomes an option, then of course you need to know about this. And I'm guessing you will want to know specifics too, some of which I am happy to discuss now, others may need to wait for a while."

It wouldn't matter; he would have already decided by this point. In fact he'd probably have stopped reading after the previous paragraph. Foretelling the inevitable made it no easier; rejection was inescapable.

It was one of the hardest emails I'd ever written. I paused while I contemplated for one last time the trans-Atlantic bubble of life with Pel that I was set to burst. I pressed send. My outbox had a little check mark to show that the email had gone but I knew the consequence was going to be a cross against me: I was also about to be deleted.

Pel emailed me back that evening. He was surprised—not least because he had never met a trans woman (knowingly anyway), and he admitted to not having a clue how to proceed. But I knew what he would do; perceptions are always transformed on the disclosure that I was born with a penis.

After one more email exchange, Pel announced that he didn't want to see me again. I had already pre-passed through the sad stage of rejection as soon as I sent him that initial email, so his lack of real-time acceptance was merely a formality. It was apparent from our evening out that his testosterone levels were sky high and steaming away in his trousers. In his eyes I suddenly wasn't female anymore, and with my revelation, the magnetism he felt for me was nullified. I wasn't angry at him—he was very civilized in his rejection—just intensely sad at the outcome.

Over the next few days I tried to re-examine the event. Were there any nuggets of positivity from this relatively whirlwind, almost-dating experience? It was definitely a plus-point that I could pull in a guy who was very attractive and a seemingly good catch. That part felt good, though I couldn't be sure whether he had seen me as future relationship material or just a mark on the bedpost. It was immaterial; once again I had been rejected not for *who* I was, but for *what* I was. It was that sentiment which stung the hardest.

It also made me doubt any potential for any relationship with any person. In day-to-day life I am almost always seen as naturally female, but once it evolves into a dating scenario and I admit that I did not grow up as a little girl, rejection invariably follows. Testosterone is a potent drug and for millennia has driven the male brain to simplistic conclusions of two genders determined only by genitalia. I had been beaten down by evolution—or the lack of it.

This apparent pattern of rejection raised an even more disturbing enigma of dual standards for me: would I have behaved any differently when I was a guy and dating women? I tried to exchange the players in this demoralizing scenario. If I had thought I had gone on a date with a genetic woman, but instead this person turned out to be a transgender woman, what would I have felt? The more I contemplated this, the more I disliked what I was finding out about myself. Deep down I knew that my own reaction would have been the same as Pel's, the same as Leo's, the same as anyone else who wanted to get close but then rejected me because of what I am. In my journey of transition I found this latest revelation to be one of the worst. It was both cynically reassuring and horribly unnerving.

People tell me that things happen for a reason but I've always found that concept hard to accept. Likewise, I've never believed in fate yet in the course of my transition, many things fell into place. This time serendipity occurred in my inbox. There were two emails side by side, received just minutes apart. One was the final rejection from Pel, and the next email in my inbox was from Thailand, from Dr. S, the SRS surgeon I'd met in Bangkok. His assistant offered me a date utterly different from the one I'd just had with Pel: a date for surgery that could change my life. October 24th. Did I want it?

The synchronicity of receiving two emails, side by side, seemed uncanny. Two distinctly different emails were pointing me in one obvious direction.

To Pel's email I replied, "I appreciate you being civilized, thank you and goodnight."

To the SRS email I replied, "Yes."

Chapter 33

The Summer of... Meh...

I love summer in New York City. Whether it is dining at sidewalk restaurants, enjoying outdoor concerts, or lazing around in the parks, the city feels brighter and greener. Waiting on a stifling subway platform in the middle of summer can feel like being in a rat-ridden sauna, but the subway trains are a means to a happier place. Occasionally in this season, the unthinkable happens: New Yorkers will crack a smile. It's also the time for tea to become iced. But this year my emotions were mixed. On one hand I was feeling more comfortable than ever in my own skin, yet in tandem with this was a growing sense of alienation from the world outside. My date for rebirth had been confirmed but I still couldn't drum up happiness. I had assumed that having decided upon the procedure, surgeon, and date, a weight would be lifted from my shoulders, like the relief Atlas must have felt (albeit temporarily) when not holding up the sky.

Instead I was in a deep funk with a mental malaise. I resented that I was transgendered.

"It's not your fault!" Kiki said to me at work one morning, when she could see I was not my usual bright-eyed, bushy-tailed self. I hadn't thought of my situation in such clear-cut terms, but I suppose it wasn't my fault nor anyone else's that I was trans. Regardless, that reassurance did little to lift my spirits.

Pel's rejection had hit me harder than I'd realized. It heightened my insecurities and reaffirmed my unease. The following weekend I went to Portia's house party. There were some old friends, some new friends, and some old, old friends who knew me before in my male days, but had yet to be introduced to the new me. It went well and I considered myself the ideal party invitational; fun, cute, well-traveled, easy to talk to. But I still felt bruised and alone. It should have been so different; Pel should have been there so he could have seen the wide circle of friends that I have. That would have proved to him that it didn't matter I was different. We should have been holding hands on Portia's terrace staring into the full moon. Or each other's eyes. Instead I felt very, very isolated. I had been assimilated into the female delegation but I was seemingly inaccessible to the guys I wanted to be with. This deep divide highlighted a profound sense of frustration I'd not felt before: whatever state my body was in, it would never be adequate.

I wondered if the timing of my announcement to Pel was partly to blame for his rejection. I discussed this with one of Portia's uncles who was at the party and who had known me in my former days.

"Should I have put my cards on the table sooner?" I asked him.

"Certainly not," he replied. "These days, after recovering from prostate cancer, I need Viagra, and I don't tell any date that sort of information until they need to know—definitely not until further on in any relationship. Mine is not first date subject material, and neither is yours!"

That advice helped but also highlighted different perceptions between genders. Although the scenarios are not analogous, a woman would likely have accepted that a little blue pill was acceptable for a cancer survivor, but how many men would risk becoming involved with a transgender woman in a little black dress lest it imply that they have suddenly turned gay? That ridiculous premise of assumed gayness is one of many misconceptions that trans women are confronted by in a potential partner.

After I left Portia's apartment there was one of those crazy, unexpected, never to be repeated New York moments. I was walking back towards the 6 train subway station and made eye contact with a fellow walking in my direction. Actually, he was the one who made eye contact but it was returned by me. Ten strides on, he stopped and looked back at me. As I did to him. It was bizarre mutuality. He walked towards me.

"Hi, I'm Tim." Or Tom, or Tam, or something like that. The name was irrelevant.

"Do you want to get a drink?" he continued.

"Um, well, maybe…" I replied. I felt vulnerable after a frustrating party and needed affirmation of gender and confirmation of femininity. We walked together for a couple of minutes, before he approached his stoop and opened the door to his building.

"Come on in," he said.

Ah, that wasn't the sort of drinking establishment that I had imagined when I accepted his invite.

"I can't," I replied with resignation. "It wouldn't end well."

I walked away, and feeling more dejected than ever, I kicked my heels towards the subway home.

Chapter 34
Bullets Over Broadway

A couple of weeks later Portia dragged me out for cocktails to vent about her latest man dilemma. She had met her own Mr. Big when we were hanging out at Whiskey Blue one time and now they were having issues of fidelity and communication—a lack of both. I remembered the first time they met and he definitely had eyes for her. What I hadn't realized was that those same eyes had identified me as trans. This was revealed when Portia told me of one of her later conversations with Big.

"Oh, and he asked me if you were transgender."

My heart sank. I accepted that some people will *make* me but I really hadn't thought this suburban traveling salesman would have the faintest inclination of my inner self. Just like at the awkward speed dating evening, I felt offended hearing the truth.

I mentioned this to Navi at my next session, who suggested that I should "do some work" on possible layers of "transphobia." I knew

193

I had begun to resent being transgendered but surely this didn't equate to feeling antipathy or animosity towards others of my tribe?

I started going to a group meeting that Navi had put together. There were five or six of us, all squeezed into her small consulting room, seated on various chairs or the main sofa. (One time I even got the rocking chair, which seemed like winning the lottery.) I was surprised how interesting it was hearing the perspectives of other trans women, especially as these people seemed to be at the relative start of their transgender journeys. Everybody seemed to come from a different walk of life and no one looked the same. Some were in their early 20s, others in their 40s and 50s. However there was a defining thread to all of us: a point had been reached where we had identified something irrevocably female within our inner selves. They were all still living in male mode, be it for work, personal, family, or whatever other reasons, and that inability to express their inherent inside to the outside world seemed to be verging on the intolerable for them. I could see real pain.

There are some trans folk who know there is something out of synch before they hit puberty. For other people it hits in the teens, or twenties, or at any other time through later life. There needn't even be an obvious trigger that brings these sensations to the fore, either. It just happens. Imagine these thoughts in the bottom right hand corner of the brain, just underneath the staircase, behind a pot of paint that's not been used for years. Then just like termites, those feelings grow and become harder to ignore. You have to take notice of them lest the fabric of the house deteriorates and becomes unsound. But once you do, and the issue is addressed, then the house becomes more stable. Hiding these thoughts, allowing them to fester, or hoping that they'll just go away by ignoring them, leaves you with structural issues that can only get worse. Of course I'm not comparing being transgendered with having termites, but you can't sweep either condition under the carpet.

As I was the only member of the group living my life completely as a woman, the others tended to focus on my experiences and how it was for me—not that I saw my life as any type of transitional template.

"What is it like living as a woman all the time?"

"Do you feel relieved?"

"Are you happier now?"

I was happier, yes, certainly more than I was in my latter-day man life. And looking around further at the other members of the group I sensed their disquiet even more, their blights of fate exposed in different ways. Maybe I felt lucky that I hadn't experienced the same stark inequity of balance; my own journey hadn't been so agonizing. That time was yet to come.

In the days after the group sessions I wondered how their future lives would pan out and what degrees of transition they would attain. Would they be able to transition as they wanted? Did they even have an end game? I certainly didn't know my goal when I was at that stage.

A couple of the group members told of times when they had been verbally abused, or worse. To the outsider, New York is one of the most cosmopolitan cities in the world, but not all residents are as accepting as some might imagine. There have been times when I have been subjected to verbal abuse and wanted to crawl into a crack in the sidewalk just to get away from it.

I am lucky living in the part of Queens that I do, as most people accept me for who I am. One of my dear friends in the neighborhood is Carmine. What makes him special is that he shows movies in his back yard during the summer for anyone who wants to be a part of the occasion. Why? Well, because he can, and so why shouldn't he share his back yard with total strangers? There are, of course, a hundred reasons why he should not host people in such a way; selfless friendship like his is a dying sentiment in this increasingly cynical world.

I met him a few years ago when I was coming back home one Saturday night and I walked past his yard when he was showing *Bullets Over Broadway*. There were Tiki torches lit around the garden and a large fabric tablecloth draped over his balcony which doubled as the screen. It was the Woody Allen script that made me pause at the gate.

"Come in, come in!" Carmine said.

"But… I don't know you," was my defensive, somewhat British reply. I did go in and subsequently became a regular at his weekend screenings.

One evening during my summer of malcontent Carmine showed *Tootsie* in his back yard, the story of a hard-to-hire actor played by Dustin Hoffman who became far more successful using the empowering female persona of Dorothy Michaels. Were there parallels in my life? No, I was not engaged in role-play. Still, I empathized with all those things that a natal man has to do in order to be seen as a natal woman—hair removal, voice, poise, posture, everything. Our motives were completely different but seeing the process on screen did make me smile. I must have seen *Tootsie* soon after it was released, but back then the parallels in my life had yet to unfold. This time its projection was lifelike.

Chapter 35

Countdown to Realization

As summer persevered, I counted down the days to when my anatomy would be changing for good—and for the better. On the calendar it had started off as being four months away. Then suddenly it became just two. I had booked the flight and arranged the hotel, but there were still details to sort out. I needed to tell my landlords that I would be away for a month (I didn't want to say why) and I'd need to ensure that the utility bills would get paid. I still found it incomprehensible that there really would be a day when I would step on the plane to start the trip. Then a time when I would arrive at the clinic, and a moment after that when they would administer the anesthesia for the operation. Ever since confirming the date, this occasion had been a vague yet certain event that was set to happen at *some* time in the future. But soon it was going to be *"next month."* Then *"next week."* And then *"tomorrow."* I couldn't grasp this definitive actuality.

Of course this happens to everyone, for everything, on every single day, but this was set to be the single most important event that I would ever elect to do. Coming to terms with the ticking clock as the days passed became an obsession. This countdown realization manifested itself in different ways. I was still shooting up with estrogen twice per month, but that needed to cease four weeks prior to surgery. And although I knew there would be some ongoing estrogen dosing after V-Day, the existing regimen would end. A more amusing aspect of the countdown regarded my laundry. Each time I went to the laundromat to wash and dry outwardly unsuitable but sadly practical undergarments, I was reminded again of what I was not. It was a constant embarrassment having all these pairs of man's underpants displayed on the folding table. They were not mine, honestly! But the end of those days was in sight. I began looking forward to underwear shopping for real, proper, feminine lingerie for my post-surgery anatomy. The whimsy of knickers helped me address my nerves, but those apprehensions were never far below the surface.

As the specter of SRS drew closer, the more I found myself consumed by its enormity. I couldn't focus at work or relax at home; all I could hear was this ticking clock in my head. The logic of my choice was unequivocal and I knew I should be elated by the prospect of becoming more female. So why couldn't I embrace it more?

I also started to think about death. Not as a consequence of botched surgery, but as the inevitable end to life. Perhaps this was a part of my required process of letting go. Even so, dwelling on death worried me even more.

With this deepening gloom, my perceptions of the outcome changed. Whenever I considered the realities of the operation I was about to have, I saw it as a mere compromise: a least worst option. I would never have a natal vagina. Or know how one really feels. Or experience female orgasm. Or truly sense my womanhood. My cynical self again questioned the whole point of SRS. Why was I going through with it? Was this just a superficial change? No. My logical self reassured me that surgery was an essential way to move forward. Besides, it would be infinitely preferable to my status quo.

Then it got worse. Fear began to overwhelm me. I became supremely anxious, positively afraid of what would soon be happening. Still I couldn't understand why a process I wanted to happen had become so terrifying. I tried talking it through with Navi, who explained how deceptively deep the human mind is. Like an iceberg, 10% visible on the surface, but the 90% below the waterline is the most powerful. We carry on with our visible lives, but it is the invisible nine-tenths of the mind that directs us, sways us, and is the hardest to control. It appeared to be the nine-tenths of the iceberg that was giving me the most trouble, albeit for reasons that I couldn't quite fathom. I hoped it wouldn't be my undoing.

Navi wondered whether the surgery I had accepted in my practical mind was not yet in sync with my emotional side. Certainly the logic of my decision made sense and the schedule was sound, but was I ready for this titanic change on an emotional level? Navi raised the possibility of postponing surgery for a few months, or even a year. The same thought had crossed my mind too, but hearing those words from someone else only reinforced my resolve. No, there would be no delay; I would proceed as planned.

I also reflected on the remarkable rate of change that my life had undergone. It had been barely three years since my day-to-day existence had been in male mode. At that point Nicky only came out at weekends or after dark, with a wig and terrible make-up. Was that pace of evolution accentuating my anxiety?

I tried to look for other parallels but they usually made me feel worse. Was being transgendered like being Pinocchio? The wooden puppet strived to be a real little boy but could never achieve that dream. SRS was going to take me closer to who I am, but I also started to appreciate that being a *real* female was impossible. Pinocchio would never be a living, breathing little boy. I would never be a true woman.

My unease deepened. Fears lurked like poison ivy, slowly creeping through my body and getting stronger as the days passed, poised to suffocate me.

One night I was watching *Pretty Woman*, the 80s movie with Richard Gere and Julia Roberts. It should have been a feel-good chick flick, but all it did was amplify my frustrations. I wanted to be so many of the things that Julia's character was, yet in actuality I was everything that she was not. Not the hooker, but I wanted to be appreciated and admired and, yes, loved. In the movie, Gere wanted the pretty woman to be something she was not, but she struggled to maintain that manifestation. Was that a distorted metaphor for me? Was I not desirable? It didn't matter; I could never be the person that men *first* see in me. I am always discarded as an unwanted freak following the dawn of revelation.

For a while I actually thought I was a woman, I really did. This was but a tantalizing dream cynically fashioned out of my subconscious mind, almost tangible yet always an inch out of reach. The fictional hooker from Sunset Boulevard and the misguided transgender person from the posher suburbs of Liverpool: we were both naïvely deluded. In the end she got her Richard Gere and he got his fantasy woman but their acceptance was just a popcorn mirage of reality. Deep down we all know the movie was just a fairy tale. My life was a nearly tale.

So bring on surgery! Bring on the new me! It can't be any worse than the misguided hopes, desperate dreams, and foolish fantasies of who I almost was! Forget truth, ignore reality, live life! But the poison ivy prickles my throat as I exhale.

I.

Will.

Never.

Be.

A.

Woman.

I drifted off into a restless sleep; until I woke in the middle of the night.

That was when the panic struck.

Part Two

Chapter 36

The Morning After

Intense panic had hit me in the middle of the night. I was woken from sleep by a five-alarm fire in my head. Images and words and colors all bounced around. There was noise in my head, too. I couldn't breathe, and abstract thoughts were out of control. It was beyond confusing: I felt suicidal. I remember getting up and walking around but still my mind teetered on the abyss. Helpless and afraid, my turmoil was absolute.

I don't know how I survived those pre-dawn hours but perhaps the human spirit is stronger than we give it credit for. I did make it through daybreak; the overnight vampires couldn't survive beyond sunrise. It was 8 o'clock and I hadn't slept since sometime around 3am. I'd probably slept a couple of hours before then, not that it was restful at all. I felt utterly drained after the overnight mental pummeling. I brewed my pot of morning tea extra strong, and with successive sips, strands of rational thought returned.

I managed to get dressed, apply some make-up and walk to the subway. I stumbled into Kiki's for my regular receptionist duties, though I can't believe I functioned at all that day. I took care of the practicalities that my job entailed, but on this day they all seemed so trivial. My mind had capsized, so little or nothing made sense except for one stark message. A semaphore signal had been raised by all the red flags waved in my head overnight.

Thankfully it was Thursday, and so I had my scheduled afternoon therapy with Navi. She immediately sensed my anxiety and I told her of the events of the past 24 hours. That session ended up being more Band-Aid than permanent solution. We discussed ways for me to foster calm, but just talking about those dark overnight events helped me appreciate ways in which I might get beyond them. Then we touched on what I knew was the core of my anxiety: delaying my date for surgery.

My decision to go through with SRS had evolved; I hadn't seen it as a requisite finishing line when I started my journey. Instead it had become apparent halfway through the race, sometime after the starting pistol had gone off. But the overnight panic had changed that perception and it was now clear that I couldn't proceed with this life-changing schedule that was merely weeks away. However in defiance of logic that seems incomprehensible now, I still couldn't accept that truth. I had felt the demons pounding inside my head—they had nearly killed me that dark September night—yet still I wanted to overlook their elucidation of fact.

Instead I focused on the immediate short-term to prepare for the ominous ogre of the night ahead. I invested in some nasal strips that help to reduce snoring. I don't think I was snoring when my panic was brewing, but any way I could make my breathing easier might ward away shortness of breath. My nose had been stuffy and so I also got some decongestant. So with anti-snoring strips, a nasal spray, and half a Valium that I found in the back of my medicine cabinet, I hoped I would be prepared for the uncertainties of the next twelve hours. I was half expecting the panic to return, but that night I managed an uneasy sleep.

Over the next few days I even felt better about myself and almost managed to ignore the impending surgery that was looming over my future. Yet however much I wanted to mask it, my discomfort was clear to others. Dr. Rose had been a pillar of support for me ever since I had seen her that first time with a suspected case of medieval bubonic plague. As soon as she saw me for my scheduled appointment, my obvious disquiet became her immediate concern. She was reluctant to give my surgery her renewed blessing.

The next meeting with Navi sealed my fate. It was a very downbeat, extremely upsetting therapy session, the worst I'd ever had. My lucidity had gone completely and I was dreading my rebirth. Even the hints of false hope that I'd fabricated post-panic evaporated. At the end of that session I felt numb but I made the inevitable decision.

It took ages, but that evening I composed the email to Dr. S in Thailand. I told him that I wasn't able to make the surgery date. I had no idea what the financial implications of this decision would be, but dollars were the least of my concerns. It was heart-wrenching to press 'send' as this seemed like 'end'. Then I cried almost uncontrollably. I took myself to bed and rolled myself under the bedclothes, trying to banish thoughts of what I had just done. Remarkably though, I slept.

With the morning I felt a calming sense of relief, yet one lined with empty disappointment. After planning everything out so well, I had let myself down. The schedule had been faultless: surgery followed by legal name changes, so that in just months I would have been officially, legally, and utterly female. All the travel obstacles would be gone. 'F' would replace 'M' in my passport and my US visa would finally show a female face.

In our therapy session Navi had proposed a revised time line of six to twelve months. I wept at the idea of such a long wait. Would it really take that long before I was emotionally prepared to physically move on? We concluded what we had previously suspected: my emotional mind hadn't agreed with my practical brain. That imbalance had led to a mental chasm that could only be filled by anxiety—thus the panic attack. I didn't like hearing those words though their meaning made sense.

In another restless (but thankfully not panic strewn) night, I tossed around the idea of a three-month delay, but maybe Navi's suggestion of at least six months was more practical. A new self-recognition appeared and it made me feel worse: I was clearly not as advanced in my journey as I'd imagined. My future was starting to show cracks in the pavement and forks in the road. SRS suddenly became an elusive option and not a definitive solution. Might it ever happen at all? I cried again. I never wanted all the mental paraphernalia that comes with being transgendered, but nobody who is transgendered ever does.

My email to the clinic in Thailand canceling my surgery received no reply. Little did I know that there had been severe storms in Bangkok that week and their Internet was down.

Chapter 37
The Discotini Weekend

The brain, as any scientist will tell you, is extraordinarily complex; the mind, even more so. Buddhists see the mind as a formless continuum that joins our body for this life before passing to the next body. Others consider it more as the repository for hopes, dreams, and memories. Science may never uncover all its possibilities, nor will mental health professionals ever know the entirety of its secrets.

My mind had built a Jenga tower of concern which had been toppled once my anxiety removed the crucial block. The virtual debris lay strewn around as I tried to piece together a new foundation. I had finally accepted that SRS was premature and made the monumental decision to postpone surgery. As a result my feelings were an unholy alloy of bitter disappointment and palpable relief.

I had already arranged that my friend Grace would come visiting from Providence that weekend. When we had planned her visit it was set to be a fun celebration to help me on my way to Thailand. I texted her to say that there was no need for her visit anymore as things had changed. I grieved even thinking in those terms but she insisted on coming the next day as planned, possibly on the promise of a few basil-infused martinis to be sipped on my deck. When she arrived I told her of my decision and we hugged each other. Then we talked. And talked some more.

It was a beautiful September evening with just the hint of a chill in the air. Over the summer I'd had my crop of rhubarb, the raspberries had been spectacular, and the honeysuckle made a takeover bid for the space occupied by the tomatoes. The family of American robins had fledged long ago, though some came back to revisit my birdbath. I liked to think they were the same ones anyway. The back yard was in a state of conclusion; all the plants that had been set to bloom or fruit had done just that. There were still leaves aplenty on the big ash tree overlooking the yard but it wouldn't be long before it started shedding for the winter. On the deck we consumed cocktails as I utilized the last of the season's basil, cut fresh from the small wooden planter.

With every *Discotini* I mixed up (Discotini = basil-infused martini enhanced by accompanying cheesy 70s & 80s disco tunes), we talked more about feelings and gender and sexuality and all the things that had been weighing so heavily on my mind—issues that had snowballed into a huge icy chunk of mental anguish. We discussed my day-old decision to delay surgery and talked over the reasons behind it. She was neither delighted nor disappointed, just concerned; Grace would support whatever decision I made. What had promised to be a gloomy, angst-ridden time turned into a wonderfully happy occasion, washed down with plentiful Discotinis and fueled with pizza from Joe's restaurant on the corner of my block. The heady combination of vodka, pizza, and dear friendship washed away many dregs of distress. We talked some more, drank some more, and had another slice.

By the end of the evening the noose around my mental state had loosened and my thoughts had settled like the basil sediment at the bottom of the martini glass. I knew that this variety of updated clarity was likely to be accompanied by a post-Discotini hangover in the morning, but this seemed acceptable collateral damage. Yet along with that increasing lucidity were one or two tinges of regret for things bigger than a vodka overdose.

I was right; Sunday did dawn with hangovers, but my morning Typhoo eased the haze. I mused on my newly remixed emotions that seemed to ebb and flow by the hour. Had I been too hasty in postponing surgery? No, surely that decision was correct. Or was it? I felt like a sailboat that had become disconnected from the rudder; my direction wavered in the breeze.

The day after Grace left the strangest thing occurred, and it changed my life. I had been out with my downstairs neighbor for an early glass of Cabernet at a local wine bar. I wanted to meet up with her, but one glass was quite enough after the Discotinis of the weekend. After I returned home, I settled in for the evening to watch some TV that I'd recorded: the deliciously dark *Dexter* followed by *Homeland*. That was when it happened. Someone in the episode of *Homeland* said to the lead character, "You're ready." It was actually about preparing for a covert espionage operation inside Beirut, but all I heard was the words "You're ready." They stood out and flashed in bright neon over my TV; the actors were talking to me.

"You're ready…"

"YOU'RE READY."

It was true.

I WAS READY!

I didn't want to wait another three months, or six months, or a year.

I WAS READY FOR SURGERY.

I wanted to do this NOW!

Whether it was the conversation with Grace, the Discotinis, the actors from *Homeland,* or a combination of all three, surgery was back at the top of my agenda and seemingly throughout my whole mind as well. I would immediately contact the clinic in Bangkok to tell them. No, my practical self insisted that I sleep on it, knowing that I shouldn't retract another decision too impulsively. It had taken many months to make the initial decision to go ahead with SRS, followed by weeks to then rescind it, and so I didn't want to retract that rescinded decision without letting this newfound enlightenment distill further. I waited until morning.

When I woke, I remembered that I'd not received confirmation from the clinic of my decision to postpone. What would happen if I checked my email and they had already allocated my spot to someone else? I was nervous as I checked my inbox—which I did even before boiling the kettle for my tea. Thankfully there was nothing from the clinic and so I quickly updated them on my decision, and that surgery could happen as originally scheduled. After that there was an excruciating delay while I waited for a reply from the other side of the world.

The storms over Thailand subsided, and the clinic was back online. It took another restless 24 hours of waiting, but their email reply then appeared. Everything was fine and I was reconfirmed. October 24th was set to be my new birthday, the day my life would hit reset and everything could start again. I still had nerves, but not worries. I felt grateful for the storm systems over Thailand and the synchronicity of fate. Not only that but my emotional side had made up with my logical side; perhaps they too had been out for Discotinis.

Chapter 38
The Calm Before the Calm

ays went by and my sense of purpose strengthened. The
anxiety and confusion that had subjugated my thinking the
week before had been banished, almost in their entirety. What
concerns remained regarded the purely physical. I was nervous about
being under anesthetic for eight hours; the subsequent four days
confined to bed with minimal mobility didn't sound much fun either.
The 48 hours of bowel-emptying colonic cleansing in preparation for
the operation filled me with dread, and I couldn't forget the two
hours of intensive dilation exercises that I was soon to embark on
and that would then dominate my life for the foreseeable future. But
with my unexpectedly swift change of heart, these practicalities
became less daunting. I viewed them as hurdles to jump and not
impassable trenches. The chasm of unease that I had been peering
into before had been reduced to a mere scratch on the surface. I
started looking forward to surgery. Looking forward to it! I'd never

felt that emotion, not even in the pseudo-giddy days after making the decision initially. I started smiling again as the dark storm broke and my inner light shone brighter than ever. I can't attest to spiritual guidance but I found this new sense of direction positively inspirational.

It became increasingly easy to talk about my future status with others. I wasn't going to place a full-page advertisement in the *New York Times*, nor break the news to those who weren't a close part of my life, but there were people that I did want to bring into the loop. In one instance that was a co-worker at Kiki's. I had worked with her for more than a year and so I wanted to tell her why I would shortly be absent from the office for several weeks. I felt this was going to be a fairly straightforward announcement, but I never knew what others' reactions might be. So over a herbal tea in the office lounge one day I told her I would soon be heading to Thailand for surgery.

"But you look so feminine!"

Those words still make me smile. If I had said, *"I'm going to have open heart surgery next week,"* a similar response might have been, *"But you dress so stylishly!"* It was the right answer, but to a different question. In fact, I think the 'feminine' comment was a delayed reaction to the "by the way, I am transgender" statement from earlier in our conversation, but those words hadn't been absorbed by the time I mentioned surgery. I shouldn't have worried about her reactions, as we have been firmer friends ever since.

However responses are never straightforward. Usually I feel relief once I tell people about being transgendered, eased from keeping one more secret. Yet along with that liberation I often lodged an irrational fear that the same person wouldn't respect me as before. In this instance, did my co-worker really have no idea that I was transgendered, or was she just being polite? It had been a terminal surprise for the men in the two failed dating situations I had experienced, but I always assume women have a sixth sense about these things, that they can sniff an impostor to their ranks at 50 paces—not that I have ever felt like, or been treated as, an intruder. Sometimes I feel that women *know* even if they don't let on that they do. I occasionally experience a look from women so direct that it almost pierces my soul. Not with hostility, but perhaps a virtual assessment of my genes to determine if there is an X or Y in play.

I also appreciate that women are far more inclined to share personal matters with me as a women than they would have been if I was a man, something that comes with being in the sisterhood. I remember having cocktails on my deck with a new-ish friend earlier that summer, and she told me of the time with a recent lover when she'd had the most intense mind-blowing orgasm of her whole life. Men don't share like that. They might brag about their sexual exploits (though I never did), but this would usually be covered in general terms, not with intricate intimacies. I liked being included in the sisterhood and enjoyed the new parity it seemed to bestow.

One thing my workmate asked me after I broke the news to her was whether I thought my own feelings would change after surgery. Nobody had ever asked me that in such straightforward terms, nor had I questioned myself in that respect either. I supposed it would be inevitable that my emotions would change, though it was impossible for me to conceive in what way. I guessed SRS would make me feel more complete, but that too was an intangible emotion. How might I change? That was yet to unfold.

One material thing I was really looking forward to changing with my updated anatomy was the way to conceal it. For the 50% of the world's population who wear women's underwear (and that's a rough estimate, not including tribespeople of the Amazon who wear stylish unisex loincloths), the procedure is simple. You visit a store—online, at the mall, or on Main Street—and buy whatever knickers or underthings you like. (As a Brit, the word "panties" just doesn't sound right, it is too Americanized for my ear. I could never imagine the Queen saying "panties".) It's a pretty straightforward procedure, rarely heralded by cause for celebration. The purchase might be to replace something that has fallen into threadbare disrepair, or due to one iron too many (some people do iron their undies you know), or perhaps in preparation for some impending hot date, when the underthings are the seductive precursor to the main event. Up to that point my day-to-day panty routine consisted of wearing the somewhat male type, the ones I felt so awkward displaying at the laundromat. Soon they would be gloriously redundant, so now was the time for an expedition to Victoria's Secret.

Of course I had been to one of these ubiquitous temples of femininity before, but nothing had fitted as it should have. That would soon change, and so this trip took on a new significance. I chose the Fifth Avenue store near the office, and as I approached I felt I should be cutting a ribbon at the entrance to welcome me across physical and metaphorical thresholds. A pink ribbon, naturally.

Entering this Aladdin's cave (or, more gender-specifically, his wife Princess Badroulbadour's cave) a new world of luxurious choices was on display. It was like pulling back the stage curtain before a performance by the Rockettes, but this was to be a performance that I would be involved in. I'm sure my eyes must have popped open wider than a Disney princess and I felt like dancing and twirling through the store as Giselle might have done in *Enchanted*. Scarlets, and blacks, and stripes, and frills, and lace… an endless array of slinky undergarments was on display, and soon they were going to fit.

Oh, but what would fit? I had a conceptual image of what I would be looking like in a few weeks, but the practicalities of one panty style over another had yet to be tested. Bikinis or hipsters?

Which ones might ride up, and would thongs would be a small strip of fabric too far? (Or too little?) Hedging my bets I invested in five different styles so I could decide, over time, which design was the best fit. How perfectly practical! I was longing to see how they would fit, and how the thinner fabric would feel against my skin, but that experience would just have to wait. Finally, I was impatient.

Chapter 39

Sorority Bonds

I can always rely on my mother to speak with supreme simplicity, even if there's potential to cause offense in the process. Many people find this blanket ability to speak her mind an endearing trait, but it can be alarming to the uninitiated—and even to me, after all these years.

"If there's one good thing to come from all this business with you," she said to me on the phone one weekend (with "this business" referring to the whole transgender equation), "then it is that you get along better with your sister now."

She was right of course. This thawing of sisterly relations between Sue and me had been a highly unexpected bonus, though I'd like to think that it is not the only positive result from all "this business." But not only does Mum come from an era where the concept of anyone being transgendered is completely alien, she had also known me as male for quite a few decades—and she had given birth to me as a boy, after all. Substantive change like this does not come easily to her generation, and the fact that she'd come so far in accepting the new me in such a relatively short time made me immensely proud of her. It still does. These days she will also tell me if my make-up is excessive, my hair is a mess, or if a dress is too short—which remains the remit for all mothers around the world.

Even so it was unforeseen that Sue and Nicky would develop this strange new bond; frankly it confused us both. The fact that she and I talked about it in those terms, and accepted it as a new start, was nothing short of remarkable as well. I rather like having a big sister now.

Two weeks before I was due to leave for Thailand, Sue came to visit me. She had a scientific conference to attend in Washington DC, and thought an extension to New York for a few days would be a good idea. That way we could test the water of the two new sisters being together. Without a doubt it was a good idea, and similarly we were both nervous at the prospect too.

Sue had never been to New York City before and so had all the official sightseeing to do. Thankfully she is as staunchly independent as the rest of our family, and so all she needed was a subway map and a few tips before she headed out to explore the big wide world of Manhattan. Even so, her trip was always about more than experiencing the view from the Empire State Building or the skyline from the Rockefeller Center Observation Deck—which was just as well, as it rained for most of her visit. We had dinners in the city (and talked), walked along the High Line (and talked), and watched some TV together (only talking during the advertising breaks). There was a lot to discuss, but after many years of not wanting to talk to each other at all, that was hardly surprising. I even found out what she does for a job ("Research Manager") and that she takes her tea decaffeinated. We were able to rekindle our relationship. Drawing on the past yes, but sharing those memories like never before. I was also able to talk with complete candor about my upcoming surgery. That put her mind to rest and I found it a surprisingly settling dialogue too. It was a remarkable few days of reconnection that nurtured the roots for a much healthier family tree.

Sue had originally hoped to traverse the United States by train on this trip, but her schedule ended up being too tight for that expedition. We raised the idea of doing it together at some time in future: two sisters on a journey of mutual discovery across the continental self, a long-distance conversation through the Rockies that would have been simply unthinkable a year earlier. But Sue had a proviso for the trip if we were to make it across America together:

"If you meet someone," she spelled out in uncompromising fashion, "then you need to go to his cabin. I still need my bunk bed, however lucky you get."

Perhaps Sue is under the grandiose delusion that the Amtrak California Zephyr is akin to the Orient Express. Sadly she would need to forget filet mignon and soufflés, and downsize to the realities of burgers and fries instead. But this comment made me realize that Sue had inherited our mother's sense of honest pragmatism. She is her mother's daughter just as, perhaps, I am now too.

Meanwhile, things between Mum and me continued to strengthen and become easier, with one exception. Ever since we had discussed the possibility of surgery when sitting by her fireside several months before, the subject had remained out of bounds. However, she had still donated to my SRS fund, regardless of her feelings about the money's use. But whenever we talked on the phone, as we did most weekends, surgery was never mentioned. I think she understood that I would be going away, probably to Thailand, at *some* time, and during that time I would likely have life-changing surgery, but she didn't want to know any more than that. No dates, no schedule, no nothing. She only wished to be informed when the deed had been done. I appreciated that ignorance can be bliss, but it was also very impractical—once I left for Bangkok there would be silence from New York. I addressed the unspoken subject during our final phone call before my trip.

"Mum, I need to tell you that I won't be around for our Sunday phone calls."

"Oh really? Are you going away?"

"Yes, I'll be away for a while."

A pause while I sensed the long-distance penny drop.

"You are going away for that?"

We both knew what "that" was.

"Yes."

"To Thailand?"

"Yes."

"I see."

More awkward silence and I could sense her getting upset.

"But you will be on email?"

"Oh yes, of course, though I'm not sure how frequently."

"Well, do keep in touch, love, won't you?"

Now I could feel tears brewing inside.

"Yes, yes, we'll talk on the phone sometime. And email. We'll be in touch…"

We said our fractured, emotional goodbyes, and as the phone line closed I'm sure we both wept. For ourselves and for each other.

Chapter 40

Final Impressions

Wednesday dawned bright and clear. It was an early fall morning in New York City and this was my last day working at Kiki's—for a while, anyway. In 48 hours I would leave for Thailand. I particularly wanted to look chic in the office that day so I found a pretty silk top in Express which I matched with a cute, cropped, charcoal gray jacket and scarlet knee-length skirt. Black pumps set it off and I was ready: businesslike but sexy. I had a spring in my step as I walked to the subway station before taking the R train into Manhattan.

My final day started off in much the same way as my other days working there, dealing with correspondence, arranging appointments, and handling the steady flow of clients. I tried to put the temporary finality of the occasion to the back of my mind lest I become too emotional. I had stopped my hormone therapy three weeks previously, as a prerequisite for surgery, and so I knew the propensity to turn any event into a tearful one was precipitously high. When

Kiki gave me a card signed with love and best wishes from everyone in the office, the floodgates opened. But it wasn't enough for me to start crying just on receipt of the card. It happened when I tried to thank any of the team for their thoughts. It happened again when I was accepting a UPS delivery. For goodness sake, it even happened when I was taking out the garbage. I was having some serious problems in keeping it together. Thankfully I was wearing waterproof eyeliner, so at least the make-up repercussions weren't too apparent.

I had become extremely open with Kiki about my impending surgery, and consequently felt much more relaxed about it myself. It even became a source of unexpected humor.

"Will you be doing anything for Halloween, Nicky?"

"Yes, I'm going to scare people with my new vagina!"

It beat trick-or-treat.

I had also been talking to Kiki about the chore of masturbation. The balance between male orgasm and feeling completely female had grown increasingly dysphoric for me. Whenever I tried, which was rare, I felt guilty and the process became increasingly weird. The advent of hormone therapy 18 months earlier had dropped any desire to pleasure myself to almost zero. Navi told me of the school of thought that contended frequent masturbation prior to surgery was a good thing, so the brain wouldn't forget the sensation. I was already a lost cause in that respect, as my brain had long since forgotten any expectation of fun below the equator. But Kiki reminded me that I really should make the best use of it while I could, and that was when I had a remarkable brainwave. I remembered my friend Cat, who had started a project amassing penis molds of past lovers, thus creating her own hyper-personalized silicone dildo collection. She claims that this is for artistic purposes, and that a local gallery will be exhibiting her mammoth member collection when she has enough examples to fill the shelves. Personally, I suspect that the collection is also to keep her from boudoir boredom on dreary winter nights in Hoboken.

But this struck me as an amazingly good idea. I should create my own penis cast! That way I could be immortalized in silicone: a memorial to something that would be gone the following week! Besides, I'd need to exercise my new vajayjay frequently, and what better way to do this than with an exact copy of its predecessor! There would also be the amusing bonus that in the future, if sometime told me to go fuck myself, I could say that well, yes, actually I already had.

I conducted a frenzied Internet search of local stores that might have a suitable casting kit in stock. There was no time for mail order delivery, as I would be leaving town the next day. Thankfully the classy SoHo erotica store Babeland had one available, and so Kiki agreed to go shopping with me as soon as our last client left.

Buying sex toys with another girl was fun. I was amazed at the selection as I looked around at the array on display. Apart from a plethora of phalluses in a rainbow of colors and assortment of sizes, there was clothing for intimate occasions along with more dominatrix-steered ones too. Gift packs and toys were tastefully shown, often with specifications and guidelines. The store was scrupulously clean and clearly trendy; a far cry from the tawdry images that had crossed my mind when I had imagined such an establishment. We duly found the molding kit and Kiki kindly bought it for me—something I felt she should pass off as a legitimate business expense. Before we left, I examined the dildos on the shelves and I wondered when I might be making friends with one; though that concept was still perplexing.

I slept well overnight. This would be the last night I'd be sleeping in my own bed for quite a while, and probably one of the last times I'd be sleeping without any discomfort for some time. But then I remembered: I had the penis mold to fill. It had been such a long time since I had any sort of mold-worthy occasion that it was hard to envision how I could make this happen. Charmane in the office had suggested a good female-centric Internet porn site, but I couldn't imagine that making a huge sea change in my ability to fulfill my self-induced obligation. But I tuned in online and found a video of a good-looking couple having fairly attractive sex. Still, I wasn't sure if I was aroused, and looking at the man and the woman on screen added to my uncertainty. I wasn't equipped as she was, but I certainly didn't feel like he seemed to either. In which half of the act did I belong?

The instructions on the molding kit noted that once the compound had been mixed, there were just 90 seconds to make the impression. After that, a further two-minute wait when there should be no moving at all inside the mold. This seemed impossible. There was extra pressure too as I knew I would only ever have a single shot at this; the kit could only be used once and there was no chance for refills. Besides, the process held zero pleasure for me, and I didn't want to expend any more time doing this than was absolutely necessary. But with a little visual stimulation and a heck of a lot of willpower the deed was done. The two perfectly formed porn stars continued their unwavering performance on my laptop, oblivious to my task, but I had filled the mold. I hoped this occasion would be my last obligation to manhood; I wanted no further part of it.

Chapter 41

The Vagina Diary

I left new York late that evening in a remarkably serene state of anticipation. The surgery that I had initially embraced, then feared, and finally welcomed was about to happen. I'd made the long flight to Thailand many times over the years, but this time it felt the most special; it wasn't a journey, but a destination. When I arrived in Bangkok I was thankful that there were no identity issues when I passed through Immigration as there had been the last time. Walking beyond the arrivals area and into the sweltering air outside made me feel welcome once again. Whether it is due to dust, humidity or just its unique soul, I'm sure Bangkok smells different than all other cities. A driver from the clinic picked me up and took me to the hotel that would be (with the exception of a few days for the surgery itself) my home for the next month. I wondered how other trans girls coming for the same procedure feel coming all this way, to a strange country, so far from home. But to me it *was* home.

Although I'd not stayed in the Dusit Princess Hotel before, I immediately felt comfortable in the surroundings, and with the people who would become unofficial members of my support team. From the greetings that the bell captains in the lobby gave me on arrival, to the constant friendliness of the food and beverage staff in the restaurants, their warmth and unwavering smiles pulled me through the following weeks.

Hotel rooms tend to be soulless but this one didn't seem to be. In addition to the electric kettle and selection of slightly disappointing teas, it was very comfortably equipped with a king size bed (and sheets that were changed daily), a large writing desk, marble bathroom, and a wide picture window that overlooked the swimming pool at the back and a shopping mall to one side. Further away the landscape was nondescript, but it was distant enough that I never felt hemmed in. Occasionally I could see planes circling before landing at the airport, and I often thought of the stream of travelers coming to the city. What were their stories?

Bangkok is a noisy city, but my room was surprisingly quiet. Air conditioning kept it cooler than the 90 degree heat outside, but I liked to open the windows every so often so as not to lose my sense of reality. Birds sometimes perched on the ledge outside my window which made me think of home. I wondered if they knew my American robins.

Throughout my time there I kept a diary, a journal of events and feelings. I didn't log these accounts daily, but I tried to note the most thought-provoking times. Usually I recorded these thoughts on my laptop, but sometimes I dictated them into my cell phone to transcribe later. I knew the experience would be life-changing, even though I had no idea what would unfold. One thing was certain however: this would never happen again. These are my unadulterated thoughts.

Three Days Before...

I always overpack. I did it in my 'past life,' but I have the tendency to do it even more in my current one. But what self-respecting woman wouldn't want to add that extra outfit into the suitcase on the off-chance that it might be worn for 30 minutes at some time within the next 30 days? Assuming that I might be taking new things home with me (in addition to my genitalia), I wonder if I will have enough packing space for the return journey. That is my only concern at the moment, such is my continuing state of calm.

The program for SRS patients is clearly structured by Dr. S: four days in the nominated hotel prior to surgery, then four days in his clinic, followed by at least 18 days recuperating back in the hotel. During that time of recovery there will be daily visits from his nursing team (Sundays excepted) and for the first five days I will be confined to my hotel room. So I will be making friends with room service. Only after that are limited treks allowed around the hotel, and maybe, just maybe, further afield too.

Ever since arriving in Bangkok yesterday morning I have been on a strictly liquid diet. Prior to this trip a liquid diet had merely entailed choosing between a trusty Cabernet or a more adventurous Malbec, but this time it is all about sloppy yogurt, broth soups, and juice. But I must enjoy this lackluster diet while I can; tomorrow I can't have the yogurt anymore. I already feel deprived. But it then gets worse. Tomorrow I have an enema. The following day I will have the unbridled joy of taking such a strong bowel-cleaning laxative that the bathroom should never be more than 20 seconds away. On the day of surgery I can have nothing to eat or drink whatsoever prior to the operation, which is due around 3pm. So at least I should be able to feast again after surgery, right? Wrong. The broth liquid diet continues for another couple of days before I can advance to thicker soups, maybe even the luxury of a piece of toast to go with it. It is only when I am back in the hotel in seven days' time that I can eat what I want again—a free menu that suddenly has the lure of gastronomic paradise.

I know I will be in some discomfort when I return to the hotel post-surgery, though I've no idea how that will be. It will mean that I need to sit on a donut-type cushion to ease the pain in my newly remodeled nether regions, a cushion that needs to go everywhere I do. The three or four times a day dilating sessions start after I return to the hotel too. I now appreciate that nobody in their right mind would do this surgery unless they absolutely have to. Yet even with all these hassles to look forward to, I am still excited. My new future is unwritten yet poised to happen, like a new country waiting to be discovered, peeping over the horizon.

Two Days Before...

The highlight today was my first pre-op enema. The effects were startlingly immediate. I also experienced intense nausea followed by a general feeling of upset stomach unease. So for the first time since arriving here, I am feeling decidedly unwell. Tomorrow's repeat enema and enhanced bowel cleaning is set to be even worse.

One Day Before...

I've just had my final consultation with Dr. S. It was good to see him again. I have signed all the consent forms, handed over X-rays, EKG reports, blood tests, and other documentation. This included referral letters from Navi, Dr. Rose, and a psychiatrist whom I only met once—but was still required by the Thai legal system to confirm that I was of sound mind. I'm probably not of sound mind on many matters, but on this issue I certainly am. Dr. S explained the procedure more, and went through any questions I had. My concerns were mostly about scarring, the actual shape of what he will create, and how I will feel afterwards. I think that is my biggest unease: my mental state when I wake up following the anesthesia. But Dr. S is an expert, his team is very experienced, and so I should just rely on them to make it happen.

Forever my own devil's advocate, I have reminded myself again that there is no point in keeping my genital status quo. I can never imagine using that equipment in the way that it was intended, ever again. I might even be able to have some fun with my soon-to-be-forged lady-parts. But outweighing myriad factors many times over, I know I will *feel* more complete. I will be able to embrace my life completely, and not just be on the sidelines of it. People are straight, or gay, or male, or female, or any of countless categories (which shouldn't be categorized anyway). Maybe they were born that way, maybe not. I am transgendered. It's taken me a long time to appreciate that, but I now do.

Although I will be legally and anatomically female from tomorrow, I still have my past, and I will still be a post-op transgender female; I will not magically morph into a genetic female. The bulk of my life was spent in male mode and I recognize that without bitterness. However, since accepting and embracing my femininity, the happiness I have felt has doubled, or tripled, or increased exponentially. I am a woman inside, and from tomorrow, I will be a woman on the outside too.

The Day Itself

I am now waiting in the hotel. In about one hour, someone from the clinic will collect me and take me there for surgery. This is the day that will change my life.

I have been overwhelmed with positive thoughts and support from friends and family all over the world. I feel humbled. If there is a spiritual support network, then the strands of support I have received will keep me afloat on an ether of positivity.

I was outside on the hotel grounds earlier. I noticed a gnat gliding with ease across the goldfish pond. My life is not apparent to him, nor relevant either. This is the biggest day in my life, but for others, just an ordinary day. Billions of individuals across the globe live lives irrespective of others yet intertwined in some bigger picture. Whatever that is.

I have no great beliefs in the afterlife but of course I wonder. My father died when I was three and so I never knew him. He remains a source of support to my mother, who never remarried. But if his spirit is around, I hope that he too will keep a watchful eye on me over the next 12 hours. I hope as well that he is not offended by my actions, and can help guide my mother through her ongoing process of understanding and acceptance.

I came out of the shower this morning and looked at myself in the mirror one last time, imagining how it will soon be. The more I have progressed on my transgender journey, the less I have liked to look 'down there.' I now see what I have as an untenable anatomical anomaly. That needs to be fixed.

I still don't like to think of the specifics of the actual procedure that I will be going through in a few hours' time, but I don't like to imagine the process of any medical procedure. So I will just concentrate on my own 'before' and 'after.'

I had the pleasure of sitting next to a lovely couple from Mexico on my flight from Hong Kong to Bangkok. We were talking general pleasantries, and then they asked me why I was going to Thailand. For some reason I wanted to tell them my reasons and so I did. For complete strangers, they were totally unfazed and charmingly supportive. One thing the woman said to me really struck a chord: "So you will be like a phoenix; the same person, but reborn through your own type of fire."

I have considered many metaphors for this process I am going through, but the concept of the phoenix is one that had eluded me—and the one that I like best. I would rather not spontaneously self-combust on the operating table, but the figurative end result is the same. Rebirth. A new life, but with the values, memories, and history that remain.

I, the phoenix, shall rise again.

...The Day After

(dictated and later transcribed)

I am lying in bed in the clinic with my legs apart so not to damage anything. I feel pretty out of it. I am not in any pain, but I am pretty uncomfortable. The process before and after surgery itself was quite good. I had no panic beforehand and I didn't worry when I was given the anesthesia. When I woke up it was much better than I had anticipated. But as I have just discovered, the surgery went on for much longer than anticipated, around 11 hours, and that was because Dr. S came across a problem. Apparently there was some inner scar tissue that could not be separated. He worked on it for several hours, but to no avail. Any longer would have put me at increased risk. Dr.

S says the appearance is good, the sensation should be too, but the depth is not great. This is not something that will improve over time.

I have had lots of messages of support from my friends, and Mum called the clinic twice last night. The first time she called I was still in surgery. Then she called again and I was in recovery. So at least she knows that I am OK.

...Two Days After
(dictated and later transcribed)

Today I am feeling more... human, I suppose, and slightly more mobile, though I have to stay in bed. The hours go by fairly slowly, and I'm still just eating broth type soups, but I'm not very hungry anyway. I feel disappointed as I am reminded that the operation has given me limitations. I believe there is a further corrective procedure I could undergo, but even that wouldn't come with a guarantee of success. Is it worth doing anything else? I guess I should just focus on the positive.

...Three Days After
(dictated and later transcribed)

I continue to feel more normal as the hours go by. It's a strange sensation lying here as I've not seen the results of the surgery. I may not see that for a day or two yet when the bandages come off. I don't consciously *feel* any change in my anatomy. I know it *has* happened, and I know the surgeon is happy with the likely sensation and the look of things, but it's so hard for me to visualize who I now am.

I spend most of the time resting, sleeping, and drifting between TV channels, not really watching any of them. The room that I'm in is fairly small and simple, with plain white walls, a small cabinet for my clothes, some storage space for medical supplies, and then a clock and a flat screen TV on the wall at the end of the bed. I think there are three other rooms with three other girls recovering, but I have not seen anyone else or heard anything either. In fact it is remarkably serene here, with just the gentle hum of the air con to ease the silence. Nurse Nin keeps an eye on me through the day. She's pretty tiny, even by Thai standards, her long black hair wrapped up in a green medical hair net. I wonder if it was unleashed whether it would reach the ground like Rapunzel. She feeds me liquids (mostly juices, no tea), gives me medication, and checks my vitals at regular intervals. I sense a happy aura around her as she bustles around, chattering with me whenever she pops in—our conversations restricted by language, never by intent.

I am relatively comfortable and so perhaps the enormity of the last three days hasn't truly sunk in yet. I'm trying hard to focus on the optimism I read in emails from friends. Yes I guess I have just been through a huge change. I sometimes I forget the enormity of that. Surgery was largely successful and now I can move on with my life. Still, I still feel a bit muddled.

...Four Days After

I've just seen myself, the creation that Dr. S has put together. I feel like Dr. Frankenstein's monster, but with infinitely superior surgical technique. It was a weird sensation looking at my new self for the first time. And I had to brace myself for the occasion. In fact did I actually want to see it at all? What if it didn't match my expectations?

This morning I awoke feeling better than I have in days. I am getting some appetite back and starting to feel more alive. I will also be heading back to the hotel today. I'm looking forward to that. The vaginal packing will be staying put for another few days, and the catheter and urine bag that follows me around will continue to do so as well. In fact, that is one of the more acceptable sides of the operation at the moment. I quite enjoy not having to go to the bathroom every so often, as instead the urine collects in my bag which gets emptied once or twice a day. I don't even know when I pee, it just collects in the bag. Whenever I've been to the bathroom before I've never quantified the process and so seeing it as the contents of a bag that slowly fills up over the course of a day is quite sobering. The other thing I hadn't realized was how much strapping and bandages I had over my nether regions. They were mostly out of sight as I have been largely horizontal since surgery. I presumed that these outer bandages might be staying on after I returned to the hotel, but not so. This morning it was time to strip it off! One of the nurses snipped and swabbed and removed all the outer layers of protective bandages. That left me feeling bare, though I know I still have a catheter tube coming out of *somewhere* down there. Dr. S then arrived, armed with a swab. I knew what that meant. He was going to poke around at the clitoral area and see if there is any sensation. And the result was… ouch! It wasn't a very pleasurable one, but there most definitely was sensation. As a result Dr. S seemed pretty happy, but did I want to see what was down there? Yes, it was time. He handed me a mirror.

It's certainly not anything like I had before! Is it a perfectly formed babelicious porn star magnet of a vagina? No. It is a rather swollen, rather unattractive collection of bits that I can vaguely make out from a doctor's anatomical chart. But these are very early days and I know there needs to be a lot of healing in the weeks ahead. Appearance will improve over time. But I did smile. For the first time in days I smiled a huge, relief-filled smile, that this, now, was me. I had done it.

...Five Days After

I am back in my room at the hotel. Even though everyone at the clinic was wonderful, it is good to experience the semblance of normality that is a hotel room. I have also just had my first post-op care visit from Nurse Cee. She was assisting Dr. S during the procedure and will be visiting me every day for the next few weeks. Cee has a predictably slight Thai frame, cropped black hair, and a smile that seems to extend beyond her mouth. I don't feel the same friendly warmth as I had from Nin, and I wouldn't like to get on the wrong side of Cee. I imagine she would have quite a temper. I suppose, too, that from here on I have to get used to lying on my back with my legs apart and having health professionals stare into my vagina. Cee was well-equipped for the occasion. She was wearing a strange contraption strapped to her head with a light at the front. It was something like a miner's helmet and I felt she was more appropriately kitted out to be digging a coal seam than checking out Dr. S's workmanship.

Now I realize the biggest difference in viewing one's own genitals for the different sexes: as a man I could always see what I had down there—obviously. As a woman, I now need a mirror. Such a simple adaptation but this seems weird. Really very strange. However I'm still reluctant to look down there again and check myself out. I can't figure out why.

...Six Days After

I feel extremely uncomfortable and sitting down in any position is a very delicate process indeed. But with any luck that will improve today when the surgical packing comes out of my wound. And it is easy to forget that it really is quite a big wound and as such needs a lot of time to heal. Today is also the day when I will actually get an indication of depth. I know it will not be good news, but at the moment I can't imagine doing anything further about it.

It will soon be time to start my dilation regimen. Again, not something I am looking forward to. The thought of sticking anything 'up there' at the moment fills me with dread, as it sounds like a particularly painful proposition. I've not looked at the area for the last couple of days—just one time since surgery—and it remains something I don't relish doing. That kind of surprises me as I'd thought I might be gawking at myself at every opportunity by now. But today is Halloween, so maybe (just like I joked in the office before I left New York) I should be scaring myself with my new vagina.

"Just try to relax," said Nurse Cee wielding the fiercest-looking solid Perspex dildo that I have ever seen in my entire life. "It will hurt more if you don't relax."

Relax? I thought, *RELAX?!—are you kidding! That thing is the size of a Kamikaze plane and you want it in my newly created Pearl Harbor?* So with me clenching my butt, fists, and seemingly every other muscle in my body, she did slip the beast in. And quickly out again.

"Good," she proclaimed. "About the same as most natal women. But it would be better if you relax."

I could have slapped her on hearing that, but lying on my back with my legs in the air put me at too much of a tactical disadvantage. She still had her miner's helmet on too.

Just prior to that, she had also pulled the packing out of the wound. You know the magician's trick of pulling a string of handkerchiefs out of his sleeve? I felt the same procedure was being done to me, but instead they were coming out of my new lady-parts. It was a nasty, smelly mess of surgical packing that I am very happy to see the last of. Does it make me feel more comfortable sitting down now? Possibly.

But wait. She said I was about the same as most natal women. That was a welcome surprise. Does it put my thoughts to rest about further surgery to increase vaginal depth? Probably. The actual result, measured in the same way as checking oil level in a car engine with a dipstick, was actually a lot better than I had feared.

So that was it: the first time that I could experience the concept of something being inside my new vagina. A surreal perception, and although it hurt, it was all mine.

...Seven Days After
(dictated and later transcribed)

Dilation (dy-**ley**-sh*un*): *The widening or stretching of an opening or a hollow structure in the body.*

I can't describe how I feel at the moment. Unbelievably emotional yet I can't identify what those emotions are. The two nurses from the clinic have just paid me a visit—Nurse Cee and Nurse Jay—and together we did my first real dilation. Twenty minutes of extreme discomfort. I can't imagine having to do that for the rest of my life, and even less as part of a future sexual experience.

Isn't that supposed to be fun? I know it will get better but at the moment I can't even think of tomorrow. Discomfort, pain, and emotionally blind. I feel like crying all the time.

When the nurses were here they also removed the catheter from me, and so for the first time since surgery, I have no tubes or anything else connected to me. But removing that catheter was also horribly painful. The discomfort over the last day, and the last couple of hours in particular, has confused me. I know I have just had major surgery and I know things will improve, but I'm struggling to feel happy. I can't think of anything.

…Eight Days After

Last night I had two beautiful dreams. Ever since I confronted my transgender status, I have tried to identify whether I saw myself in dreams as male or female. Sometimes that is clear, like the department store dream a few months ago, other times less so, but for these two nights I have most certainly been female.

In the first dream I was taken by a couple of European gentlemen (with beards I think, though I can't recall the rest of their appearance) on a trip to, probably, Boston. They didn't speak much but we ended up on a glorious, grassy, cricket-type playing field where we spent time together. It was a perfect summer day, and I could sense the birds chirping and the luscious smell of fresh-cut grass, sensations that were blissfully real. The sense of journey was there in the dream; the end point was happiness. The second dream was about me making close friends with a wonderful woman, I think named Katie, who had an adorable little daughter in tow. I'm not sure where we were, but the daughter wanted me to come home with them as there was a mountain of home-baked cookies at their house.

Then they evaporated, grass, cookies, dreams and all. In my current state, I feel that looking for any existential meaning in these dreams is largely pointless—unless I am set to end up being a follower of European male cricketers or a closet cookie lover. However, the abiding emotion in both dreams was one of blissful contentment, and certainly in the second dream, one where I felt genuinely disappointed when I woke up and realized that it was just a dream. "Oh, Katie," I heard myself saying disappointedly when in that just-arousing-from-sleep mode, and realizing that I was in my own bed in a Thailand hotel, and not in someone's kitchen with my hand in the cookie jar.

After my excruciating and emotional time with the visiting nurses yesterday, the physical process of dilation today was significantly less painful. Also, as I had blubbered through the entire nursing visit yesterday, the two had consulted with Dr. S, and he had agreed that it would be OK for me to restart my hormone regimen. Normally it would be advisable to wait until long after I had returned home, but my emotional blathering was enough to convince the doc that I should start again now. I nearly cried on the spot with that good news. In fact, I think I probably did.

...Nine Days After

The idyllic dreams of yesterday have instigated thoughts about the next steps that will become possible. Now I will be able to update my legal gender. I will also change my legal name to Nicola Jane Chase. My past, however, will always be the same. Strangely though, I find that quite reassuring. I am one of the luckier transgender people who was not desperately miserable in the 'wrong body.' Of course I was upset at the instances of rejection, and losing one of my best friends along the way was sad, but I am a strong woman and I will get beyond that. The process of acceptance for Mum was hard for us both, yet we stuck with it. Friendships have been cemented and strengthened. I'm not even upset that I took my time to get to where I am now. In many ways it would have been easier to have come to terms with it earlier in life, but I don't even know whether I *was* transgendered in my 20s and 30s. Every transgender person needs to find a position in their lives where their past doesn't become a yoke and their future is cleared of internal conflict. Very few of us reach that point, but I am more hopeful than ever that that place is next on my map.

Each morning, if I wake early enough and look out over the street beside the hotel, I see Buddhist monks walking serenely along the sidewalk collecting alms. Their vibrant saffron robes make them stand out from everyone else, which almost seems at odds with their obvious inner calm. I wonder if such calm is heading my way.

...Ten Days After

Yesterday was completely exhausting. Holding a solid Perspex dildo inside you for 30 minutes, three times per day shouldn't be draining, but by the end of the third session I felt bushed. However I will need to negotiate wider gauges and endure the process for longer periods of time in the weeks ahead so that I can be prepared to meet a real penis in the flesh and throw down a suitable welcome mat.

Today saw another semblance of normality as I went down to the hotel coffee shop for breakfast. I was around groups of people again for the first time in ages. This was just as welcome as the enticing buffet and fresh brewed coffee—which is a refreshing change from the pale tea I can make in the room. In the immediate days post-surgery at the clinic, Nin was there to look after me, and since then, here at the hotel, the housekeeping and room service staff are always friendly when they come to my room. But just to share an elevator with a couple of guys, and for them to ask me what floor I wanted, made me feel feminine again; especially when they invited me to exit the elevator first. Unfortunately there was also bad news loitering with gleeful intent at the breakfast buffet: a large jar of Nutella. This is a very troubling proposition, lest I am to return to New York with the unwelcome legacy of a larger dress size.

...Twelve Days After

I am half a world away from home and so friends and family can't come visiting as they might have done if I were recovering at home in New York. But being the independent person I am, that status doesn't concern me. I had wondered about bringing a friend with me for part of the duration but I would have felt an obligation to entertain them rather than having them help me convalesce. So instead I brought a DVD player along with a supply of movies and TV programs. I have the classic comedy of *Airplane* (both I and II, and both of which still tickle me), the complete collection of *The Fast Show* (one of the sharpest British comedies of the 90s), along with a full boxed set of *Inspector Morse*, which I am slowly working through. The hotel also has a selection of international TV channels which, although limited, at least enables me to keep abreast of Premier League soccer from the UK, as well as the seemingly endless array of cooking shows that are available around the world. So between drama, comedy, missed penalty kicks and wondering who will be kicked out of the kitchen next, I have been keeping myself amused and entertained.

Apart from limited trips to the hotel coffee shop, I remain confined to quarters in my room. Rest is still the best solution for recuperation but I have never felt alone. I have also been Skyping with Mum. We have been in regular contact and her calls to check on my welfare on the day of surgery meant more to me than she could ever know. There is a seven-hour time difference so we have to be organized in our Skype scheduling, but we can see each other and I can show her my room and the view outside. I love the familiarity of seeing her and the ability to share my perspectives. Our conversations are wonderful, and I am amazed at how comfortable I feel talking to her about every aspect of my recovery, from the discomfort of sitting on anything but my pink donut cushion, to the trials and tribulations of daily dilating. This connection seemed inconceivable just a few weeks ago. I feel truly, deeply, blessed.

...Fourteen Days After

Good marketing always impresses me. In this respect I really admire the branding that Dr. S's plastic surgery clinic has achieved with its products. Not only are the Perspex stents used for daily dilations all embossed with the website address of the clinic (though practicalities of multitasking would make web-surfing tricky when being used), but the canvas tote bag I was given is also branded with the clinic name. It boasts that the clinic does SRS and FFS (Facial Feminization Surgery). The bag is extremely well-made and was given to me on my arrival in Bangkok. It contained a month's supply of KY jelly (which is quite a lot) some cleaning materials like baby wipes (yes it can get messy), and one scary-looking balloon-like syringe that seems to be for the future douching process. The bag also included my first batch of... what's the correct euphemism here... 'feminine hygiene products' which I seem to be going through at a rate of knots. It is a very useful and much appreciated bag, but it will later test my loyalties and willingness to promote the services of the plastic surgery clinic in public. I'm not sure how much I want to be seen walking down New York's Fifth Avenue with a bag that proudly shouts *"Hey, look at me! I've done SRS in Thailand!"* Which is a great shame as it is a particularly high quality tote.

There was splendid irony contained inside the canvas bag, too. As part of the welcome kit, all SRS patients are issued a hand mirror to help us see where everything now is. Remember that up until now in my life I've been able to see my genitalia directly; a vagina is not the same. That concept remains surreal, but the mirror helps. However, unlike the personalized tote bag, the clinic did not provide a bespoke mirror but instead an off-the-shelf number. It is branded with a Japanese cartoon character that has swept Asia over the years, and amazingly, other parts of the world too. One that initially seemed cheap and tacky but now I see it as utterly appropriate for any transgender women seeing their new vaginas for the first time, even though the smutty innuendo might be lost on the clinic itself. The mirror is one branded by the *Hello Kitty* logo.

...Eighteen Days After

Since arriving in Thailand I have seen some incredible thunderstorms, bigger than I've ever seen before. They seem to grow with looming intensity as they approach from the horizon but I feel no anger from them. Forks of dazzling lightning pierce clouds that are almost black. When the rain comes—which it does in torrents—it seems bountiful. I'm sure I'd think differently if I were caught outside in the downpour, but behind the tinted glass of the hotel windows I actually feel replenished. Dry but somehow nurtured.

Unfortunately that replenishment hasn't been reflected in my physical recuperation, which has hit a bump in the recovery roadmap. Although I have no terms of reference for how I *should* be feeling at this moment, I could tell that my newly coutured nether regions have been swelling up and not swelling down. Pain and discomfort has also increased. So yesterday I headed back to the clinic for an inspection by Dr. S, which then led to a minor surgical update. It was bizarre returning into the operating room where so much had happened two and a half weeks ago. This was also the first time I'd had my legs up in the stirrups—without being under general anesthesia anyway. I guess I'll need to get used to that gynecological position.

Dr. S went to work by giving me a local anesthetic in the danger area while Nurse Jay soothed my often-furrowed brow. I could sense some work going on with the occasional prod and poke, and I think I felt stitching being unwoven and re-weaved, but it wasn't painful. A lot of anxiety even so, and I found myself shaking like a leaf.

This glitch has messed up my recovery schedule and put my return trip to New York on hold. The doc wants me around for a further two weeks, and so my flights back home—booked for five days from now—have been scrapped. Home now seems suddenly more distant. I also have the return of my dear friends the catheter and urine bag to keep me company; collectively they are as welcome as a herpes outbreak on date night.

...Twenty-two Days After

There are many degrees of embarrassment that any of us can suffer but I'm sure the risk of being seen to do something stupid is amplified as a woman. How many of us have left the washroom feeling fine, but only later realized that we have been trailing toilet paper stuck to the bottom of our shoes on the way out, just like the puppy on the TV commercial. Or that the back of a skirt is stuck where it shouldn't be, thus proffering the world a fine view of what layers of undergarmentry are being worn.

Ever since I renewed my reluctant kinship with my catheter again a few days ago, I have been trailing a urine bag around with me like a poodle. In my hotel room this is not so bad. I can sit and read, or lie down and sleep, or watch TV, and the bag minds its own business nestling on the floor. But for any adventures out of the room, a more complicated arrangement is required. The four feet of plastic tubing between body and bag has to be attached to my person, either wrapped around my waist or tied in a big loop, and then the urine bag itself can be hooked on my knickers. This arrangement is topped off with a loose-fitting frock so the camouflage is complete. Nobody can see the urine bag or the associated plumbing, but I have a preordained fear that something will happen. It wouldn't take much for the bag to slip its moorings and then plummet down to the floor for the whole world to see. The bag of urine would rupture spectacularly, sending a yellowish flood, worthy of Noah's Ark, gushing over the glistening marble hotel floor. Even though the bag and associated tubing is of industrial strength, doubtless there will be a flaw. Or I will trip on an upturned fork and puncture it that way. Or have a confrontation with an army of knitting needles. Or suffer an attack by a staple gun. This conceptual banana skin is well-poised for me to slip on, however much I remain on my guard.

Or maybe I'm just going stir crazy living in my hotel room 20 hours per day.

…Twenty-eight Days After

It was 4 weeks ago today that I had surgery, and six days since my last journal entry. My higher spirits have dampened. According to my original schedule I should have been back in New York by now, and perhaps even back at work. Instead I remain in Bangkok, still in the same hotel room and still trailing my catheter and urine bag around. If there are no further hitches, I should be stepping onto the plane home in three days' time.

Never in the last month have I had any doubts about my actions in coming here—not one iota—only the practical disappointment that the healing process has taken far longer than I'd hoped. I know I have to remain a patient patient and accept that these weeks of recovery here in Thailand will enable a solid foundation for my long term recuperation.

My body is finally in sync with rest of me; now it is just the healing process that has to catch up. Returning to a normal life is on the horizon.

Chapter 42

Back Home... and Down to Earth

I left bangkok airport in a wheelchair. (Well, in a plane obviously, but I was taken to that plane in a wheelchair. It wasn't some magical Mary Poppins flying wheelchair.) It was a process I found both humbling and surprisingly pleasurable too. I remember the first time I saw Mum come through airport immigration in a wheelchair and I was dismayed that my previously agile mother had come to this. But now I appreciated it more from her perspective; there are a lot of advantages! These wheels come with the ability to jump the queue, avoid walking the country mile between check-in and gate, plus the pleasure of boarding first. There were also airplane transfers in Hong Kong and the arrival at New York to consider, both of which would have been beyond exhausting if I'd not had someone pushing me around. This ease of transit became such a treat that I may well consider breaking my own leg before my next long-distance trip.

On the plane I surprised myself by sleeping a lot of the 16 hours from Hong Kong, before arriving in New York at 6am on a Sunday morning. With no immigration lines at that hour, and wheelchair assistance to boot, I was home by 7am. It was barely light outside and all was tranquil in my apartment, which had been in eerie hibernation for the past month. It felt reassuring being home but also slightly strange; everything was familiar yet nothing had been touched for all that time. The cards wishing me well in advance of the trip were still on the shelves in the living room and my tin of Typhoo tea had a hint of dust on the top. My life had changed completely, but everything else had not. I sat quietly for a few minutes, the faint buzzing from the long-distance flight still ringing in my ears. I looked out at my garden, but the remnants of green that were there before I left had all disappeared. It was early December and so it had started its seasonal hibernation. I was about to do the same.

The rest of that day, like any arrival after a long-haul flight, was a woozy, discombobulated mess. It was good to be home yet I found it hard to appreciate the enormity of what had just happened to me, half a world away, in Thailand. I had been there just 24 hours earlier, but the relative immediacy of travel made memories of four-star hotel comfort seem like last night's dream. The highlight of the day was a delivery of flowers from Kiki and company at the office to welcome me back. I put them on my kitchen table and cried. I felt overwhelmed.

The New York weather didn't help. Although it was only late fall, it seemed like the bleakest of midwinters. I felt cold like never before. There was also the tiredness. The first time I attempted the previous routine 12-minute walk to my local subway station, I almost fainted with exhaustion. The initial days back at Kiki's were thoroughly draining too. A mix of nausea and fatigue persisted until I completely got over jet lag and finished the remaining industrial-strength antibiotics I had brought back with me. Both conditions seemed to last forever. Then there were subsequent days of withdrawal symptoms from those same antibiotics. I needed to refamiliarize myself with the place that I call home but all I felt was listless and sad. Even the trappings of the holiday season that make this city so exciting at this time of year made no difference to my mental slump. I had been through the biggest event of my life; being home again felt like a huge anticlimax. I was cold and alone, yet not wanting any company.

Still, it was a pleasure to see Dr. Rose again the following week.

"Welcome to your first gyno examination on US soil!"

She appreciated all the weird emotions I was going through, but I still felt sore and grouchy. The thrice-daily dilations in my cold apartment seemed ugly chores. Not only that but whenever I had an audience with my new self, I didn't enjoy the perspective. I knew that I was still swollen and my appearance would improve but I still couldn't feel proud of my new baby. My ambivalence confused me further.

December brings out the party spirit in New Yorkers but I didn't feel like socializing; all I wanted to do was stay home. When friends asked me how I felt after surgery, the answer was simple.

"Tired."

"Yes, but how do you *feel?*"

"Tired."

"Really?"

"Yes, bloody, freaking, frustratingly tired, all the time. Get it?"

Perhaps they thought I should have been dancing on clouds of elation, having scaled the pinnacle of personal synchronicity. Maybe some post-op transsexual women are like that, but I definitely wasn't.

"Any regrets?"

Apparently that is one of the most common questions post-surgery. Regrets? Regrets that I had gained a vagina (albeit a rather high-maintenance one) and found personal equilibrium?

NO!

NO!!!

NO!!!!!

I knew that my recovery would entail many additional months of convalescing but it would improve—*I* would improve. I had predicted that there could be months of not feeling well post-surgery, but anticipation of a future emotion doesn't make it any easier to greet when it actually arrives. For quite a few weeks I felt like crap.

Christmas was advancing. Kiki was joking with me in the office one time, asking what I wanted from Santa Claus this year.

"Well, I have a vagina now; I guess I'm kind of done."

So much for being naughty or nice.

My mother also came to visit me for Christmas. We'd scheduled that earlier in the year, prior to her knowing my SRS schedule. Once she knew, Mum promptly offered to postpone the trip so that it wouldn't be a strain for me. But her visit gave me something to look forward to, though I still couldn't figure out why I needed something to look forward to anyway. Why was I feeling the comedown and not the joy of fulfillment? Was this post-natal depression from my new baby?

Mum and I ended up having eight really lovely days together. Central Park is stunning whatever the season, but we had a beautiful walk one cold, crisp afternoon. This time I had trouble keeping up with her. We also paid a visit to the 9/11 Memorial, which seemed to echo our own microcosm of grief and acceptance.

One time during our neighborhood strolls my mother really surprised me with a totally unexpected comment.

"You would have made a good father."

I was taken aback. Mum is not very child-centric, and contrary to most mothers is not yearning to be a grandmother. I pondered more about being a parent: what would have happened if I had become a father? Although there are instances where fathers became successful women, those cases are rare. The more frequent scenario is a family broken up when the man addresses her transgender self. In that respect maybe I was lucky to have stayed single, not that I can rewrite history. Now, I can't imagine how it might have been if I remained in denial and kept my feminine self locked away. You can't avoid being transgendered, however much you might want to hide in the corner. Those termites will always make themselves known.

I thought back to my failed date with the great Dane, Pel, and how I had easily envisioned his children as part of our trans-Atlantic life. That seemed easy and something I wanted to embrace as a woman. Maybe one day it will happen.

"Have you done your exercises yet?" my mother would question me lest I miss one of my regular dilation sessions. She often sat with me on the sofa while I was doing them too, cup of tea to one side. It was such a complete turnaround of acceptance and understanding. We also shared a sofa when we had another joint therapy session at Navi's. This time she also managed to refer to me by the correct name and gender; I felt so proud of her. As we were leaving, Navi also mentioned a couple of points that seemed to help my mother's understanding of The Situation. First, I was probably female long before I realized it myself. I'd not considered my situation in such detached terms before but it did make sense. Also, she suggested that

Mum should try not to think of my SRS as any sort of male mutilation; there is no man alive who would not faint with terror at the thought of what my surgery involved. It is only us transgender females who require surgery to correct the twist of fate that we were dealt. By my mother's own admission, she may never completely accept everything about me as I am now. I'm definitely not a son anymore, but am I a daughter? That's something that neither of us can quite figure out.

We spent a relaxing Christmas Day in my apartment. This time the reminiscences were fonder as there was no backdrop of the Ghost of Future Yet to Come. In addition to another pot of nail polish in my Christmas stocking, there were also a couple of pairs of earrings! So much had changed.

I also received a present from the Queen, although she probably didn't wrap it herself. My new passport arrived. Apart from being a nice shiny maroon color on the outside, my joy at seeing Nicola Jane Chase on the inside was immense. This was now my legal name as determined by Her Majesty the Queen and her government in the United Kingdom. It felt like a royal decree, a representation of everything that I had gone through but a confirmation of so much more.

Mum left for England just before New Year's Eve. Like me, she has few fond memories of that evening. The time allowed me to dwell on the remarkable 12 months that had encompassed far more than life-changing surgery. That had been the highlight, as it had allowed me to reset my life—but it nearly hadn't happened at all. I felt so glad that it had. Now I was moving forward. The dating rejections from earlier in the year slipped into paler insignificance. I started appreciating that the world was opening up to me again, especially with my new passport. Perhaps I could be on someone's arm as we traveled. Obstacles from the past started to be replaced with opportunities for the future. I began dreaming in real-time. Countless bridges still needed to be crossed, but I was able to approach new horizons with an inner strength and confidence as never before. My physical recovery still needed time but my mental wellbeing had already taken greater strides forward. A spring tide of positivity started washing up on my shores.

Chapter 43

Pants (Trousers) and Statements

T he first weeks of the new year also brought on some spring cleaning: physical and metaphorical closets needed to be cleared out. It was easy for me to forget that there were people in vestibules of my life who were still unaware of my updated self. I decided that the best way to correct this would be to send out "New Year / New Me" cards. I'd skipped sending Christmas greetings this season—I'd had neither time nor inclination since returning from Thailand—and besides, I liked the metaphor of starting afresh with New Year cards. I chose some attractive cards and decided that I'd print out a note that I'd slip inside which would contain all my news. I needed to boil down my thoughts and emotions into two sides of large print 5" x 8" paper that would fold, conveniently, into the envelopes. For that task I once again brought in my toughest editor: my mother. Through a sequence of emails, we settled on a composition that we considered the right balance between enough knowledge and too much information. I wanted to explain, in a nutshell, how I had realized I was transgendered, and that I am now unequivocally female. I also included a photograph of Mum and me in New York from a few weeks before. I felt such parental endorsement would help show that my status was not changed on a whim.

Having decided on a text and a format, I then had to decide who would receive these 'Statements,' as Mum liked to call them. Just because I was full of the joys of spring didn't mean that everyone in the global phone book needed to know about my change. I was not going to track down the postman from 20 years ago, or everyone I grew up with at school, or even some dissolved acquaintances from my more recent past. In fact, most of the world could happily exist without this extra burden of information. I compiled a list of old friends that I'd not seen for years, plus relatives from parts of my family that I was vaguely aware of but never saw and mailed out statements to them. I sent a few extra copies to my mother so that she could distribute them as needed too. I thought back to when I first told Mum and realized again how much had changed in just two years. Then she was bereaved; now she was the one helping me draft announcements of my rebirth. I love you Mum.

After I sent out the statements I breathed an expansive sense of relief for exhaling the larger truth. Responses from the traditionalists came via snail mail, but the trend was to email me, usually accompanied by virtual gasps. The degree of support was not universal, but the essence of appreciation was. Two cousins praised my honesty. A former girlfriend said she cried tears of joy when she read the statement. (*"I always knew you were different!"*) A DJ friend in the Middle East emailed me with words of support though he admitted struggling to find the right phraseology.

"I reckon 'congratulations' doesn't really work. Here's the thing… I kind of realized as I read your letter that you seemed to be happy… and that perhaps hadn't been for a good while. So it didn't take long to think, 'Good On Yer'. But that seems a bit trite and to be honest a bit shit, too. 'Nice One!' didn't seem appropriate. Nor did, 'Get your tits out for the lads'."

So he just settled on "cheers." I appreciated that too.

For most people this news was a relative bombshell. For me, that bomb had been ticking away at my front door for some years and I'd already had a sustained period to diffuse it. By this time I had also gained more experience in knowing what to expect when I told people. Emotions were complex—both theirs and mine. There was the unburdening factor from my side, but this revelation also had the potential to set back old friendships, either by degrees of time or levels of discomfort. There were one or two old friends who didn't reply to my statements, and only in later correspondence did they acknowledge my news (either by a change of name on an envelope or revised email address within a generic festive email). What did they feel? Had this information overload caused me to be ostracized from the Venn diagram of occasional friendship? Or, conversely, did their lack of response signify a deeper acceptance, as if my news wasn't the shock I had imagined? I never found the answer to that.

Along with notes inside my friend rolodex, my non-euphemistic closet also needed updating. This process had started while Mum was here for Christmas.

"You should wear more trousers," she'd said. "Women wear trousers all the time. If you want to be more of a woman, you should wear more trousers!"

Of course her uncompromising advice made sense, but I still couldn't accept this irrefutable logic. However in my defense, another reason why I had spurned pants in the past was that they hadn't fitted well. Post-SRS that would be different. I decided to do as Mum suggested. Knowing that I'd need considerable moral support if I was to make this leap of fashion faith, I roped in my friend Grace, who happened to be visiting New York that weekend. She could at least reassure me that my butt did *not* look fat, regardless of whether it did or not. The shopping experience didn't end up being traumatic at all and I even enjoyed trying on different styles. I found two pairs of jeans in Express that seemed to do the trick: one traditional denim and one black and red snake print. When I came out of the fitting room Grace said all the right things and so I charged them to my AmEx card and brought them home. The next day I took the snake print pair out for a test drive. Matched with knee-high boots and a long coat these things called 'pants' were not so bad after all. I even managed my own *camel toe*!

Next it was time to consider my wardrobe space. I had known this day would come for a long time but I wasn't sure when it would arrive or what form it would take. I certainly hadn't foreseen that the stimulus would be my pants reawakening. For a few years I had kept my old and never used man-clothes vacuum packed in bags at the top of the closet, waiting for... well, I'm not quite sure what I was waiting for. Waiting for the right time to say goodbye, I suppose. In the past, when I envisioned this day, I thought it might be a rather emotional time and assumed that everything I wore in my past life needed to be expunged from my new one. I had heard of other transgender women who celebrated with grand bonfire ceremonies of their man-clothes as a purge of their history. To me, though, it was more about creating hanger space for the phoenix's closet than deleting my past. I meticulously went through everything and turned out all the man-clothes that would never work for me. Yet a few things caught my eye as I considered their future. Some woolly sweaters were fairly unisex, so they could stay. T-shirts from bands or concerts, too. Then I noticed a beautiful old shirt with embroidered gold flowers. I'd seen women wearing men's shirts (mostly in movies, when sharing a morning orange juice at the breakfast table with a new lover), so maybe I could too. It didn't work. The collar was weird, the buttons on the wrong side, and the sleeves far too baggy. The fit wasn't good enough on so many levels. I even tried on a suit again, just for old time's sake, but had to laugh at how ridiculous it looked. I was simply not the man inside the man-suit anymore.

The historical clear-out resulted in four huge bags which were later collected by my local Salvation Army thrift shop. All those clothes had some tales to tell, in the same way that thrift shop purchases I have made must have had histories too. They can't narrate those yarns themselves, but they all have a past interwoven through the fabric. If I wanted, memories of times wearing a particular outfit could remain with me; they didn't need to be donated to the thrift shop of history at the same time.

I have no idea where those garments ended up, but I smiled at the idea of them being found by a trans man who appreciated my past sense of sartorial style and wanted them for his journey of apparel discovery. In addition to the woolly sweaters and band T-shirts, one other item had to stay: a bold black shirt with gaudy pink flamingos on it. I fondly remembered purchasing this on a visit to see Louise in Minneapolis in 1989. She mocked me at the time for buying something so flamboyant, but it later became a staple in my club-DJ wardrobe. Besides, it might have a tough time finding a new owner from the Salvation Army clothes racks, especially as it had lost 10 shades of color following a run-in with a hotel laundry some years earlier. Although I can't imagine ever wearing that shirt again, neither can I shut the door on the poor flamingos; it would be like kicking a sick puppy out onto the street. But if, in the years ahead, you see someone wearing a faded pink flamingo shirt bought from a NY thrift shop, then it might have come from the American Midwest before going on a trek through the Middle East (where it had the argument with a hotel laundry), to Asia, and back to New York. A veritable round the world trip worthy of any avian migration. But if you can imagine a better history through fact, fiction, or fantasy, then that is fine too.

Chapter 44

Dream Attack

J anuary lumbered into February. These are the months when the weather is grimmest in New York City. After the glittery excesses of the holiday season many New Yorkers fall into a chilly lugubriousness but I felt unseasonably warm. I had embraced an uncompromising sense of serenity, further enhanced by an upsurge of self-confidence. I felt truly happy. I even went a little crazy and had the occasional hot chocolate and not just my default English breakfast tea. Of course I have been in high spirits at many other times in my life but this was different; it was much deeper. In fact the degree of calm was almost unnerving—oxymoron excepted. I felt *authentic* for one of the first times in my life.

Although I knew my transitional journey wasn't over, I began to experience an emotion I doubted I would ever feel: I was transgendered and it didn't matter anymore. I didn't care if people stared at me, perhaps wondering what I was. It didn't bother me if people thought or knew or guessed that I was trans. The outward perceptions of others had always been so important to me, but they were becoming increasingly irrelevant. I still worried about all the things that most women fret over (wrinkles, weight, and if I looked fat in a dress) yet now my disguise had fallen away. One gender was not masking the other anymore. Though for this self-acceptance to be complete I had to release one final legacy of my past.

When I moved to New York in 2007, it was with a leap of faith: a fairly measured hurdle, but still a jump into the unknown. I had become unsettled with my life in Hong Kong. Perhaps I needed something—or to be someone—that I wasn't yet aware of. Was that disquiet my inner-self starting to grapple with being transgendered, subconsciously bubbling under my daily existence? I'll never know.

I had moved to New York with the support of Radio Television Hong Kong (RTHK) and became their radio correspondent here. I felt that this could be a stepping stone to radio or other media here that would immediately embrace me as the latest British transplant with an adorably cute English accent. It didn't turn out that way, and it wasn't long before I realized that radio in the United States is a dying art form. There are myriad reasons for that, and the music industry has itself partly to blame. Restrictive formats, outdated music policies, and newer ways of music delivery all contribute to the statistic that fewer people choose to listen to radio here. National Public Radio (NPR) is a dim beacon of hope, yet largely impotent.

At this point, my life had been entirely in the feminine for three years. Apart from adopting the androgynous model for travel, the one glaring exception to my femininity was over the airwaves. It was only for a few hours each week, but radio was a necessary part of my life. If nothing else, I needed the money. Every week I had to dig deep to find a male persona, don my male voice, and either report live or record other programming. I feel that I produced some great features and unique radio programs over the years and I loved the kudos of earning a living within the media. However, in terms of radio recognition, I was a man. As I was working from home I didn't have to *look* like a man while attempting to *sound* like one—that was some consolation, at least. I suppose I could have broadcast in a ball gown, though I don't think I ever did.

That reverberation of my former self was becoming impossible to maintain. I guessed that the radio station would have embraced me as *Nicky* Chase, but this was not something I wanted to put to the test. To be in radio you need a voice. My male voice was quite good for that medium, my female voice was not.

Voice remains one of the cruelest elements of transgenderism, as I'd learned from the Cable Guy Incident early on in my transition. Then I had looked somewhat female but been perceived as male because of my voice. Pitch, vocal style, sentence construction, cadence and flow all contribute to the perception of gender through voice. The anatomy of women around the head, neck and larynx is different from that of men, and that is not something which can be reliably tweaked with surgery. As a result, all trans folk—male and female—need to adapt and train their voices if they want to sound the way they feel. Thanks to all the classes, group lessons, and efforts to embrace my inner Marilyn, I had gotten better at sounding female, but radio is a much tougher critic. In person, or on TV, the appearance of femininity helps tip the balance towards female discernment; remove those visual clues and vocal recognition becomes more ambiguous. If I had continued with radio as a woman, the listener would likely have found it harder to judge whether I was male or female. So I made the decision that until the time when I could make radio programs and be perceived as unquestionably female, then I needed to stop making them as someone arguably male. I resigned from RTHK.

The civil servants in Hong Kong were surprised at my seemingly irrational decision, especially as I had fudged the specifics of why I needed to do this. I said that I needed to take an extended break, but that maybe I could work for them again at some time. Maybe I can, and I'd rather not burn any bridges to the future. The evolving formats of the way people receive content, along with their perceptions of what they want from it, are fascinating. The ties between traditional news, music, and information dissemination will doubtless loosen still further, and for media to survive in any guise it needs to constantly reinvent itself. Perhaps I can be a part of its re-genesis. However for now, quitting radio was a requisite end to the last part of a life that I had known for many, many years. My previous leaps of faith hadn't resulted in me slipping into a crevasse, and so I could only hope that this one wouldn't either. Even so, I worried about what would take its place. Not only would there be a financial gap, but a creative one too. I didn't know how I would cope with either. But leaps of faith are, by definition, jumps into the unknown.

I prepared myself for recording that final radio program from my home studio. This was one last chance to play some of my all-time favorite tracks. So there had to be something from the Cure (I chose the blissfully gloomy "Bloodflowers"), Britpop from The Charlatans and Teenage Fanclub (neither band ever put out a bad album), and highlight tracks from The Veils and The Verve. There was also Talk Talk, The Church, The La's, and Echo & The Bunnymen. And I had to include the wonderful Kirsty MacColl whom I had the true pleasure of interviewing just a few months before she was tragically killed. Newer tracks from Foster The People, The National, and Silversun Pickups also expressed the wealth of talent from this side of the pond. I enjoyed this last hurrah but it had to end. I signed off on air and closed the mic for one last time. I wasn't emotional but I felt the finality. There was relief, too, at not having to maintain a part of me that had left the building a long time before. It wasn't an Edward R Murrow moment, nor a Casey Kasem one, but it was a significant line drawn in the musical sand. A final track from New Order ("Dream Attack" from their still scintillating 1989 album *Technique*), and I was gone.

Chapter 45

Questions and (a few) Answers

The brutal New York winter persisted. My inner glow of well-being continued to grow, along with the satisfaction of dealing with one less gender. However, I couldn't forget the practicalities of my new anatomy; I needed to devote a good two hours per day to my dilation exercises and this regimen seemed to dominate the whole day. But I was always diligent in that respect and those two hours were sacrosanct. I developed them into personal *Nicky-time*. I could put my feet up, or read, or watch TV, or do whatever I wanted to do without personal reprimand—albeit in the semi-reclining position that the deed dictated. I never resented this necessity and these exercises weren't the ogre that I had imagined they would be prior to surgery. In fact, they reaffirmed my feminine form each time.

That time on the sofa (or occasionally in bed) gave me time to reflect on deeper aspects of my transition, along with musing over other questions that friends asked me.

"How do you feel?" was still the main one.

Did I feel differently having passed through the veiled ordeal of SRS? Apart from my ongoing fatigue, I suppose I did feel a greater balance within my personal equilibrium. I was the same person as from a few months ago but I was surprised that the actuality of surgery had affected me so overwhelmingly well. Maybe that was just the obvious consequence, though I hadn't expected it. Before surgery, however much I tried to ignore what I had below the waist, each time I had a shower or visited the bathroom my dysphoric past was on display. Now that had changed and I was not reminded of what I wasn't anymore. Was it as simple as that? I knew my hormonal balance had shifted slightly with my updated anatomy, but I didn't consider that to be a fundamental reason for my updated peace of mind. The psychological effect of surgery seemed to have benefited me quite profoundly.

I thought more about surgery and how this tends to be the main association that pops into people's heads when they hear the term *transgendered.* Of course being transgendered doesn't necessarily mean having sex-change surgery; some trans people will go down that path, others will not, but we are transgendered nonetheless. Societal norms deem that the genitalia we were born with define the gender we are. Every transgender person needs to rewrite that software program within themselves while nudging the bigger perceptions of society at the same time. We have realized that our inherent sense of *being* has defined our gender, regardless of the genitalia we possess.

Something else was bobbling around in my head as I contemplated the gender equation. When I'd told friends or relatives that I was transgendered, there was one platitude often spoken in reply, which seemed to be as much for their benefit as mine.

"But you are the same person!"

Of course I was the same person—or was I?

I discussed this with Mum a few times and we agreed that I was inherently the same *soul*, but did that make me the same *person* as before, now that I was physically a woman? We couldn't find an answer between us and I still find this aspect of my change one of the most fluid enigmas.

Most of my physical body is much the same as years before, even though body hair has been banished, I have female curves, and my vagina has been retro-fitted. Adding and subtracting hormones has also contributed to my outward femininity. I consider that I now look as female as ever; I certainly feel that way. However, even before I started hormone therapy and yet was living my life as Nicky, others noticed something else; I was *behaving* like a woman. I remember one time when I was Skyping with Corelli and he pointed out that my mannerisms were distinctly female. I hadn't noticed these in myself, but being the actor and director, these traits were singularly feminine and clearly apparent to him. I'd not *tried* to turn these characteristics on; they just happened.

I recall early times in my cross-dressing days when I left the apartment and made a conscious effort to walk in a more womanly fashion. "Don't stoop," I'd read in an online blog. "Women walk more erect than men." So I tried to walk with my shoulders back, butt in, and heels forward. Occasionally at female voice classes we received tips on how to sneeze, and cough, and giggle. These didn't seem as relevant to me, as I felt I sneezed, spluttered, and tittered as a woman would anyway. I rarely felt any need to train myself in adopting female attributes as those seemed to come naturally to me. Furthermore, if I were now asked to assume the mannerisms of a man, I wouldn't know where to start. I suppose I would then need to feel guilty if I were lost and had to ask for directions. Some things are so much easier as a woman.

The more I considered it, the more peripheral differences I saw in myself. I rarely enjoyed clothes shopping before, but now my closet has grown to twice the size it was in male days. My tastes in music have changed: less indie, more clubby. Although not irrevocably drawn to chick flicks, I do watch different movies and TV programs now: not so much Law and Order, but more Friends and Ally McBeal—if only on re-runs. My pleasure watching these programs isn't because they are stereotypically female; I enjoy them more because my tastes have evolved.

The most unanswerable question I asked myself was whether my *thinking* had changed. I find it impossible to remember *how* I thought before, and whether it might be different to now. My rational streak remains (not least in considering these changes), but not all blondes have to be ditzy ones. I suppose my thinking must have changed, as all other aspects of my life have altered, but beyond the outward aspects of fashion, music and TV, specifics are trickier to pin down. As I noted at the start of this book, people ask me when I knew that I was transgendered. I still find it hard to answer. When I sensed feelings of femininity within me initially, I expressed them in the form of cross-dressing. I didn't expect or plan for those emotions but they were there. I didn't promote them, but neither did I stifle them. That led to my day-to-day existence as a woman, hormone treatment, and ultimately, sexual reassignment surgery. No stages of my personal evolution happened because I felt they were things that I *should* do to be a woman; they were simply an organic progression of who I am.

So am I the same person as before? When I look in the mirror, I see only the me of now.

Chapter 46

Not Support, Just Encouragement

My love is guaranteed. No, let me correct that: my *vagina* is guaranteed. This was one of the many factors that made me feel so sure in choosing Dr. S for my SRS. Unlike the latest Cadillac, this vagina assurance is not a 50,000 mile warranty for service and spare parts; the doc wants all patients who have had SRS with him to be completely happy with the results. So to that end, he will perform corrective surgery if needs be. I had been saddened by the issue of disappointing depth immediately post-surgery, but it wasn't nearly as bad as I'd feared, and I have since come to terms with it. However, four months after surgery, I was not completely happy with the esthetics down there. Maybe I was being too superficial, but I thought that she could be a little prettier, even though I knew she'd never be Grade A porn star material. I explained this to Dr. S by email, and he agreed to do a minor revision surgery under local anesthetic. I felt this could be a big confidence booster for me. Of course I hope that in the years ahead someone else will fall in love with my lady-parts, but first I needed to do that myself. (Cue Whitney Houston singing "The Greatest Love of All.") And I wasn't there yet. (Eject that CD then!) This would entail another trip to Bangkok, but I never need any excuse to return to that part of the world. Besides, this time it would be different: I could now travel under my new name and with new passport. No disguises, no identity crises, no chance of a fracas at Immigration.

There was something else on my agenda too. Having renovated my basement, it was time to consider updating the mezzanine. I remember talking to Grace about boobs even before I committed to SRS.

"I don't wear a bra for support," I'd said, "just encouragement."

Hormone therapy had given me a nice lift but to give me the shape that I aspired to meant wearing push-up bras. Although I didn't mind that, I preferred the idea of having the push-up *under* the skin and not over the top of it. It would be so much more convenient that way.

I'd often thought that I'd get a boob job, though I hadn't been sure when it might happen. So one of the things I did just before leaving Bangkok post-SRS was to have a chat with my provisional breast doctor, the wonderful Dr. N who gave me my more feminine nose the previous year. I wanted counsel as to the best size of boobalicious upgrade. Would one cup size be best? Or maybe just half a cup as opposed to a whole beaker? I've often felt that there is something weirder about trans women with unnaturally large implants than natal women who choose to upsize their boobs beyond reality. Maybe it is a knee-jerk reaction, that having lived without breasts for most of our lives, we trans folk want to make up for that with overly ambitious cup sizes. Of course natal women and porn stars can also be overzealous in the boob department, but transgender women can fall into the same titty trap too.

I wanted a bit more oomph in my Oompa-Loompas, but not much. Not to the extreme that I would be ogled on the street by builders and bricklayers who would gasp, "Wow, look at the bazookas on that babe!" My boobs needed to be somewhat subtle; the supporting act (that didn't need that much support) as opposed to the show-stopping main event. So I visited Dr. N before I left Bangkok to talk breasts. He explained all the options. I had no idea that there were so many factors! It's not just a matter of choosing a cup size, as you also have to consider the pros and cons of rounded ones or shaped teardrops. Then there is the matter of projection, which sounds like something you'd have in a movie theater but actually refers to how much you want them to stick out. So there's the basic size plus the shape, and how aggressively pert you want them to be—if you want them to have the ability to cut glass on a cold day for instance. There's also the width to consider, which is dependent on how wide your chest cavity is. Many surgeons will make all these decisions on your behalf, but I wanted to be part of the decision-making process. I went prepared with an oversized bra so that I could simulate options with Dr. N's ever-resourceful nursing team. Unfortunately the test bra I had brought with me was too voluptuous in style. Each time we tried slipping in an implant, it would pop out like a slippery fish. We resorted to using one of the reserve bras in the clinic, but as they were usually for Thai patients, they were a tad small for me. We found a size 36, only a couple of inches short of what I'd usually wear, and that gave me some idea of how the future might be as we stuffed in different implants sizes. Dr. N only works with the firmer gel-type implant, not the flimsier saline variety. That's just as well; the fit was so tight under the small-sized bra that the salty fishes might have ruptured and met their watery grave.

After about an hour of discussions, fittings and deliberations, Dr. N suggested the best option. Then I dropped down a further size as I was still wary of being too top-heavy. Having agreed on a size, shape, projection, material, and program for surgery, all we needed was a date. We agreed to keep that schedule open so that sometime in the future I could return to Bangkok and we wouldn't need to go through the size-determination process again. Now the time was right for completion. I liaised with Doctors N and S (they actually do know each other), agreed on a timeframe for both procedures, and booked my flights to Thailand.

My decision to return to Bangkok coincided with the first inklings of spring in New York. I felt that it also marked the end of my personal winter. Since returning from SRS I had mostly been in hibernation. I stepped out of my cozy isolation for work, groceries, and pants shopping but little else. I considered my healing process to be paramount, and while there could have been room for both socializing and recuperating, I wanted to concentrate on the latter. Besides, the time constraints of at least two hours per day being taken up by my exercises (as Mum still euphemistically refers to them) meant that I really didn't have much time outside of my work routine. Although this exercise regime needed to continue for many more months before it could slack off, the start of spring signaled a time for me to venture out of my cocoon.

I also started to see the bigger picture. A final point of transition started to become visible on my mental horizon. I could almost hear the cheering crowds as I ran through the virtual tape on the invisible finishing line. Come the summer, a new butterfly would have pupated. Someone as physically complete as her dreams had hoped for, but with a status she never dared to expect. Someone with the mental strength of mind to accept what she is, and not be ashamed of her past or of being transgendered. Someone ready to embrace the world in a completely revitalized way. Virtually complete, I was almost ready to fly. And, who knows, maybe go pollinate too.

Chapter 47

Oriental Orientation

This was the trip I had dreamed of making for years. This was the flight when I could finally dress as I wanted. This was the time when I could wear heels, even though I knew I would have to remove them when exiting the plane down one of those inflatable chutes in the event of an emergency. (Yes, I do read the aircraft emergency information cards located in the seat pocket in front of me. Likewise I always put my seatback and tray table in the upright and locked position prior to take off and landing without being prompted to do so.)

I had the broadest smile as I handed in my officially female passport at check-in. Even passing though security control was a delight. Others cursed the inconvenience of having to remove shoes, belts, and dignity when passing through the body scanner, but for me, this was pure pleasure. I had primed and prepped myself before I left for the airport. Sure it was going to be 15 hours on a plane, but this time I wanted to look unquestionably female and feasibly glam. My hair was blowing prettily, just like in one of those shampoo advertisements. I'd chosen an uncharacteristically long skirt but it was swirling á la Stevie Nicks. Also a black embellished T-shirt and a broad belt, worn high on my waist. My confidence was brim full.

"Look at my heels!" I wanted to shout out. "I am Nicola Jane Chase, a woman, and I have the passport to prove it!"

In the end I thought it wiser to keep some vestige of cool lest I be carted off by security for being crazy.

Walking between the security checkpoint and the lounge I remembered how the Mexican couple had described me on the plane to Bangkok. Yes, I was the phoenix and now it was time to let her fly. Unfortunately financial practicality deemed that this had to be in economy class again at the back of a Cathay Pacific Boeing 777.

I waited in the lounge prior to take-off, where I had met Pel the year before. The seats where we had talked over wine and cocoa had been changed; I appreciated not seeing the same scene again. Memories still lingered of our Italian dinner together, with remnants of hurt too, but I brushed them aside without a tear. It was his loss, not mine, and the world was my oyster once again. I felt a greater satisfaction of promise as the pearl within the shell.

The flight was called and I made my way towards the boarding gate. Horrendous lines. Even my frequent flyer pass didn't act like a magic wand. I glanced around. A tall fellow brandishing an American passport appeared to be looking for the same solution. He found an airline agent at the same time as I did and we were both directed to the slightly shorter of the huge lines. But in the process of Q&A with the airline agent, I caught him catching a stare at me. Actually, more than a stare. It was a look that started at my head, and then continued to survey me all the way down to my heels. And back up again. I probably should have been turned off by this overtly sexual once-over, but I was lapping it up. I was the hot chick looking my best boarding the plane and I was game for attention. I exchanged a few words with Tall American Passport Man and he appeared interested in continuing the conversation.

He told me that he was heading to Hong Kong for the Rugby Sevens, a spectacle that I had wantonly spurned throughout my 12 years living in that city. The event seemed to put greater emphasis on beery socializing than on watching the game. (And why do people feel the need to show support by painting their faces in team colors? I could never understand that aspect of popular sporting fan culture.) We filed onto the plane together and Tall American Passport Man found his spot in business class. Before he sat down we briefly mused on the fact that there would be little to do for some hours on arrival as the flight was due to arrive in Hong Kong at 5am, and most of the city is not in dim sum mode at such an early hour. I continued my trudge down the aisle towards the cheap seats at the back of the plane. I was just getting myself sorted out, when he walked down from business class to find me.

"By the way, my name is Todd," he said, handing me his business card. That's right; he hadn't actually introduced himself before. "If you ever find yourself in Boston…"

"I'm Nicky. I shouldn't think I will," (oops, that was wrong message to give!) "but thank you. Maybe we can touch base again when we get off the plane. Grab a coffee or something."

"Great, I hope you can get some rest in the meantime."

I actually did get some rest, though not before I'd mused over a non-date coffee rendezvous after touchdown. I definitely felt a tinge of excitement when he'd come to find me. I must have been high on emotion too, as I'd suggested coffee and not tea. No, he was American and so I had to speak in refreshment terms that he could equate with. Had I been too forward or played it too much like the man? Not this time. And without doubt, the heels helped.

On the other side of the world (and on the other side of Customs & Immigration at Hong Kong International Airport) I did meet up with Todd again. It was good to have a more leisurely chat and a frothy cappuccino with him. (I actually did have coffee.) There had been minimal maneuverability for creative flirting when boarding the plane while others were attempting to fit hand baggage the size of a grand piano into the overhead bins. Todd asked for my email address which I duly gave him. I wanted to leave the ball in his court and not pine over whether I'd ever hear from him again. Besides, I wasn't even sure if he was my type. That made me wonder what *my type* actually was. I knew that tall was good, and that well-traveled was a bonus, but beyond that I found an image of my perfect man hard to visualize.

Another reason for this trip was to update my legal name and gender status in Hong Kong. Having worked in that city for a continuous period of seven years through the 90s and 00s I had earned the right to permanent residency there. (How much simpler the US Immigration system would be if they adopted such common sense measures.) The only condition for maintaining that residency status in Hong Kong is that I pop by the city at least once every three years—which isn't burdensome at all. The city has an extremely practical smart identity card system too, and that was the document that needed updating. I had booked my appointment with the HK Immigration Department in advance, and duly went to their offices in Kowloon with all my paperwork. Different countries have different requirements for accepting the change from 'M' to 'F' for legal and immigration purposes. Some require that you have lived in your 'acquired gender' for a certain period of time, others deem SRS a requirement for updating your legal gender. Hong Kong belongs in the latter camp and so I made sure I had brought the certificate from Dr. S with me. It is actually a very good looking certificate, one clarifying that I have been through SRS, and I wondered if I should have framed it on my wall or hung it above my bed. But it is also quite medically explicit, and I remember showing it to my New York-based immigration lawyer one time and he visibly paled as he read through the details. The color literally drained from his face as he absorbed the minutiae of the surgical procedure I had been through. It is not an operation that men do.

The updates in Hong Kong went without a hitch and I felt a deep sense of satisfaction seeing my new name stamped again by officialdom. Perhaps immigration officials are trained to accept transgender people with civility and normalcy, for that is exactly what happened. And that sense of equality is all that trans people like me ever wish for. We don't ask for special favors or procedural shortcuts—simply to be accepted in the same way that we perceive ourselves. I felt proud of the city that will always hold a special place in my heart.

The stopover in Hong Kong was just for half a day but I got everything done, and I arranged to pick up my new ID card on the return leg of the journey. So with my business there complete, it was time for the short two-and-a-half hour hop back to Thailand!

It was lovely being back at the Dusit Princess Hotel. I felt I was among friends once again. In fact when I went down to breakfast in the hotel coffee shop for the first time, members of the serving team greeted me in no uncertain terms.

"Welcome back Madame," said one, with a lovely welcoming smile, typical of the smiles that the country is renowned for. "It's good to see you again!" I felt exactly the same.

The hotel is used by patients of Dr. S, so there will always be some trans folk around, either immediately post-surgery, or for subsequent check-ups, or even for a surgery-free vacation. Over the next 10 days I enjoyed meeting other transgendered people and those who had traveled with them.

I briefly talked to one girl who was almost certainly there for surgery but apparently hadn't achieved complete openness about her situation. I mentioned how enjoyable I found it lying by the swimming pool. She said, meanwhile, that she had "forgotten to pack her swimsuit." I smiled inwardly at the apparent euphemism and chose not to suggest that she could buy one in the mall next door if she wanted. It also made me wonder how else anyone could explain why they were staying in the hotel for such an extended period of time and yet be confined mostly to their room. Full disclosure is not for everyone—I know it took me a long time to get anywhere near that level of comfort.

There was an Australian couple from near Melbourne. They married as man and wife many years ago, but for the last decade have been wife and wife. Being a couple of typical Aussies, they brush off the magnitude of this achievement, but I remained in awe at each of them for intertwined but complementary reasons. It is easy for me to forget that the people intimately connected with trans folk also have monumental hurdles to overcome. They have to come to terms with a partner, son, daughter, or loved one who isn't quite the person they first knew or fell in love with. And yet they are. Oftentimes circumstances like this don't work out, and so to see this example where it had been a success was truly heartwarming. We often chatted over corn flakes and croissants at breakfast, and I always looked forward to hearing their Aussie brogue in the morning. They also drank tea.

Another girl I met was from deep in the American heartland. Justy was a beautiful and confident young lady who had just been through SRS. We talked about many things but one of her concerns was the level of care she would be able to receive back home in Kansas. How many medical professionals have enough transgender experience there, or how far would Justy have to travel to see one? I immediately appreciated my own situation more; as a New Yorker I have an excellent LGBT clinic close by in the city. Justy's experience also made me wonder about the countless other trans women in states where anything beyond perceived normalcy is considered almost deviant. How many had to remain in stealth mode just to escape verbal abuse—or worse?

There was another factor in Justy's story that I found compelling. She was traveling with her mother, Tessa. They had both traveled halfway across the world so that the legal but inapplicable 'he' could become the physically correct 'she.' The more I considered this feat of bonding, the more it overwhelmed me. A mother had given birth to a child that, by genital qualification, was a son. However as that child grew and experienced increasing dysphoria, the mother reached an extraordinary point of recognition where not only did she accept her child's revised gender, but wanted to be there for the surgical correction. This feat of familial approval didn't happen overnight, but I hope Tessa appreciates how incredible her act of acceptance was.

I was fascinated to hear these backstories as we congregated in a faraway land. Each of us shared a connection, though our paths to this destination were unique. This deep interest in the passage that other transgender people had navigated also showed me something further about myself. In the past I tended to set myself apart from other transgender people, and was perhaps even aloof to them. I often felt that I looked better or that my timetable of transition was better. I rarely wanted to be seen with them, and maybe I even doubted that some were trans at all. However now I was experiencing more empathy with my tribe; I was engaged by their stories and wanted to help others by volunteering my own story. I wondered if this new sense of parity had been enhanced since my own SRS. I hadn't remembered these more balanced perceptions prior to surgery, so was this another unexpected mental consequence of my physical change?

Many times throughout my transition people have called me brave. I often felt confused and a shade embarrassed when I heard that. I never *felt* brave, not in any traditional sense, as I was just being myself. There were stages early on in my cross-dressing experiences when it was nerve-wracking to leave my apartment in wig and heels, but the more I accepted my female self, the more that dressing accordingly seemed the norm. I see courage in others, though.

Every gender-questioning person needs to pass through a process of realization to accept who *we* are. There are often similarities in the narrative, but no experience is the same. For some, the process of self-acceptance is straightforward as they act upon their inner messages. For others it requires incredible fortitude, perhaps in the process of self-determination itself, or in the ability to act upon that sense of identity. Some, sadly, will never be able to get to the stage they desire, whatever stage that is and however deeply they wish to change. Inner demons can be too strong, let alone the power and importance of approval from their family or peers. Culture, religion and society all play parts in the degrees of self-acceptance and being accepted, regardless of any physical or anatomical change in the individual. It can be difficult to accept the messages from our inner self; but for some, acting on that deep sense of true identity can be the hardest decision of all. Now I understand why others call us brave.

Chapter 48

One Last Anesthetic

I had returned to Thailand for completion, physically and perhaps spiritually too. Returning to the clinic where I had my SRS was vitalizing. The previous occasions I had been there were for the surgery itself and then the subsequent adjustments. At the time of the initial surgery I remember feeling that I just wanted to be done with the process. I had been on a mental rollercoaster over the preceding months, and then after arriving in Thailand the bowel-cleaning process prior to surgery was a nauseating ordeal. By the afternoon when I was due to be picked up at the hotel and taken to the clinic prior to SRS, I felt weak and hungry. Maybe that dissociated feeling helped to dispel my nerves. The follow-up visit to fix the healing glitch had been necessary but laced with the disappointment of delay. So this time I felt much happier, even though I knew I was going to have another surgical repair job with my legs in the stirrups. However it was strangely affirming too: the environment was familiar and it was wonderful to see the people who had changed my life five months before. Before he scrubbed up I got a big hug from Dr. S which reaffirmed that I had made the right choice of surgeon—not that I had ever felt in any doubt. My nether regions were quickly numbed by a local anesthetic and he got to work. I was even able to chat with him during the process, though I didn't like to joke too much lest an errant laugh from him caused an irreparable misstep. After he had finished snipping and stitching he showed me the results. Wow! My vajayjay looked better than ever! It still makes me smile that I need a mirror to view my new genitalia, but these reflections were joyous. It would entail a further few months of healing, but I could finally feel proud of myself and my appearance. This part of my transformation was complete. In the months that followed I occasionally needed to remind myself that I hadn't been born this way. How soon we forget.

Before I left New York I had become really excited about the other reason for this visit: my upcoming boobification. However, in the run-up to this final procedure I felt peculiarly nervous: concerned about the procedure, the anesthetic, and how it would turn out. I had the utmost faith in the surgeon and his team, but this process involved a lot of personal choices. Would I like my new boobs and my new shape? Might they be too big or had I been too conservative? I felt my chosen options were about right, but this couldn't be confirmed until the operation had been completed. And then it wouldn't be like exchanging a pair of shoes; this selection was going to be with me for many years.

I wondered how a more rounded bosom might affect my daily life. I assumed that I'd feel better about myself and my figure, but would there be any downsides? I didn't think I'd topple over, but I assumed there would still be a shift in mass. Although I had experimented last time with Dr. N as we tried to find the optimum size of implant stuffed in a bra, I figured it must be a completely different sensation when the implants were under the muscle. How would they actually feel?

Maybe I should have gotten used to receiving an anesthetic but perhaps it is such an unnatural process that one can never get used to it. I rested in the pre-op room of Dr. N's clinic and waited for a chat with the anesthetist. I hoped this would be my last operation in a long while. The previous time I had been here for the nose tweak, the anesthetist had once done a work placement at a hospital in Queens. So there had been the surreal experience of chatting about us both living in New York while I was about to count down from 100, waiting for the drug to kick in. This time the anesthetist was different, as was my sense of pending conclusion. While SRS was arguably essential for my personal wellbeing and mental health, it wasn't the same for breast augmentation. I didn't *need* to have bigger boobs, but this was something that I really *wanted* to do. This was not an operation solely for trans women after all; it has bolstered the self-esteem of millions of genetic women in countless countries over many years. But for me, this was set to be the finishing touch to all I had achieved.

Anesthetic-induced sleep comes instantly like the thud of a heavy dream. Waking up from its illusory spell is more complex. Drowsy, dopey feelings that the real world has returned, but not completely. I remember waking up after SRS and trying to look at the clock on the wall but it wouldn't stay still nor could my eyes focus on the rapidly moving hands. On that occasion I had been asleep for around eleven hours and I didn't appreciate until later the remarkable skills the anesthetist must have had to keep me in a perfect state of suspended animation for such a long duration. Was I aware that I was asleep for that length of time? Did I detect a passing of time, or would I have had the same sensation if the anesthetic lasted just minutes? This time I assumed it should be shorter, and I think I presumed that when I woke up from the anesthesia, but all I could sense was that it was dark outside. And quiet; everything was very quiet. I could detect some movement around me—one of the nurses, I guessed—but I wasn't aware of much else. I was thirsty, but I had difficulty getting my mouth to make enough words to ask for water. But the nursing angel was there and she soothed me with sips of water. I drifted in and out of post-anesthetic slumber for the rest of the night.

In the cold light of day the following morning (actually the blissful air conditioning in the blazing heat of Bangkok) other sensations became apparent. Whenever I moved my arms or torso it was really painful. After SRS it was awkward and uncomfortable but I don't remember much pain. I knew that the process of getting sub-muscular breast implants would likely be much more painful. It was. Yet that is another remarkable facet of the human body: nobody can actively remember pain. You can remember how it happened, or when it occurred, but not the actual sensation of pain. Consequently it's hard to prepare yourself for it. You know something is going to hurt, but beyond that, it's a matter of waiting for it to happen. In this case, lying down in bed was fine but any effort to raise myself out of the virtually horizontal into the practically vertical... OUCH!

Dr. N came visiting later that morning and seemed perfectly happy with the way the operation had turned out. His nursing team hovered around as I reacclimatized myself to life in the real world and gingerly started to walk around the room. Although it seemed an impossible schedule when I had woken from anesthetic (not that I thought in such logical terms) by late that afternoon I was ready to head back to the hotel. It was still awkward to move my torso, but most of the muscular pain and discomfort I experienced earlier had eased.

I then had to wait a frustrating 48 hours before returning to the clinic for the grand unveiling ceremony. I walked from the over-ground subway station along the quiet lane towards the clinic. It was baking hot—it always is in Bangkok—but I enjoyed this. Even so, I couldn't imagine having to work outside in this climate. I could see some construction in the next block and workers there were swathed in protective clothing, which must have made it feel even hotter. There was a small food cart selling noodles halfway along the lane, but the vendor appeared to be fast asleep. I was pleased that it wasn't the type of cart that sold crepe pancakes as I can rarely say no to those. A couple of stray dogs meandered listlessly into a rare garden that seemed like an oasis. I ambled along to the clinic, and was eager to see what my new frontage looked like. By necessity it had remained under wraps post-surgery. I felt it was like giving birth but then having your newborn popped back in the womb for safe keeping.

There are multiple ways to *guestimate* what new boobs can look like, but this was the time when I would discover if the choices I had made, and advice I had been given, had resulted in the shape and appearance that would please me. I'd already established that I didn't want huge, but what would these look like on me? The nurses carefully unraveled the bandages like an Egyptian mummy to reveal my new self. And the outcome? Cute! I thought they were kind of cute! Underneath a T-shirt they probably wouldn't appear outwardly different from my previous padded bra state, but these were all mine! Still sensitive, swollen, and requiring much convalescence, but all the planning and estimating and guesswork seemed to have paid off. Ladies and gentlemen, I now had cleavage!

I left the clinic that morning with a distinct glow, and not just from wearing insufficient sunscreen. For the next few days I had a brace of thin plastic tubes coming out from under each newly enhanced breast. These drained fluids out of the wound area and delivered those fluids into two plastic vacuum-bottles. Sometimes I carried these around in a convenient shopping bag but I could also loosely strap them down with tape just below my waist. Then they could be hidden under flowing skirts. I felt I had kangaroo testicles swinging from side to side, but at least they were only hanging around for a few days. How strange and unwelcome it was to have something dangling below the waist once again. But with these bottles—or rather the anatomy that they were connected to—I started to feel a deep sense of achievement.

The following few days in Bangkok saw my recovery continue and my sense of wellbeing blossom further. I enjoyed the ongoing conversations with my newfound transgender friends in the hotel, along with their partners and parents. The Bircher muesli at the breakfast buffet became a firm favorite with me as I continued to be strong-willed against the draw of the Nutella jar. I headed out of the hotel more often and into the city that I love. One of those excursions was to the remarkable labyrinth of discovery that is the weekend market of Chatuchak. Hundreds of stalls selling everything from… well, just everything. The shopping maze is mostly enclosed, but that's not always a blessing. Outside it can reach over 100 degrees, but inside, the oppressive humidity takes over. A few of the tiny shops have air conditioning, but the owners must be wise to the fact that foreign shoppers often come in for a blast of cool rather than to pick up ornate jewelry. The heavy air of Chatuchak is filled with smells and sounds that are intoxicating and addictive, from the dusky scent from the area that sells leather goods, to the clattering from the stalls that have every size and shape of crockery imaginable.

The places that sell clothing seem hotter still, unless that is just an illusion from seeing an infinite number of clothes hung across hundreds of stalls from ceiling to well-trodden concrete floor. Alleyways are barely wide enough for two people, yet almost always have three jostling past each other. Of course there are multiple food stands too, so you are never more than a few minutes away from a Pad Thai or green curry, cooked by chefs who were surely born on the sun. Nobody else could tolerate the incessant heat and five-star Thai peppers that make jalapenos seem bland. Still they smile. That's why I love Thailand.

My shopping experience was relatively subdued this time. I picked up a rose-patterned knee-length skirt I was just able to squeeze into, a couple of pink T-shirts, and a selection of three-pairs-for-a-dollar earrings. I also had my first run-in with the type of Asian bathroom that is often found in less salubrious parts of the region: the infamous squatting toilet. I'd met one before in my male days, but using it then was simply a matter of aiming down a hole. Squatting with a skirt on, with no assurance of where everything would go, was a completely different matter.

Back at the hotel I was relieved to sit and not squat. I became increasingly delighted with my new boobs, too. They remained tightly ensconced, double-wrapped in both a sports bra *and* a support bra, but on the occasions when we showered naked together we got along very well. It would still be weeks before I wouldn't need to wear the double bra set 24/7, and until that time of complete healing I also had to sleep solely on my back, which I didn't find easy or restful. But this was a temporary situation. I knew that by the New York summer, I would be out in a T-shirt and shorts and feeling pretty, sexy, and completely in sync. The inner and outer me were finally at peace.

The two surgeons I can never thank enough; they changed my life forever. Beyond that, they helped give me the inner calm that I never knew existed. Their respective teams also reminded me of the absolute dedication that nurses and caregivers have. I knew I would be back in the City of Angels again, but leaving Bangkok this time also marked the most defining moment for me yet. I felt close to my finishing point, balanced by an exhilarating sensation of a new journey about to begin.

Chapter 49

New York City Spring

I returned to New York feeling like a new woman. The enduring process of pupation I had gone through was almost complete, and the lengthening days of spring mirrored my own sense of personal growth. In the six months since SRS, my prevailing emotion had been of waiting. Patiently (impatiently at times) waiting for the healing process to reach a point where I could resume my life. I had now arrived there and my blossoming sense of achievement was almost dreamlike.

There were practical things to take care of. For a start, I needed to go bra shopping. Nothing in my lingerie top drawer fitted my personal top drawer anymore and so I needed to restock. I appreciated that this experience would likely become more fun as the soreness, aching and inflammation around my two new best friends reduced, but I had an immediate need to find a new bra that kept everything in place until I was fully healed. That meant spurning whatever was pretty inside the Victoria's Secret catalog, and instead embracing granny bras. Imagine the most un-lacy, un-cleavage-revealing, unflattering, and definitely unappealing bra on the shelf, and that is what I needed to find. If my grandmother were still around, even she'd have thought that style a tad frumpy.

At least I could go bra shopping and understand the sizing. It was a simple process of visiting JC Penny and finding something that I felt comfortable in, even if it wouldn't have set the fashion runways abuzz. It had been different in Thailand. Just after my arrival in Bangkok, the day before boobification surgery, the nurses at the clinic told me to go and buy a sensible bra for use with my soon-to-be enhanced figure ("just leave the tags on in case it doesn't fit"). But in Thailand they use the metric system for lingerie.

"Get a size 85. With an E cup. 85E."

"E cup!" I gasped, "I don't want to be an E cup—let alone be a size 85!"

I had panic visions of overflowing breasts that would make me so top heavy I'd be unable to stand up without toppling over. Or I would have to arch my back like a pregnant scorpion. But it could have been worse: in France, the same sized bra is called a 100E. That would have made me feel positively gigantic. But the nurse was insistent, and so I went searching for an E cup bra in Bangkok. That is the equivalent of a DD, and it is tricky finding a selection of DD bras in a country where the average cup size is an underwhelming A. I went to the biggest department store in the city, and they had a grand selection of two bras to choose from. I could either select ugly and expensive, or slightly less ugly and more expensive. I revel in the shopping experience in Bangkok as most things are so wonderfully cheap, but not when it comes to bras in atypical cup sizes. So I went for the slightly less ugly, albeit pricier, alternative.

"It's for my friend," I protested to the cashier. She just smiled back at me.

Of course the nurse was right, and although I was definitely not getting DD breasts installed, I needed something that would accommodate the post-surgery swelling. Thanks to the American obesity epidemic, large bras with big cup sizes are readily available in the United States, and although I hoped I would never need an 85E (38DD) ever again, at least I knew there were more stylish options available if I did.

Being told to buy an 85E bra was another example of the unexpected good times I've had in the years of transition: nightclubbing in Bangkok long before I even considered surgery, high octane, high speed traffic dodging on the back of a motorbike on the way to meet Dr. S initially, the pleasure of seeing my new passport, flying for the first time as a woman. These had all been incredible experiences and highlighted different stages of my journey. The acceptance from friends and family had been a heartwarming revelation, and seemed to strengthen previous bonds. Above all, the relationship I have with my mother is better now than ever before. It was at this point when the biggest realization of all became apparent: the joys of being a woman outbalanced all of the many setbacks I had experienced and suffered to get to this point. Everything became blissfully worthwhile.

Looking out my window in Queens I saw the daffodils blooming and the big ash tree overlooking my back yard was already sporting noticeable green hues. All final traces of snow had gone and the grassy lawn seemed to be waking after the long winter. I'm sure I spotted a pair of American robins making plans for their future and I wondered if they were from last year's brood returning home. It was clear; spring really had sprung. Inside, I echoed that sentiment and my future was also set to bloom. For years I had focused on physical changes and mental readjustments. Now I had gotten to a point where those unsynchronized aspects of my life were balanced. I too was at a seasonal threshold; spring was on my doorstep and I was heading outside.

Chapter 50

As One Door Closes...

His email came as a surprise. Todd, the guy I'd met while boarding the flight to Hong Kong some weeks ago, had got in touch. He was visiting New York and wanted to know if I'd be up for dinner one night. Sure, why not. We'd got on well enough at the time, and so it would be good to touch base with him again. I wasn't sure if I felt chemistry around him when we had met for coffee in Hong Kong, but that had been after enduring a 15-hour flight, so who knows what sense either of us made. Dinner is scheduled for this evening.

There was another notable date I'd had with someone else whom I had met at JFK Airport. (Note to self: try to find men in places other than airport departure lounges.) That was with Pel, but this time I know it won't be the same. I am now in a different state than when I met Pel, personally, emotionally, and physically. I suppose I have grown up.

I try not to have a checklist of requirements for any potential date, but having traveled the world is a huge plus on the date's résumé. And by that, I don't mean Manhattanites who make it off the island once in a blue moon to try a new Brazilian restaurant in Queens. If I am to have a solid relationship with someone, then they need to have a passport with plenty of stamps in it. It's not the travel per se that is important, but I feel that once anyone has experienced life in other countries, it broadens their outlook.

There is a deeper subject that I return to though; one that brings me back full circle to the first few words of this book. As a male, I considered myself heterosexual. As a female, I also consider myself heterosexual. This is one of the strangest aspects of my transition. Before I found women *sexually* attractive, now I find them *empirically* attractive. It is the biggest of all the changes that I didn't see coming, and the one that made me address my sexuality along with my gender—which again, going back to basics, are two distinctly different things.

In my dreams I see myself as a loving wife to a successful man, probably with a family, and then growing old with him. The dog and white picket fence scenario. My transition would then be absolute. I would have met someone who embraced me completely; a man who knew of my past and accepted it as the past. But even greater than that, he would *love* me. I don't really know if any past girlfriend truly loved me when I was male, or if they did, it was too long ago for me to remember. So the concept of a partner loving me—yes, me— seems almost ethereal.

There was no significant other during my transitional time from male to female, whenever I consider that clock to have started. So what might it be like to be half of a couple invited over by friends? I can almost hear the casual conversation that refers to me.

"Yes, Nicky and ***** are coming over for dinner tonight." It sounds so simple, and it's what millions of couples around the world regularly enjoy, but this basic aspect of social interaction has been missing from my life for many years. I vaguely remember doing this as a man with past girlfriends, but it never felt completely right, and those hazy memories are now distant. What *will* it be like?

It is strange looking back to who I was. I don't begrudge all those years spent in man-mode, though I wonder how it would have been had I recognized my inner self sooner. But that assumes my inner self was female all along, which is a premise that I don't even know is true. Was the relative lack of success I had dating women as a man due to my deepest inner self knowing that I was trans, but my outer self not hearing those whispers? It seemed that I often dated people who were unsuitable; was that significant too? We'd just lumber on, developing a nice enough friendship yet with minimal sexual spark, before it eventually fizzled out.

I remember with great retrospective amusement trying to date a girl named Lucinda. We were in a sort-of relationship for a few years, but I'm not sure if either of us truly acknowledged that. She was American-born Chinese and we were both living in Hong Kong at the time—though separately, of course; I've never actually lived with anyone when in a pseudo-committed relationship. Another early signpost along my pre-transitional road maybe. I met Lucinda through magazine back-page dating which was all the rage at the time; full blown Internet dating was still in its infancy. Our problem was that neither of us stopped the dating process even when we assumed, by default, that we were dating each other.

"You are always looking for someone better, for Cinderella," another ex used to tell me. "She doesn't exist." But does that mean you should accept assumed second best, or is it better to keep looking, just in case? Is the glass slipper an opaque expectation? The answer becomes less relevant as I now search for Prince Charming.

But back to Lucinda. There was one time when we were still notionally a couple but I was feeling that she wasn't The One. So I browsed other anonymous ads on the back page of one of the free *What's On* type magazines—probably the same magazine that we had used to find each other in the first place. One person sounded quite interesting so I thought she might be a potential Cinderella. I sent a witty and creative message to her. However, as I was casually looking over Lucinda's shoulder when she was checking her email the following weekend, I saw the very same message *I* had written to that anonymous person in *her* inbox! It was *her* ad that *she* had posted! Awkward! There is a track from 1979 by Rupert Holmes, *"Escape (The Pina Colada Song)."* It was the tale of a bored couple that sought excitement out of their current relationship only to find each other again. That was us. Two Pina Coladas on the B side.

"I bet you're gay," she once said when I really wasn't in the mood for lovemaking—which I rarely was. "Or bi. Maybe you're bi."

Well Lucinda, I'm transgendered. Maybe you picked up on something that even I didn't appreciate at the time. Our escape didn't have the same happy ending as in the Pina Colada song, as there were no renewed vows of friendship nor cracking open the champagne on the beach at midnight. But it was an appropriate ending as we did break up—eventually, anyway.

At the moment, medical science doesn't have any definitive answers as to why a person is transgendered, when that switch turns itself on, or whether it is always on and we just take time to notice it. Many believe that something happens in utero, possibly as a result of some chemical or hormonal imbalance. Or perhaps it's due to an external factor which caused something to change in the fetus. My mother was pregnant with me when she received the awful news that my father was ill, and possibly terminally so. I wonder if this might have been the trigger that was in some way responsible for me being transgendered. I will never know, nor does it matter to me. Maybe one day we will understand more about the medical, genetic, or biological aspects of being transgendered, but it will never change the fact that there are countless people like me who have experienced this trick of being, and have had to react to it accordingly. Some are able to manage their shifting life with guts and determination, while others experience deep depression that can often end in suicide. There are transgender people who identify the issue very early in life and can accept their inner identity before puberty kicks in. For others it only becomes apparent in later years. I was one of the latter. Whether I knew the truth about myself and repressed it, or whether it just wasn't there for the first 30-something years of my life, will probably always be a mystery to me. Yet this is not a puzzle that I feel any need to solve.

A while ago Mum said that she almost envied the position that I was in, as I have a singular perspective on plurality through gender. However, I see it a different way: not a blessing nor a curse, but a compromise. For the first half of my life I was relatively content being a man; in fact I remember being very happy at times. But that pales in comparison to the deep sense of inner peace and true fulfillment that I feel now. Yet part of me remains an *almost-woman*; some experiences will always be out of reach. I can only imagine what it would have been like to go through puberty as a girl, or to go to the high school prom, or have that first kiss, or lose my virginity. Many women might scoff at any suggestion that these were enviable times, but they are points within a rite of passage that can never be mine.

The biggest gift that any non-transgender natal man or woman has is actually something they *don't* have. They have no need to worry about the gender they were assigned at birth, or a change that happened later in life, and the complications of accepting a mismatch. That is a luxury that no transgender man or woman will ever experience.

I've done virtually everything I can to fix the shuffled deck that life threw at me, and I've spent countless thousands of dollars to get where I am now. I dread to think how deep the transitioning money pit has been, but what would have been the alternative? Buy a yacht and sail around the Caribbean as a *man*? The concept is ludicrous. To have missed out on this liberating sense of authenticity would have been the saddest loss of all.

"How could I *not* love you?" my mother said recently when we were re-discussing The Situation from a touchingly warm retrospective. I am so lucky to be blessed with the family and circle of friends that have supported the emotional bridge to my new self. Unfortunately, there are far too many within the transgender community who do not have the same unconditional love. They will be stigmatized and abused, whether physically, verbally, or emotionally, by friends or family, and by people they never even meet. We didn't ask to be like this; all we ask for is acceptance. Understanding can come later.

I never anticipated being part of a group that suffers discrimination. I grew up in white suburban England, and so the verbal stones of abuse tossed in my direction since have been a new experience, one to shield against but not cower away from. This is my welcome to the other side of the tracks. Prejudice is ugly, but millions have tolerated discrimination in multiple scenarios over countless years. Sadly, millions more will endure the same fate in the future.

There are many groups that fight for *rights* within a million categories under and beyond the LGBT umbrella. While I appreciate the need for this dialogue, I prefer to remain an advocate for transgender *understanding*. After all, it wasn't many years ago that I too had no idea of what that term meant—let alone realize I was part of that very same group.

Doubtless there will be detractors of my story—there are in any open society—and I know I will have to be thick-skinned to weather the zero-out-of-five review scores that this book will generate in some quarters. Of course there will also be misguided opinions that with the right "treatment" I could have been "cured" of being transgendered. Some will always see me as a freak of nature, or a person who mutilated a perfectly good male body. There will never be complete understanding by everyone. I share my experiences with the wish to foster a greater understanding within a larger community. The more barriers are removed, the more acceptance becomes possible. My biggest hope is that my story resonates in such a way that stigma and prejudice are reduced in those who once knew less, but now know more.

I am a transgender woman and proud of my accomplishments.

Ah, it's getting late and I have just finished the tea that I have in front of me. It's the mug with Chinese dragons wrapped around that I brought with me from Hong Kong. I also have a date to go on this evening. I almost forgot about Todd in composing these final thoughts. A date. Well, sort of. Something I have not experienced in many months, and certainly not since SRS. I suppose I'll need to have The Conversation again. No, maybe this time it can wait.

A single woman in New York City, I can sense the twists and turns set to unfold as the dating world opens up in new ways. I am not so different anymore. I have a past, but everyone has that. Who knows, it might even be me doing the rejecting next time, not that I am looking for that. I hope excitement will find me, love would be even better, though if I end up being the bitching old spinster sitting in the rocking chair doing my knitting, I will still have tales to tell. Regardless, I am now a part of where I want to be. This evening exemplifies my new self. I bring no expectations, as this is simply a date between a man and a woman. Just like the millions of others that have happened for the amazing people of this incredible city.

One last look in the mirror. A deep breath. I drop the latch on the door, and pull it closed behind me.

About the Author

Nicola Jane Chase grew up in the suburbs of Liverpool, northwest England, as a passionate music lover—and as a man. The first of many changes was quitting a stable career in retail management for the more adventurous, if insecure, life of a globetrotting club DJ playing dance tracks for the international jet set. She (albeit then still a *he*) then shifted direction and spent a decade on the airwaves of Hong Kong delivering cool indie tunes to a dedicated fan base. In 2008 she relocated to New York, the city she now calls home.

Music has since taken a back seat, yet her knowledge of 1980s tracks remains impressive, and her pleasure from listening to them rarely wanes. Now unreservedly *she*, her focus these days is on fostering greater transgender understanding and acceptance. To that end, she is a popular speaker at public and private events, and welcomes media inquiries.

An avid tennis player, she lives for the warmer days of summer when she can play on the outside courts in New York City. When not writing, speaking, flicking through rare 12" vinyl, or working on her backhand slice, she can often be found in her Queens back yard tending rhubarb and arguing with her gooseberry bushes.

Visit the author website:
www.nicolajanechase.com

Follow the author on Facebook:
www.facebook.com/TeaAndTransition